QUOC PHAM'S STORY

THE WORLD LOOKED AWAY

VIETNAM AFTER THE WAR

For Huynh Trường Lê Hiền

Never give up hope

Khóa 1/70

Sinh viên Sĩ quan Thủ đức

Quoc hyp

March 2018

by DAVE BUSHY

For Debby Le -

To know why we lived in the USA

ARCHWAY
PUBLISHING

and became the USA Citizen

Grand Dad

This book is a work of non-fiction. Unless otherwise noted, the author and the publisher make no explicit guarantees as to the accuracy of the information contained in this book and in some cases, names of people and places have been altered to protect their privacy.

Cover Photo: U.S.S. San Jose crewmembers in rescue of Quoc Pham's boat, January 20, 1980. Records of the office of the Secretary of Defense, courtesy National Archives Research Administration.

Maps created by Hung Pham

Archway Publishing books may be ordered through booksellers or by contacting:

Archway Publishing
1663 Liberty Drive
Bloomington, IN 47403
www.archwaypublishing.com
1 (888) 242-5904

Because of the dynamic nature of the Internet, any web addresses or links contained in this book may have changed since publication and may no longer be valid. The views expressed in this work are solely those of the author and do not necessarily reflect the views of the publisher, and the publisher hereby disclaims any responsibility for them.

ISBN: 978-1-4808-5236-5 (sc)
ISBN: 978-1-4808-5237-2 (hc)
ISBN: 978-1-4808-5238-9 (e)

Library of Congress Control Number: 2017917214

Print information available on the last page.

Archway Publishing rev. date: 01/08/2018

Publisher's Cataloging-In-Publication Data
(Prepared by The Donohue Group, Inc.)

Names: Bushy, Dave.
Title: The world looked away : Vietnam after the war : Quoc Pham's story / by Dave Bushy.
Other Titles: Quoc Pham's story
Description: Bloomington, IN : Archway Publishing, 2017. | Includes bibliographical references and index.
Identifiers: ISBN 9781480852365 (softcover) | ISBN 9781480852372 (hardcover) | ISBN 9781480852389 (ebook)
Subjects: LCSH: Pham, Quoc Tan, 1946- | Boat people--Vietnam--Biography. | Vietnam (Republic). Hải quân--Officers--Biography. | Vietnam War, 1961-1975--Personal narratives, Vietnamese. | Vietnam--History--1975- | LCGFT: Personal narratives. | Biographies.
Classification: LCC DS559.914.P43 B87 2017 (print) | LCC DS559.914.P43 (ebook) | DDC 959.7044092--dc23

To Xuong and Vo, who raised Quoc.

To Kim-Cuong, who sustained him.

And to Duong, who encouraged
him to tell his story.

CONTENTS

LIST OF VIETNAMESE NAMES USED IN THIS BOOK

Throughout this work, the author has used common English for names of the individuals mentioned in the story, omitting Vietnamese spelling and accent marks. The Vietnamese language and pronunciation of names in particular is highly dependent upon accent marks. For instance, Kim-Cuong and Quoc named their son Phạm Quốc Hùng. The last name, in English – Hung – is spelled the same as Kim-Cuong's father's name, Dương Thành Hưng. The variations in accent marks create a changed pronunciation and thus a different name. This can be confusing for the non-Vietnamese reader.

Below is a list of the Vietnamese people mentioned in this story, with a brief description of who they are or the role they played. The common English spelling of their names, as used in the book, is on the left. Their full Vietnamese names, with accent marks, are included on the right. A few individuals, only mentioned once in the book, are not included in this list.

Quoc Pham	Phạm Tấn Quốc
Duc	Lt Đức (Quoc's commander)
Kim-Cuong	Dương Thị Kim Cương (Quoc's wife)
Xuong	Phạm Văn Xương (Quoc's father)
Vo	Huỳnh Thị Võ (Quoc's mother)
Sinh	Phạm Minh Hùm (Quoc's First brother)
Lan	Phạm Ngọc Lan (Quoc's Fourth sister)
Phuc	Phạm Hữu Phước (Quoc's Fifth brother)
Nga	Phạm Ngọc Nga (Quoc's Sixth sister, who died)
Hoang	Phạm Minh Hoàng (Quoc's Seventh brother, Army NCO)
Loc	Phạm Thiên Lộc (Quoc's Eighth brother, Air Force private)
Cuu	Phạm Trường Cữu (Quoc's Ninth brother)
Toan	Toàn (original team leader from Apartment Complex)
Vong	Vọng (original team from Apartment Complex)
Minh	Minh (joined Quoc's team at reporting center)
Son	Sơn (joined Quoc's team at reporting center)
Thai	Thái (spy-ring leader)
Thach	Thạch (spy)
Hoang	Hoàng (suicidal prisoner)
Quang	Quang (executed prisoner)
Chu Tu	Chú Tư (District Chief)
La Tu	La Tư (First boat owner)
Y (like "E")	Phạm Văn Y (Quoc's cousin)
Khuong	Phạm Thị Khuông (Quoc's cousin)

Dong	Dương Thị Phương Đông (Kim Cuong's sister)
Nga	Dương Thị Hằng Nga (Kim Cuong's sister)
Dung	Trần Anh Dũng (Second mechanic)
Di	Di (Second boat owner; boat used in escape)
Lam	Lâm (militia member)
Thong	Thông (experienced sailor)
Loi	Lợi (First mechanic)
Hung	Phạm Quốc Hùng (son)
Kim Ngan (Amanda)	Phạm Quốc Kim Ngân (daughter)
Kim Khanh (Connie)	Phạm Quốc Kim Khánh (daughter)
Cuong	Phạm Quốc Huy Cường (son)
Hung	Dương Thành Hưng (Quoc's father in law)
Tot	Võ Thị Tốt (Quoc's mother in law)
Ut Duc	Út Đực (Kim-Cuong's uncle, National Liberation Front (NLF) follower)
Muoi	Phạm Thị Bạch Tuyết (Quoc's Tenth sister)
Hong	Võ Thị Tuyết Hồng (Kim Cuong's aunt)
My	Mỹ (Hong's husband)
Hong Ngoc	Nguyễn Mỹ Hồng Ngọc (Hong's daughter)
Hoang	Hoàng (Hong Ngoc's brother)
Thieu	Nguyễn Văn Thiệu (S. Vietnam's Second President)
Huong	Trần Văn Hương (S. Vietnam's Third President)
Minh (Or Big Minh)	Dương Văn Minh (S. Vietnam's last President)
Duong Nguyen	Nguyễn Thị Thuỳ Dương (Quoc's Second Wife)

PROLOGUE

This is the true story of Quoc Pham, a South Vietnamese Navy officer, and Kim-Cuong, the woman who loved him. It is about the enduring strength of family and the human spirit. The story is set against the backdrop of a victor whose leaders chose brutality and economic punishment towards a people who had taken up arms against them.

After the Geneva Accords in 1954, South Vietnam had been established as an independent nation, divided from North Vietnam by the 17th Parallel. In the following five years, South Vietnam had been relatively prosperous and had known peace. Then in late 1959 the conflict began anew, as the North began its efforts to take over the South and create one combined nation. Though it was always seen on the world stage as a fight by a free country against a Communist aggressor, to Quoc and his fellow countrymen it was simply a fight against invasion. Ideological dogma was less a part of their thinking than was patriotism. As patriots, their belief was that they fought to keep their country free and independent.

America's decision to enter the war and how it was fought will be debated forever. That involvement, however, ended in 1973.

Victory by North Vietnam did not end the suffering and death of war. It changed the venue. Nearly two million men and women are believed to have been interned in the Reeducation Camps of Vietnam after the war officially ended. At least a hundred thousand are thought to have died. Countless other citizens of the country succumbed to starvation and disease in the period between 1975 and 1985. They are still called The Ten Dark Years.

No accurate accounting exists. Stories are not chronicled in official government documents or in the history books of the world. Details only reside in the memories of families and the people who experienced them. Even today there are only a handful of articles and books about the subject.

By providing the perspective of one man who lived it, this work serves to tell the story of the years after the war. Quoc Pham was promised ten days in a Reeducation Camp. Instead, he remained in captivity for years, suffering brutality, near starvation, and continued retribution by the Communists, all while his family lived through an economic depression. Five years later, he ultimately became one of the hundreds of thousands of Boat People who escaped by sea.

This book is also about what happened to Kim-Cuong and the rest of their family while Quoc was captive. In the process, the book provides insights into what was happening to all the inhabitants of the country during the continued war with Cambodia, a conflict with China, and the downturn caused in part by imposing Soviet-style economic planning on the economy.

The Communist advances in 1975 were dutifully reported by the world's press, but after the fall of South Vietnam, there was an almost surreal quality to the reporting and in official comment from countries around the globe. Information stopped flowing. Although something was happening in Vietnam, those outside of the country had no sense of the enormity of the human suffering in the camps and elsewhere within the country. The Communist leaders also expelled most foreign journalists, which further exacerbated the dearth of information from inside the nation.

It seemed to those who remained in Vietnam that the world looked away.

In the 1980s, through the efforts of some U.S. congressional leaders, journalists, and the United Nations High Commission on Refugees, the world slowly began to turn its attention back toward Vietnam. This still did not prevent the continuing deaths in the Reeducation Camps or the loss of untold thousands of Boat People, who would perish at the hands of pirates and the unforgiving sea.

The war between North and South Vietnam lasted for more than two decades. It played out in both Southeast Asia and on the world stage, directly and indirectly involving the world's superpowers. Approximately 1.1 million soldiers were lost by North Vietnam (North Vietnamese Regular Army – NVA and NLF) and 750,000 South Vietnamese military personnel died. About two million civilians throughout the North and South are thought to have been killed during the war. The United States sent more than 2.5 million men to fight. Nearly 60,000 died.

Richard M. Nixon was elected U.S. president in 1968, vowing to end the war for the United States. He stressed the Vietnamization of the conflict and a drawdown of U.S. combat troops. Nixon nonetheless pressed forward with combat actions during the early 1970s, including massive Christmas bombing campaigns in 1972 meant to bring North Vietnam to the peace table. On the face of it, they did, and the Paris Peace Accords were signed in January of 1973, effectively ending U.S. military involvement. At that point, Americans, weary of the war, began to turn their attention away from a region that had taken so many lives and caused such domestic conflict.

During 1973 and 1974, there was limited military action between the North and the South, with the North moving slowly to bring more territory under its control. This occurred against the backdrop of the Watergate scandal in the United States, culminating in the August 1974 resignation of President Richard Nixon.

Following the resignation, Gerald R. Ford became president. He had limited political capital and was unable to abide by commitments that Nixon had made to South Vietnam promising resupply and air support in the event of aggression from the North. The U.S. Congress and the American people had effectively tired of the war and concentrated on other initiatives and agendas around the world.

The U.S. and most other countries averted their gaze. By early 1975, many must have hoped that the enmity of two decades had somehow disappeared and that peace could magically be upheld between the North and the South.

However, the Communist North had shown a commitment and patience that transcended American resolve. In January of 1975 they tested what might have remained of that resolve when a cross-border invasion was ordered to liberate the South. The Americans took no meaningful action. President Ford requested funds from Congress to aid the South, but was denied. The North continued a campaign that was as swift as it was relentless.

It was a disorienting time for the citizens of both Vietnams. Those who lived in South Vietnam continued to act out their daily lives during the early days of 1975, understanding that momentous change was occurring. They had experienced such change before and most held firmly to the belief that the country, against all odds, would survive.

By March, however, as the Communist advances continued unabated, South Vietnamese President Nguyen Van Thieu ordered a withdrawal of forces from the central highlands and two northern provinces. An orderly withdrawal turned into a general rout and by mid-April, Cam Ranh Bay fell. The South Vietnamese military forces made one last stand at a former U.S. Air Force base in Phan Rang, about 200 miles due east of Saigon. Though most South

Vietnamese still clung to hope, in reality it was no longer a matter of if the North would win, but when.

The country of South Vietnam officially surrendered to the government of North Vietnam on April 30, 1975. Quoc Pham's story begins a week before on the Vietnamese Island of Phu Quoc, located in the extreme southwestern part of the country in the Gulf of Thailand, just miles south of the Cambodian coast.

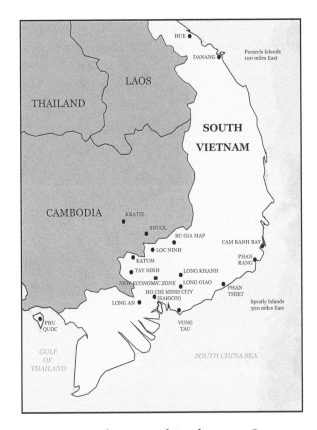

Locations of Cities and Reeducation Camps
in The World Looked Away
Map created by Hung Pham

1

WILL SOUTH VIETNAM FALL?

"The Camp on the island of Phu Quoc had been set up at the beginning of April 1975 at facilities previously used as a POW camp for Vietcong and NVA prisoners. There were at least 50,000 refugees on the island, all people displaced from the central part of the country due to the Communist advances."

Quoc Pham

APRIL 22, 1975

What military man ever thinks he will be defeated? Quoc had not previously even contemplated such a thought until that spring day. Something was different, though, when Lieutenant Duc, Quoc Pham's commander, called him to his office and said, "I've got a mission for you, Lieutenant."

Quoc replied, "What is it sir? Are there more refugees coming? I don't know how we'll feed and house them."

"No, it's bigger than that. Things don't look good in the capital. I need you to fly over today to do something for me personally."

Quoc had known Duc for only one month. They were the ranking officers in that part of the camp. Though Quoc was Duc's subordinate, they had nonetheless developed a friendship. Quoc recognized from the tone that this was an order based on personal need, not a military one. Such an order was uncommon. Even as Duc spoke, Quoc sensed that the orders might give him the chance to see his family in Saigon. He asked, "What are my orders?"

"See to it that your family and mine are taken care of. I don't know if the military situation is going to get really bad, or if the army can stop the Communists, but I want to make sure that we at least have a plan for our families to escape. I can't leave the island now, but I can send you over to Saigon to take care of my wife and children."

"Yes, sir."

"And you can take care of your family as well."

Quoc paused. "But what about our job here?"

Duc pondered and looking into the distance replied, "Lieutenant Pham, that might become less important than we think."

Quoc wondered why he had been selected for this mission. He had hesitated before his answer because what his superior had just told him indicated a dramatic shift in military thinking. Here was an officer of the well-equipped, trained, and staffed South Vietnamese Navy openly talking about the possibility of defeat of the only country Quoc had ever known.

He struggled not to let the idea of losing the war consume him. His military training had taught him to compartmentalize thinking and accept orders. But it was impossible not to let dark thoughts enter the most disciplined mind. He took comfort in the fact that the mission at least coincided with his deep desire to be with his wife and family during such a time of uncertainty.

Quoc would fly to Saigon and carry out his orders. He obtained details from Duc about how to find the lieutenant's family and what arrangements his superior had made for their evacuation. Plans were quickly made for Quoc to get a seat on one of the commercial transports scheduled to leave Phu Quoc for Saigon. No one knew just how much longer air service would be allowed to leave the island.

Quoc had been on Phu Quoc for less than a month. He had been reassigned from an advanced strategic training course in Saigon. He had been dropped off a few weeks before, near the navy base at the extreme southern end of the island. His orders then had been vague. He was told to help manage the burgeoning refugee population that had been displaced by the advancing Communist forces.

Phu Quoc was as far away from the war zone as one could get. With its beautiful beaches and stunning sunsets, it was destined to become a tourist destination. In March of 1975, though, it was a makeshift refugee camp, utilizing structures that had been built as POW internment centers for use by the South Vietnamese military.

By April 22, some 50,000 refugees were estimated to have occupied the island's seventeen camps. The facilities had neither been designed nor constructed to accommodate such an influx. Food was scarce and the basic necessities of water and sanitation were severely lacking. Quoc, Duc and their support personnel had no sleeping quarters and made do with whatever food they could find. Quoc considered himself fortunate. At least he had a sleeping bag. Though there had been no outbreaks of disease, cases of dysentery and fever were on the rise. A handful of medical personnel attempted to alleviate the suffering, but their efforts were hindered by lack of basic sanitation, medicine, and supplies.

Communication between the mainland and the island was almost nonexistent. There were no civilian phone lines for the camps. Radio communication between Naval Headquarters in Saigon and the makeshift island headquarters was erratic and infrequent. Television news, which was rare in Saigon, was not available on the island. There were some local radio stations, where regular programming was occasionally interrupted by almost matter-of-fact news reports providing information about Communist advances from the

North. British Broadcasting Corporation (BBC) radio provided the most consistent and accurate information.

As Quoc bounced along the unimproved dirt roads in the American GMC *Deuce and a half* (2 ½ ton) truck, he gazed ruefully at the old camp. He recalled how the South Vietnamese had released thousands of prisoners back to the North after the peace accords in 1973. The information he had learned was that the North in turn had released only about a hundred South Vietnamese prisoners. The rest were still thought to be in prison.

When Quoc arrived at the airport, there were long lines of refugees and a few military personnel queuing up to attempt passage on the flight. His official orders granted Quoc Pham one of the precious seats. At 2:00 p.m., he boarded the small 50-seat turboprop and sat down, a pit in his stomach. He attempted to shield any sign of worry or concern from his fellow passengers and made no conversation with his seatmate.

After a 55-minute flight, the airplane began its descent. From the west, it approached Saigon's Tan Son Nhut Air Base. From all appearances, the beautiful green countryside that soon blended into a sprawling city of three million looked just the same as it ever had. The bustle of the city below was unchanged, with the normal haze layer from the thousands of cooking fires arrayed throughout the streets of the city.

The aircraft touched down in Saigon at 3:00 p.m. The pilots parked on the ramp next to a long line of aircraft, including a U.S. Air Force C-130 Hercules – a four-engine turboprop that could easily carry three times as many people as the one Quoc had just flown on.

Quoc walked down the stairs of his airplane to the tarmac. He noticed several U.S. Air Force crewmen motioning him over to their aircraft. He also saw a long line of Vietnamese people, all of them in civilian clothes. They were queued up to board the C-130.

As Quoc walked near the line, a U.S. sergeant recognized him as a South Vietnamese naval officer and gave him a thin-lipped smile. "We've got a seat for you if you want to leave. We're headed for the Philippines. You can get out before it's too late."

Quoc sagged a bit physically. It was the tone of the American's voice and his fatalistic message. Quoc was hearing and processing something he did not want to believe. Here was the country's long-time ally – albeit one that had pulled out all of its remaining ground troops two years earlier – telling him in no uncertain terms that defeat appeared inevitable. Quoc, though, was a man on a mission. With his customary courtesy he softly replied, "Thanks so much, but I am on an assignment." He quickly added, almost as a confession, "I must get to my family."

The U.S. airman shrugged, turned and went about his business. Quoc walked off the ramp, into the terminal building. Soon he was outside hailing a cab, instead of his preferred and cheaper motorbike. He so urgently needed to see his family.

The traffic seemed as bustling as ever. Cars, motorbikes, and a few man-powered cabs crowded the roadway, horns honking, and individuals yelling for friends. The airport was like the rest of the city, with a road network and infrastructure designed for horses and carriages. It had never been adequately upgraded by the French occupiers or by the Vietnamese authorities that had run the city for more than two decades.

A small yellow and green Peugeot taxicab pulled up. Quoc threw his bag in the back seat and jumped in. He merely said, "Nga Bay Ly Thai To." It was the address of his parent's house. The driver nodded his head in acknowledgement and made no attempt at conversation. It was not commonplace to engage in discussions with strangers in Vietnam. Quoc figured the man had his own worries and concerns and he needed time to himself before he arrived home.

He looked out the car window, seeing the streets lined with stately, canopied Dau trees. He processed the various pieces of information he had gathered during the day and in the past weeks: First, his commander's stark message and mission; then the veiled message of the American airman. And, since January, news from the North of the Communist advances hung over all of them like a giant Sword of Damocles ready to drop.

Quoc had no way to predict the future. Even if he could, he was uncertain how he would react. He could only try to limit himself to the mission at hand.

Today his one mission was to connect with his own family. And tomorrow, LT Duc's. He had to sort out his options. And one of those options now included escape.

Pham Tan Quoc – Quoc Pham – was born in 1946 not far from Saigon. His given name, Quoc, means *nation* in Vietnamese. He was one of ten children. His father, Xuong Pham, was a South Vietnamese merchant mariner and chief engineer for Vi Go Lines, a shipping company registered under the Panamanian flag. Xuong was also an assistant professor at Phutho University's Maritime Program. Quoc had graduated from the school.

Quoc's mother, Vo Huynh, was a housewife who did not have a paying job outside the home. But she was much more than a housewife. Due to Xuong's repeated long absences away on commercial vessels, her children rightly regarded Vo as the matriarch of their large extended family.

As a mariner, Xuong had earned more money than the average South Vietnamese. In some circles he was regarded as affluent. As a chief engineer on a seagoing ship, Xuong was also one of the few Vietnamese who had traveled the world. His perspective was informed and pragmatic concerning politics and economics. He had seen countries without war and areas where capitalism thrived.

Quoc's wife, Kim-Cuong, and two young children, four-year-old Hung and six-month old Ngan, had lived most of their marriage with his parents. It was a Vietnamese custom for the married sons to live in their family's home, often with three generations occupying a small space. At any one point as many as 12 people occupied their home. The house was in the city, about five miles from the Tan Son Nhut Air Base.

The row house his parents lived in measured about nine by 40 feet. It had one and a half floors, one small bathroom, and a four-by-four-foot kitchen with a small natural gas stove, a sink, and a few cupboards.

Houses in Vietnam were markedly different from those in the West. Imagine outsized shoeboxes turned lengthwise on their narrow sides, sharing end walls. Only the end units had side windows. All the units lined busy pedestrian sidewalks, which invariably seemed to be a part of each home's inset entryway. Entrances to homes served a number of purposes, including access to businesses and storage for motorbikes and bicycles. There were usually sliding doors which were left open all day, encouraging air circulation within. From the entrance, a common living area included a leather couch and easy chair, as well as tiny stools clustered together where people half-sat and squatted while talking or eating. The floor was concrete, covered with linoleum. A doorless opening to the kitchen and adjoining bathroom then led to a stairway that opened to a large common sleeping area. There were no beds, just sleeping mats. For some privacy, a few thin curtains could be drawn between generations and individual family members, especially younger couples who desired privacy and intimacy.

Quoc's monthly navy income was 25,000 Vietnamese *dong* (about 200 U.S. dollars), which barely kept him and his family at the poverty level throughout the war. He had lived with his parents until he could save enough for a down payment for a home.

In February of 1975, Quoc and Kim-Cuong had finally saved enough to buy an apartment in a housing complex reserved for military personnel and government officials. It was about five miles from his parents' home. Although uncertain about the future, they had purchased the apartment through a government mortgage. However, no one had ever been completely certain about anything in Vietnam.

Quoc was a lieutenant, junior grade. He was 29 years old. He stood 5' 1" tall, with the upright bearing and countenance of a naval officer. Quoc was shorter and thinner than many of his contemporaries. Like the rest of his generation, he had lived his entire life in the shadow of war. He looked and carried himself like an older man. War made Quoc grow up fast, and he had the hardened personality and strong temperament of a veteran. His skin was normally dark but even moreso due to his continued exposure to the sun and wind in his role as a shipboard naval officer.

Quoc did not consider himself handsome, but those around him noted something about his character that made him stand out. Kim-Cuong often reminded him that the traits of strength, honor, and determination were critical for a man to lead his family, as well as to serve his country.

Quoc's daily blue uniform with collar insignia looked much like those of his counterparts in the U.S. Navy. It readily identified him as a member of the South Vietnamese military. He had worked with the U.S. Air Force as a clerk before he was drafted into the Navy. There was no question that Quoc was allied – and identified personally – with the South Vietnamese cause. He saw it as defense against invaders.

Three of Quoc's brothers and one sister had also served in the military. The older brother, Sinh, was an intelligence officer with the army. He had been captured in Quang Ngai in March of 1975 by units of the NVA. Little was known about his whereabouts, but the family felt certain he was in captivity. A younger brother, Hoang, a non-commissioned officer in the Quang Ngai local militia, had also been captured in March. He would be released in mid-May.

Another brother, Loc, was an air force enlisted man. Quoc's sister had been in training as a second lieutenant in the army when she had died tragically in March of 1975. The family had yet to learn the circumstances of her death.

Most of Quoc's time as a naval officer since his commissioning in 1970 had been on board a Landing Ship Tank (LST) and later on a high endurance cutter (WHEC) with 5-inch guns used for coastal shelling.

As the cab headed toward his parents' home, Quoc thought of his young and beautiful wife. Her deep sparkling eyes and long black hair made her stand out wherever she went. It was an image that sustained him daily. He had not seen her for several months. Indeed, for most of their marriage he had been away on deployments.

Kim-Cuong was Quoc's strength and sustenance throughout the terrible war. Today he would talk to her about the unthinkable: Escaping from the only home they had ever known. Quoc had no idea what he would say. He just knew that today he had to be with her.

2

THE MOIST EARTH OF
THE COUNTRYSIDE

"Don't listen to what the Communists say, but look at what they do."

Nguyen Van Thieu - 1923-2001
South Vietnam's Second President

JULY 1960

The black-haired, darkly tanned, 14-year-old boy ran across the dirt road toward the stream. He looked out at the dramatic difference from rice paddies to the higher vegetation near the river and the fields beyond. It was as if, when he crossed the stream, it was a different world altogether.

The waterway divided Long Kim from Long Dinh. Long Kim was where Bac Ba, one of Xuong's brothers, lived. Long Dinh was the village in which the boy's grandmother, another uncle, and cousins made their home.

But there was more to this idea of demarcation than just nature. There was a growing political divide of which Quoc was only vaguely aware that day in 1960. Before the day was over, he would have a better understanding of that division. He would come to know personally what the war was about.

The morning was clear, with a beautiful blue sky and a few puffy cumulus clouds. The air was hot and muggy in the fields, oppressively so. But once he came to the gentle slope near the river, a contrasting coolness soothed the body like a cool compress placed on the skin.

Quoc could not just smell the moist earth and the richness of the paddies. He breathed it in deeply and immersed himself in the moment. It was pungent and real. The field was not yet ready for harvest, but the rice was already high above the water of the paddy. It was July. The monsoon rains had come and flooded the water-filled paddies, the rich fields that fed a hungry country.

The bridge that crossed the river had been destroyed years before, and had not yet been repaired. Quoc didn't know why. A small boat had been substituted to serve as a ferry to carry passengers across the river, moving from Long Kim to the other side, about a hundred yards away. The boat held three to four passengers and was hand-propelled by a man standing and rhythmically rowing. His conical-shaped *non la*, or leaf hat, shielded his head and face from the sun.

There was no active war in the country at the time. Only the silent one. The collapsed bridge foreshadowed what would happen to Quoc and to the country. North and South Vietnam had maintained a cautious peace after the 1954 Geneva Accords, which partitioned North and South Vietnam into two entities, but that was soon to be challenged.

Quoc was 14, but looked much older than his years. While shorter than many of the other boys, he was more muscular and faster than most. He could run for an hour without stopping and never lost his breath. His brother Sinh, 16, accompanied him that day.

Being a child of the city, Quoc had always been fascinated by the countryside. His father would periodically load up their American-made Chevrolet and drive the 20 miles from Saigon along unpaved and neglected roads, passing countless rice fields and a few small clusters of homes. Sometimes it would take two hours to get there from the city.

The rice paddies almost always held small cemeteries, where long-dead relatives stood watch over their progeny from brightly colored ceramic containers housed by pagoda-like structures. Ancestor worship was a cornerstone of Vietnamese culture.

That day had an almost magical quality for Quoc, especially since there was so much to be gained from the adventure. The smell of the countryside, for instance, was more than an olfactory sense. It was almost a spiritual one. The pungency wrapped itself around his head and embraced his consciousness in a way that was so much more powerful than the workaday scents of cooking fires and vehicular traffic in Saigon.

Quoc was not analyzing that day. He was just joyously running with his brother to see his paternal grandmother, Muon, his uncle, and his cousins.

A trip from Saigon to visit family had been rare in recent years. The silent war had printed itself indelibly on the countryside and the hearts of men. The brewing conflict had created invisible barriers that separated families, friends, and countrymen. Allegiances were difficult to discern. Countryside or city? Anti-Communist or pro-Communist? Nationalist or Communist? South Vietnam was filled with uncertainties and mixed loyalties. A relative might maintain an anti-Communist position in Saigon while their loyalties were staunchly with the North. One never knew for sure.

Quoc had been born in Long Dinh, about 25 miles southwest of Saigon. Quoc's father and mother had relocated the family to Saigon. His father's brother remained behind in Long Dinh with their mother, who turned 75 that year.

The tug of family and the warm embrace of their grandmother, who catered to Quoc with specially cooked meals and unconditional love, beckoned. Quoc and Sinh decided to make the long trip, first crossing the river and then walking the six miles to Long Dinh. At their age the boys considered themselves to be both grown up and invincible. Xuong and Vo stayed behind, trusting in the judgment of their sons.

As the boys jumped out of the ferry on the far side of the river, they waded a distance in the shallow water. The muddy bottom squished between Quoc's toes and made him smile. As he walked, he looked down into the water but couldn't see more than a few inches below the surface. The mud and vegetation were stirred up. Seeing into that murky water was as difficult as trying to glimpse into the future.

They waded out of the river and encountered the paddies on the other side. Quoc and Sinh walked along the manmade earthen works between the fields, recognizing the route to their grand-mother's home. The village was just six miles from the river crossing. They knew they would be there in just over an hour.

As they walked along the embankment, they ran into two older boys. They all stopped and quietly surveyed each other. Each sized up the other. Clearly the boys Quoc and Sinh encountered were questioning their motives.

"What are you doing here?" one said, in a tone that carried both warning and concern.

"You're from Saigon, aren't you? Don't you know how dangerous it is here?"

Quoc answered, "Friend, we're just here to visit our grandmother and cousins, that's all. We mean no harm."

"Brother," one stranger lectured in a firm tone, "This is *not* a place for you today, believe me."

They hesitated for just a second, but being boys, they paid little attention to the admonition. Quoc and Sinh dismissed the other boys in a quiet way that was only half-heartedly respectful. They moved on, anticipating the long-awaited reunion with family in Long Dinh.

Shortly, Quoc and Sinh heard the distant sound of drums. They could almost feel the beat resonating in their chests before they could hear it in their ears. The sound grew in volume as they drew closer and the intensity of the drumming increased. The drums seemed to be announcing something, but the boys did not know what it was or whether it was a normal occurrence.

The sounds quickly blended with something else. It was acrid, billowing smoke that they could see in the sky. Their noses caught its smell. Their eyes followed its trail to the ground. The gray plume led to their grandmother's village, which was a small cluster of about 10 simple wood structures with leafed-roofs.

Even before they arrived, they heard shouting and saw people running from the village. They didn't understand what was happening, but clearly there was a developing emergency.

They did not know it then, but countless American and South Vietnamese Army and Marine Patrols would witness such scenes over the next 15 years.

The events that day were a continuation of the conflict that had started after World War II, when the French attempted to reestablish their colonial empire in Indochina. They came face-to-face with the desires by the Vietnamese people to become independent. That the struggles of the people of Indochina would be conflated with the Cold War and its own battles between Communist and Capitalist ideologies was as yet unknown to Quoc and his brother.

The boys slowed to a walk as they entered the village. They were nearly frozen into indecision, torn in their feelings, wondering whether they should run away or press on to their grandmother.

There was an obvious disruption in everyday life in the village. Perhaps their family could help them make sense of it.

It didn't take long for them to find their grandmother. She ran up to them and embraced them, with fear in her eyes. "You must leave quickly. It is not safe," she said tearfully. "The Viet Cong have just torched the house of our village chief."

Quoc could see that his grandmother was afraid and upset, but he did not immediately understand her meaning.

"But why, Grandma?"

She spoke in a quiet but firm voice, "Because they say he is a criminal who is working against the Communists. Now go. Run! It is not safe here!" Muon was weeping.

"But what will happen to you, Grandma?"

She just stared at them and didn't answer.

Torn between familial love and a warning from the matriarch of their family, Quoc and Sinh hesitated a moment. Then, at their grandmother's urging, they began a headlong run six miles back to the river. It took them less than an hour. They were still out of breath as they crossed the river on the small ferry.

The two brothers never spoke during their flight on foot or on the ferry ride. Only after the crossing, did they begin to breathe more easily as they began to understand the enormity of what had just occurred. They felt barred from their family, for no other reason than a political conflict that now was evolving into a military one.

Muon left that night, leaving her home in Long Dinh to live with Quoc's Uncle, Bac Ba, in Long Kim. She remained there the rest of her life. Her village was never rebuilt.

From that day on until well after the fall of South Vietnam the small stream they crossed that day would become the barrier to a No Man's Land for Quoc and his family and for many of those in the South. The war they had only known about vaguely was now real. It had been brought home.

The Communists and their leader, Ho Chi Minh, were committed to a reunification strategy that would bring Communism to the South. And, from Quoc's viewpoint, they would use any means to that end, including violence.

3

FATEFUL DECISION

"Your family is the only thing that matters."

Henry Ku
Quoted in *Boat People*

APRIL 22, 1975

The taxi ride took but 10 minutes. Quoc continued staring out the window, observing the busy traffic and the daily activities of the people in Saigon. He saw hundreds of people on the sidewalks, preparing food and selling their wares. He breathed in the smoke arising from cooking fires that hung over the street in small clouds before dispersing into the haze above. As he watched, he thought, "They are all going about their business as if they don't know that the country is in peril!" He pondered, "But is it? At least a dozen times in the past decade, there have been challenges to the stability and military strength of our country. Isn't this just another episode that South Vietnam will weather?"

Quoc likened the current military state to a passing shower during the rainy season. Monstrous clouds would cover the sky, drenching the earth with heavy monsoon rains. Then the clouds would suddenly part. The skies would once again open up to the sun. So it might be with his homeland, he hoped. Quoc had known no other way in his life, and he could not imagine something different. Nevertheless, his thoughts took a darker turn, "Maybe there is another future. Maybe it will be different and unimaginable, with North Vietnamese troops occupying the South, ushering in," he wondered, "What?"

At the unthinkable, his private thoughts came to an abrupt stop. Just for a second. That future seemed like a dark tunnel into which he couldn't see and, even if he could, wouldn't wish to travel. His conscious mind challenged his unconscious. "I can predict a future," he thought. Perhaps a prediction might serve as a hope. His own retort, "But I might not like that future." With that came a sick feeling in his gut. A wrestling match between his thoughts and feelings continued throughout the taxi ride, producing both uncertainty and unease as he stepped out of the cab. It was just 5:00 p.m.

Throughout Quoc's life he had lived with a fatalism that most young people in countries at peace can never know. At gatherings of his friends, there was always a sense that this would be the last time that they would see each other. Whenever one of them got a haircut, the first thing that Navy friends would say was, "So, are you getting ready for your funeral, or what?"

Grim humor was the only way to treat life in Vietnam. With it came the skill of denying reality. Too many deaths had occurred; too many tragedies for their families and friends. So it had been with his sister's death. He kept seeing Nga's face as a child and could not accept that he would never see her again in this life. Yet he could not afford the time for grieving, especially the protracted stages of grief. There was simply too much going on in the country and in his own life. Tears for Nga would come later. Most would come well after the war.

The driver stopped and nodded his head towards the meter.

Quoc paid the 10,000 *dong* it displayed. No words were exchanged. None needed to be. The fare was almost exactly half of Quoc's monthly salary.

His parent's home was steps away from the curb. Before he had even reached the entranceway, Kim-Cuong came running and wrapped him in an embrace. Her eyes were filled with tears of joy as she kissed him. But there was something else. There was fear. Her words came spilling out.

"Why have you come home? Do you know what is happening? What will we do?"

Relieved that he was in her arms, she nonetheless recognized that his appearance back at their home was an indication of something far more dire.

Quoc's mother and father quickly came rushing out the entranceway of the small home. More embraces were exchanged and a flurry of questions came, all before Quoc was able to say a single word. Amid the cacophony, all he could comprehend was, "Why are you here?"

Quoc examined those who knew him the best in the world. Their eyes were etched with concern. His mother and wife had been crying. He figured his father had been trying to calm them. Quoc recognized that this was not the time to put a good face on a difficult situation.

Now was the time for unvarnished truth: "I've come to handle some important business. My commander sent me home to take care of his family and mine. We just don't know what is going to happen, but we want to make sure you are all safe."

Quoc said the words quietly, with a strength and certainty that surprised everyone. He needed to be a leader right now – both for the Navy and for his family. He did not yet mention an escape for either himself or his family.

Kim-Cuong had always loved Quoc for his strength. He gave

it freely as a gift to her. Quoc had also come to recognize that this woman he loved had strength of character equal to his own, perhaps even greater. Today and the days that followed would test that strength in each of them.

Although Quoc and his family were not religious and didn't actually practice either Buddhism or Christianity, there was a spiritual side to him that made him recognize that faith was needed at this time. His father had often said, "Religion is something in your heart, not in a church or a temple." The faith in Quoc's heart strengthened him.

That evening, Quoc's parents, his wife, her parents, and two of his brothers, along with Quoc's two children, Hung and Ngan, gathered around him. They all shared a simple dinner of fried eggs and canned sardines. There had been no time to prepare special foods for him. Nor would it have been easy to find the foodstuff to prepare a meal. The markets were being quickly stripped of supplies with the continued news of military defeats to the north.

The conversation that evening was earnest and far-reaching, as they each struggled with uncertainties and the possible inevitabilities about their country and their own futures. Throughout the long night, family plans were made and changed. Opinions were shared, and concerns were expressed. Everything was too often settled, yet nothing was ever firmly decided. It was as if the family was a microcosm of South Vietnam, with its uncertainties and attendant pain and tears. Quoc's family reflected what was happening in the rest of the country.

During the evening their conversations were interrupted by distressing news reported by BBC, the only source of news that they trusted. After the American ground forces had pulled out, most South Vietnamese had stopped listening to Voice of America. BBC provided a ready news source and update on current events. The state-controlled television station only broadcast one to two hours each night and never seemed to have the level of detail of BBC news.

The BBC broadcasts continued to report that cities north of Saigon were falling, and the Communist NVA Army was advancing towards the capital. How fast it was advancing was unknown.

Clearly, Quoc was a focus of the conversation that evening, because any move he made would profoundly affect those around him. Based on his decisions, other actions would necessarily follow.

Xuong, as well as being a maritime chief engineer, was currently on leave from his service on a cargo ship. Xuong also had a history with the Communists. Following World War II, when he was young, he had initially joined the Viet Minh to fight against the French. His goal was to be part of a Nationalist effort to end French Colonialism. Quoc's father, however, had come to realize that by joining the Viet Minh he would be joining a Communist army. While Xuong had favored independence, he opposed the idea of Communists ruling the country. He distrusted Ho Chi Minh and his political supporters and favored a democratic solution instead. Xuong quickly lost favor with the Viet Minh and was sent to jail from 1945 to 1946. When he was released, Xuong fled with his family to the South and, when Quoc was two years old, to Saigon. There they made a new life in the shadow of war.

Most in the West did not realize that the Vichy French had essentially administered the country throughout World War II, following the directives given by the occupying Japanese. After the war, DeGaulle's government attempted to reestablish hegemony over the region, in a move that was opposite that of virtually all the other prewar colonial powers. However, the people of what was then called Indochina opposed the idea of continued colonialism by the new French government. Even then, there were distinct differences of opinion in how a free Indochina would be created.

At that time, Communism was sprouting up in countries and

regions throughout the world. Indochina was no different. A significant portion of the population, like Xuong, had favored Democracy. After the French defeat at Dien Bien Phu in 1954, the Geneva Accords had divided the country north of Hue. In the year or so afterwards, nearly a million fled south and the stage was set for a conflict that would last two decades when it began again in 1959.

Now 21 years later, the family faced many of the same dilemmas that Xuong had confronted in 1954. Only this time escape was not to a neighboring region or country. It would have to be to another part of the world.

It was clear that Xuong distrusted the Communists, so his advice to his son was explicit. But there were others in the family whose lives had given them different experiences and, as a result, different perspectives.

Kim-Cuong's uncle, Ut Duc, had served as a soldier in the South Vietnamese army. That night Quoc learned from Kim-Cuong that Duc had been a Communist spy throughout the war. Quoc was not wholly surprised. It was common for families to sit at the same table, divided in their loyalties, with supporters of the regime in the North and in the South. It was not as common for families to sit with a spy among them like his wife's uncle.

Quoc listened intently as his wife explained a conversation she had that day with her father's brother. "Uncle Ut says that you have two choices. You can come over to the Communists or you can leave."

Quoc laughed, drawing a long look from his wife, and a look of support from his father.

Quoc's loyalties were clear in his mind, family first, followed closely by country. He would never turn his back on those around him and he had sworn to defend the nation of South Vietnam. Quoc and his family knew that such loyalty came with a price. As a Navy officer, the Communists would target Quoc if the country fell. What that meant he did not know. Everyone speculated, but no one had any real idea what the penalty might be for those military personnel remaining in a failed South Vietnam.

Kim-Cuong understood that Quoc could not philosophically embrace the Communists. Her own father, Hung Duong stated, "No, Quoc, surrendering to the Communists is not for you."

The others quickly joined the chorus advising against collaboration with the Communists, even if they marched into Saigon. "It is a matter of honor."

Each intoned that word in a way that sounded almost sacred. For the Vietnamese people, there was no greater personal attribute.

The situation demanded action based upon uncertain facts. Moreover, it required an acceptance of a cruel reality that, emotionally, the family wanted to reject. This uncertainty and emotional pain felt by Quoc and his family was doubtless felt by thousands of households throughout the country.

At one point, they all began to consider the idea of the entire extended Pham family escaping South Vietnam. Xuong and Vo, it emerged, had already spent a considerable amount of time contemplating this option. Xuong still held the high-ranking position on a commercial vessel. It had plenty of room, and it was berthed a few miles away on the Saigon River. Given his stature and his financial ability to pay bribes and certain fees, he would be able to take the 20-plus people in the extended family out of the country, likely to the ship's homeport in Singapore. Xuong explained, though, that there was a serious problem with such a plan, which made it impossible for him to consider. He said he would not leave the country while any one of his children was in captivity. Sinh and Hoang were currently held captive in the North. To leave the country without them, Xuong felt, would be to sign their death sentences. Though many in the family secretly wished they could all escape with Xuong, they remained quiet and acquiesced to his decision.

Quoc's personal options began to take focus later in the evening. Two distinct courses emerged: personal escape, probably with a few family members, or remain in South Vietnam with his family, suffering whatever the consequences that may come.

To leave? With whom? And how would he escape? Quoc had no clear direction, no compass pointing towards the North Star. He contemplated possibilities. As he listened to his family, his thoughts drifted. "A South Vietnamese naval ship could carry my son, Hung, and me to freedom. I could head back to Phu Quoc, where we could escape by sea."

Alternatively, he thought, "A land escape would be more tenuous. There is a war within Cambodia that's beginning to rage. There's no certainty of safe passage and there is a likelihood of some sort of detention if I enter that country."

Quoc's only certainty was that escape could only include himself and possibly Hung. Kim-Cuong could not travel with their infant daughter Ngan, and she was not yet prepared to leave her extended family. Kim-Cuong contemplated escape as a way to protect her husband from retribution in the event the country fell.

Quoc thought of another option, "Just stay in the country and remain with my family."

What that meant was uncertain, but it would mean that Quoc, his wife and children, and their extended families would remain in the country together. His parents had instilled in him the importance of family. It was core to his being. To stay with his family may mean possible retribution, but to leave without all of them was fraught with personal hardship and challenges.

Quoc tried to think positively. If he remained in Vietnam, his skills as a naval officer and knowledge of seamanship and navigation might well be in demand. That might override any reprisals that might occur against South Vietnamese officers. No one knew.

His thoughts raced again, "They might want me to serve in their navy or merchant marine. They'll need good men. They could decide to punish anyone who took up arms against them. But that wouldn't make sense. How do you rebuild a nation if you spend your time on reprisals and retribution?"

Quoc faced a dilemma he had never contemplated. His emotions wrestled with his logic to discover the best outcome. It was gut-wrenching.

The family discussion and debate continued well past midnight. In time, each member of the family was overcome by fatigue and succumbed to fitful sleep anywhere in the house they could find a place to stretch out. Finally, only Quoc and Kim-Cuong struggled with the decision they had to make, hugging their sleeping children as if this were their last day together. The couple ran the many options over and over in conversation and, in times of quiet reflection, in their own minds.

"Sweetheart, I cannot leave you and Ngan."

"But Quoc, if you stay, the Communists will punish you."

"They would be stupid to do it."

"Quoc, take Hung with you. Get to America or Australia or wherever you can. I'll be safe here with my family until you can send for me."

"I can't live without you."

"And, if you stay, you might not be with me anyway. They could send you to jail. You might not survive."

The discussion wasn't wholly based on logic. They cried out to each other throughout the evening, with tears and occasionally heated words. Kim-Cuong was being torn apart. She desperately wanted to save the man she loved from any possible harm. And she also wanted him to continue to live his life with honor. Leaving would be dishonorable but safe. Staying would be honorable but filled with peril. Intuitively, however, Kim-Cuong felt that Quoc must escape.

They concluded that honor was not as important as survival, and perhaps leaving was as courageous as staying.

As the glow of dawn began to emerge on the morning of April 23, a plan emerged. In the pre-dawn of morning in the country that was still South Vietnam, as a few roosters crowed and the family groggily awoke, Quoc Pham and Kim-Cuong came to a conclusion. Quoc would escape the country. Husband and wife would each take a child, Quoc with Hung – he needed less care and could now travel – and Kim-Cuong with Ngan – who was still nursing and needed her mother's care. They would separate to provide the best possible chance of safety for each child. It would be a separation designed for survival.

Although he didn't know where he and Hung would go, Quoc and Kim-Cuong felt confident she and Ngan would be safe with family until Quoc could get them out of the country.

Quoc and Kim-Cuong looked at each other. Kim-Cuong began to cry. Tears welled in Quoc's eyes. They held each other for more than an hour as the enormity of their decision engulfed them.

That morning, occasional explosions sounded in the distance. They came from mortars and heavy artillery, fired from both sides. They struck both military and civilian targets, often in neighborhoods filled with innocent citizens. But to the Communists, no one was innocent in Saigon. They did not know it yet, but the citizens were all considered war criminals, and, most especially, those who wore the uniform of South Vietnam.

4

THE LAST DAYS OF SOUTH VIETNAM

"I hesitate to recall once light-hearted and beautiful Saigon back in those gloomy days of late April, 1975, the days when the South was reddened by both the blood of its defenders and the descending vengeance of the Communist invaders."

Tran Van Phuc
Reeducation in Postwar Vietnam

APRIL 23, 1975

The family stirred shortly after dawn. The night for each had been equally fitful, with an uncertain future lying restlessly upon them. Sleepy faces and yawns emerged into the small living area as strong Vietnamese coffee was shared. They squatted close together, touching each other, holding each other's elbow or arm, as was their custom. Xuong was the first to ask. "What did you decide?"

Husband and wife glanced at each other. Their eyes betrayed the decision. The questions followed suit.

"Where will you go? What will you do? When?"

"If the Communists keep advancing south, it has to be soon."

"But what if they are stopped?"

"We hope they are. Then we can all stay."

No one in the family could shake the pain and fear they felt. The years had been difficult for each of them, as war had raged between their country and the North, but this was a new sort of pain. Before, there had been a sense of country and family unity and purpose, now there were the beginnings of dissolution of each of these, sending the adults into a state of despair.

Although Quoc felt the raw emotions of the night, he still had a job to do. Ever the military officer, he washed and shaved, putting on the blue uniform that his mother had neatly pressed the night before. He was still a naval officer with a mission to accomplish. He sat quietly, sipping only coffee for breakfast. He expressed words of comfort to his wife, to his mother, father, siblings, and children, "We are strong and we will make it through this, I can guarantee you."

His gut was torn as he spoke the words, knowing in truth he could actually provide no guarantees. He could only provide the same hope he had learned from his father and mother who escaped from the North so many years ago. It had sustained him, and it would sustain all of them as they moved into the days ahead. At that point, hope was as much a religion for him as was his faith.

Quoc kissed Kim-Cuong and turned soundlessly towards the entranceway. He and his brother, Loc, embarked upon what would be a daily ritual. On Quoc's motorbike, they headed toward the Navy base, located on the east side of the Saigon River near the center of the city. Ships were tied up all along the river at docks built by the Americans during the war. The traffic was as heavy as normal. The three-mile drive took 30 minutes.

Activity at the base seemed relatively normal, but an obvious tension filled the air. When Quoc entered the headquarters building, there was only a skeleton crew on duty, with only one duty officer, an ensign. Quoc reported his mission and, to his surprise, in short order obtained passes for LT Duc's wife and their three children to enter the base. They would be allowed at the rendezvous point for evacuation, if and when it was needed. Quoc also received approval for himself and Hung to enter the base or proceed back to Phu Quoc.

As the two men left the base they began to sense a city living under an unspoken threat. The populace was attempting to go about its daily business, yet everyone wondered what the future would deliver. Reports about the Communist advance continued. There were ever-present rumors of an imminent departure of all remaining U.S. Embassy personnel. Unrest simmered beneath the surface.

APRIL 25, 1975

On the morning of April 25, Quoc headed to LT Duc's home, again on the motorbike with Loc. Duc's wife was the same age as Kim-Cuong. To all appearances, she displayed a silent strength and dedication to her husband, but beneath that veneer, Quoc saw the same concern and fear he had seen in Kim-Cuong.

While Quoc had never met her before, the Navy uniform and the letter signed by Duc established a level of trust between them. Quoc carefully relayed the instructions to her. She and her children could escape via sea on a South Vietnamese naval vessel if the country's fall was imminent. The timing was up to her. Quoc handed her the passes to the base and gave her the name of a contact at the naval headquarters from whom she could receive further instructions.

It took several hours to answer her questions and to ensure that she knew the plan her husband had made. Quoc left her home confident that he had accomplished his mission, though by no means certain whether she would leave. That was her decision. Quoc and his family had made their own.

After his visit with Duc's wife, though, some unnamed uncertainty began to simmer in Quoc's heart.

That afternoon, Quoc headed home to find Kim-Cuong and the children still at his parents' house. It was apparent that there had been a number of visitors to the home. The air was filled with nervous anticipation, occasionally interrupted by a newscast from BBC. The broadcasters continued to paint a picture of an inexorable march southward by the North Vietnamese Army. Occasionally, governmental figures could be heard on the news broadcast.

On April 21, the day before Quoc departed Phu Quoc, President Nguyen Van Thieu had spoken on the airwaves in the early afternoon. He made the briefest of announcements. He simply said he was stepping down from the presidency. His successor would be Tran Van Huong. Huong was known for his fervent anti-Communist political views and was also seen by the Vietnamese people as a sort of kinder and gentler statesman than Thieu.

Thieu had been a former general in the South Vietnamese army. He had led a military junta in 1965 to take control of the country. He was elected president in 1967 and then, in what many thought to be a rigged election, was re-elected in 1971. He had been president for most of Quoc's adult life.

The Vietnamese people were ambivalent about Thieu. There were those in the military establishment who regarded him as a puppet of the U.S. Government. As a leader, Thieu also had a reputation for timidity. Despite a decade of military buildup by the Americans – with a million-man armed force and one of the most powerful navies and air forces in Asia – Thieu often appeared unwilling to commit himself. The Vietnamese had a saying about Thieu, "He only jumped when the tide rose up to his toes," meaning he only took action when he was forced to do so.

Thieu's replacement, Huong, would last just seven days in the role of president. In the days following the Thieu resignation, everyone came to realize the very real threat to the country. But Quoc also knew that some of the best units of the South Vietnamese Army were still on guard in the capital, including the elite Paratrooper Brigade that had been one of the most effective fighting units in the war.

As he had previously, Quoc quietly contemplated the politics of the day, with announcements like Thieu's, juxtaposing them with his own strong belief in the power of the military and the determination of the people in the South. Oddly, his mind turned to an American television series called the "The Twilight Zone," where reality met unreality and where what one saw or felt might not necessarily be true.

The next few days became a blur for Quoc and his family, with a continuous stream of neighbors and military colleagues stopping by to discuss their options.

"Are you staying?"

"What are *you* doing?"

"I haven't made up my mind."

"The Communists will have to stop short of Saigon. They'll partition the country."

"Not likely, brother."

Quoc could not find solace in sleep. When he did lose consciousness to dreams, it always came at the point of exhaustion. He continually woke up in a cold sweat, weighing the decision he and Kim-Cuong had made. There was something not right about the decision, but he hesitated to revisit it by telling Kim-Cuong his own misgivings. She had struggled enough that first night. Why reopen the wounds by bringing his uncertainties to the forefront once again?

Each morning, Quoc put on his uniform and headed with Loc via motorbike to naval headquarters. It became a ritual, a touchstone to normalcy. The official conversation was always short, lasting less than 15 minutes. The real exchanges took place outside of headquarters, where Quoc would encounter officers with whom he had served for years. During those conversations he learned that the fleet was fueled and ready to steam down the river in a matter of hours, all contingent on what occurred during the Communist advance.

Berths for Quoc and Hung would be available if they chose not to head back to Phu Quoc. But, his friends warned him, he needed to be at the port when the ships set sail.

When he spoke with his friends, Quoc's rational mind affirmed his decision to leave. But the feeling was always transitory. As he drove away, his doubts would return and the thoughts that bathed him in a cold sweat each night came to mind. He was emotionally torn.

Quoc saw a continual exodus of Americans from the city. Officially, there were no more combat forces, but a number of administrative personnel – both military and civilian – remained. That number continued to decline as a stream of aircraft lifted off hourly from Ton San Nhut. This was combined with the steady sound of convoys of helicopters heading to American ships offshore.

The Americans downplayed the exodus as a part of a normal pull-down of forces. But the Vietnamese saw it differently. The South Vietnamese felt that their allies in the American government had abandoned them and were doing their best to evacuate U.S. personnel as fast as possible.

Alternate histories would be debated forever. One common theme was the role of Watergate in neutering President Richard Nixon's power and eventually leading to his resignation and resulting in the removal of a lifeline that could have provided bombing support and military power to stop a Communist advance.

April 26, 1975

Kim-Cuong was ready to leave Quoc and his parents' home with Ngan on April 26 to rejoin her own parents. There were no phones in either home, so to bid farewell was tantamount to Quoc and Kim-Cuong saying goodbye. As they embraced, Kim-Cuong held Quoc for a long minute and then looked up into his eyes, "Take good care of Hung."

It was as much of a command as it was a request. A woman in any culture is protective of her children, especially when she thinks they may be in harm's way. With the uncertainty hanging over Vietnam, Kim-Cuong's feelings of protection were amplified for her husband and most especially for her children. Quoc heard her words and tone with equanimity and an appreciation of the direness of the situation. He chose not to question the challenge. He accepted it for what it was, an expression of love. He answered, "I will sweetheart. We will all be together soon."

It was painful as Kim-Cuong packed her small bag and collected the baby's things. He watched her being pedaled away in a "cyclo," a tricycle cab commonly used for short trips around town.

As Kim-Cuong left, she believed Quoc and Hung would fly back to Phu Quoc via military transport on the 28th and then head to sea via ship. Quoc would make his way to the United States or any other friendly country and then send for Kim-Cuong and Ngan as soon as he could. Kim-Cuong's ties to her Communist Uncle Ut Duc would help guarantee her safety and her daughter's. At least that is what she and Quoc hoped.

But as he stood in his parents' doorway, bade farewell, and saw them being pedaled into the distance, uneasiness once again overcame Quoc. It was a new feeling for him, one that he could not name. It was real and it hurt and it hung over him throughout every waking hour. His restless sleep offered no respite. There was no Kim-Cuong to comfort him and to strengthen his resolve. Her absence created a hole in his heart.

The crux of his emotions rested on the fact that, while a plan was in place, Quoc clearly could not imagine leaving Kim-Cuong and

Ngan as well as his extended family. Just as Xuong and Vo could not leave while two children were in captivity, he could not imagine being away from Kim-Cuong.

To him, an escape with just Hung was a very real abandonment of the one true foundation of his life, his family.

Quoc knew Kim-Cuong was right about escaping. Her strength had helped him make the decision to leave. But now that she was returning home to her parents' home, his doubts strengthened. Absent Kim-Cuong's support, his resolve weakened.

An alternative decision was emerging. One that would change his world in ways he could not yet imagine.

APRIL 27, 1975

The morning ritual continued with the trip to the Saigon navy yard and the ride around the city.

Walking in and out of headquarters each day brought the same chance meetings, hallway exchanges and commiseration in which he had engaged all week. The common refrain, "What are you planning to do? I've got room on my ship if you and your family need to sail with us."

Quoc took comfort in the fact that his family extended beyond those of his blood relations. The South Vietnamese Navy was a family in its own right, providing stability and assurance to Quoc at a time when he badly needed it.

The time with Loc gave Quoc perspective and opportunity to spell out his insecurities and concerns about the plan. Vietnamese men don't ask each other direct questions. Nor do they face each other directly and look into the other's eyes. However, the tangential looks, comments, and floated ideas between the two brothers were illuminating.

"What do you think, Loc?"

"We'll be okay,"

"But what exactly does okay mean to you, brother?"

"You know, Quoc, we're a strong family. We'll figure it out."

Loc's reply was meant to provide reassurance, but it failed to achieve that end. Loc's expression spoke more than his words. He showed stress and concern, and his brow remained furrowed whenever they talked. Quoc knew that his own departure would only intensify those feelings for his brother and the rest of the family.

He looked long and hard at Loc as they spoke. He saw what everyone regarded as the most handsome man in the family. His friends always called Loc the lady-killer. Loc had always been the charmer and the man with a joke at just the right time. At that moment, though, he was as serious as he had ever been.

APRIL 28, 1975

When he woke up, an idea crystallized in Quoc's mind. Despite all the uncertainties, his heart was with Kim-Cuong, his children, and a family that had nurtured him throughout the war. Quoc turned a corner, realizing he would not depart with Hung that day. He could not abandon the devotion of his mother and father or the caring of siblings and the abiding love of a wife. He knew Kim-Cuong would be angry; he prayed she would understand.

With that realization, Quoc's pain stopped, and he felt a certainty he had not known since the night of April 22. Come what may, Quoc was staying in his native country with the family he loved. It was a fateful decision the enormity of which he would only come to realize when he wore the clothes of an older man.

5

THE FALL OF A COUNTRY

"During the day on Monday, Washington time, the airport at Saigon came under persistent rocket as well as artillery fire and was effectively closed. The military situation in the area deteriorated rapidly. I therefore ordered the evacuation of all American personnel remaining in South Vietnam."

President Gerald Ford
April 29, 1975

APRIL 29, 1975

The morning dawned like any other day in South Vietnam, but something palpable was in the air. A tension enveloped Quoc and the rest of the inhabitants of the city.

That morning, a South Vietnamese Air Force pilot allied with the North permanently closed the door to air traffic as he bombed the runways at Tan Son Nhut. The country Quoc had known and loved was disintegrating.

Driving around the city that day, Loc and Quoc saw a continuing exodus of Americans. By the end of the day Quoc felt there were likely fewer than 500 U.S. personnel left in the country. That was

down from a high of some 540,000 military personnel and thousands more U.S. civilians. The detritus of their departure was evident: vehicles abandoned in parking lots, equipment unguarded, and
offices left open. The departure of the Americans angered Quoc and
the other residents of the city. A sworn ally was abandoning South
Vietnam. Most of the residents said that the Americans were selling
out to the Chinese.

That day Quoc noticed the beginning of a distinct lawlessness
in the city. Tensions were rising, with a populace that now feared
the worst but had paradoxically always hoped for the best. After all,
some said, crack Army battalions, including the paratroopers, still
guarded the city.

Early that day, the commercial radio stations began playing
Bing Crosby's song White Christmas, which was known by most
South Vietnamese military officials as a secretly coded signal to
all Americans that the official evacuation of Saigon was beginning.
What followed was not a quiet ending of the war, but a tidal wave
that engulfed the country within a day.

General Duong Van Minh had replaced President Thieu's successor, Tran Van Huong, on April 28. In his final speech, President
Huong had spoken of an impending defeat of South Vietnam and
begged whoever took power to spare the lives of all South Vietnamese
military personnel regardless of their rank or position. Huong was
highly respected and the speech was emotional to hear. Quoc's
family cried as they listened.

General Minh took power and held the reins of government
for fewer days than Huong. Minh took to the airwaves to reassure
the citizenry that there would be some sort of settlement to end the
war. Some called it magical thinking, as if the North's forces would
suddenly stop their advance and allow a solution not unlike the end
of the Korean War at the 38th parallel. His words stirred scant hope

and mostly cynicism as he said, "Let us sit together and negotiate and work out a solution."

Looting began that day. Civilians initially targeted buildings vacated by the Americans. Everything from television sets to refrigerators became fair game. Fear of a Communist takeover was overshadowed by the most fundamental avarice, with the departure of the Americans widely regarded as a windfall for many.

Chaos became real, in contrast to the durability and sophistication of South Vietnam's capital city. Quoc and his brother cruised the city in a daze. They stopped by naval headquarters and noticed that exhaust was rising from the smokestacks of all the naval vessels. The turbine power plants of those ships needed time to build up sufficient steam to power out of the Saigon River into the open sea. An experienced eye could tell that fewer lines held the ships to their stays and that normal minimal watch staffing had been replaced with a full complement of seagoing personnel. Supplies were being loaded. Quoc could see Navy family members and other civilians – wealthy civilians as evidenced by their attire – climbing the gangplanks.

The fleet was ready to sail.

At home that afternoon a continuous stream of neighbors stopped by his parents' home. A next-door neighbor told Xuong he was escaping. His family had come from North Vietnam in 1954, and he was certain the Communists would retaliate against him. He warned Quoc, "You will be in jeopardy if you stay." The words stung, juxtaposed as they were now with Quoc's decision to remain behind.

No one was able to sleep the night of the 29th. Not far away, artillery could be heard pounding parts of Saigon. The sounds of the big Communist guns boomed throughout the night. On the radio, reports said the Communists were within 10 miles of the city.

APRIL 30, 1975

Early on the morning of the 30th, Quoc and Loc took their last motorbike ride. They told their parents that their intent was to escape, but Quoc realized his parents knew he had decided to stay.

Their first stop was to naval headquarters on the Saigon River. The two men were met with a sight that drained their blood. The entire fleet of 30 ships was gone. The fleet of the South Vietnamese Navy had steamed out under cover of darkness and was at this time likely in the South China Sea – called the East Sea by the Vietnamese – out of range of enemy artillery and aircraft. Likely they were bound for the U.S. Naval Base at Subic Bay in the Philippines.

Quoc looked around. There were reminders everywhere that the base had been populated with hundreds of personnel. Personal cars and motorbikes were scattered in the parking lots. Debris strewed the area. The only activity was that of looters taking what they could carry, scurrying away when they saw the men in uniform.

Quoc and his brother heard gunshots coming from every quarter of the base, presumably from looters who had stolen weapons left behind in the headquarters.

The departure of the fleet had been Quoc's last avenue of escape. His fate now coincided with his decision. It was sealed.

There were just two small ships remaining at the port, obviously nonoperational. Quoc noticed some civilian ferries being loaded, making ready to depart. People were crowding onto them as quickly as they could.

In the sky, Quoc saw two airplanes engaged in a dogfight. It was surreal. He saw each aircraft turn and bank, struggling to fire on the other. One airplane was an American-manufactured Sky Raider, the other, a Russian aircraft. They twisted in the sky in what could have been an air show, had it not been for the deadly consequences of their aerial duel. In minutes, the Sky Raider plummeted to the ground in a sickening crash, amid smoke and fire.

The air above Saigon seemed to be filled with helicopters, predominantly Hueys, as well as Chinooks and CH-46s. Quoc could see the compartments loaded with people as the aircraft struggled for altitude. They were headed for the East Sea to deposit their human cargo onto American vessels.

As Quoc and his brother neared home, they saw a Huey designed to carry ten to twelve military personnel that appeared to have dozens of people on it. At the time, Quoc thought it seemed like a hundred. It was so clearly overloaded that there was no hope it could stay airborne. Women, children, and men were packed inside, some holding onto others as they hung from the sides. Still more clung to the helicopter's skids.

Looks of fear, of desperation, of absolute panic, were all that the brothers could see. And all they could remember years later was the sickeningly show motion deaths of dozens of people.

The pilot was attempting to transition from a low hover to translational lift, where the main rotor of the helicopter's blades effectively produce lift as a disc, emulating an aircraft's wing. But translational lift takes speed, and the only way speed could be gained that day was to descend. For a craft perilously close to the ground that was impossible: the laws of physics would not allow it. The pilot likely could never have achieved enough speed to lift the terribly overloaded craft.

Quoc and Loc watched the helicopter slowly swing first to one side, then the other, in an ever-increasing pendulum motion. Then it suddenly crashed into flames. Bodies, aircraft parts, and still-spinning rotors flung around and beyond the site. The crash hit just 100 yards from Quoc.

Abandoning the motorbike, Quoc and Loc ran for their lives back to their parents' home. Inside, the family was huddled around the radio; all holding each other, with forlorn looks in their eyes. On the radio, General Minh's voice was saying, "I hereby order all military forces of the Republic of Vietnam to surrender. Lay down your arms." Quoc looked at his brother and said just two words: "We're dead." Sobs followed, sucking the air out of the home, and the hope out of their hearts. They sat immobile, unable to speak.

After some moments, Vo was the first to move. She ran to where Quoc stored his uniforms and collected them all in her arms. She walked up to Quoc and Loc, puzzled looks on their faces. She commanded them, "Both of you, take your uniforms off. We're burning them."

Quoc and Loc dutifully complied. Vo and Xuong were soon in the street, with a can of gasoline. They soaked the uniforms and set them ablaze. A funeral pyre of military identity rose into the sky, with the acrid smell of burning cotton, with thick black smoke filling the air, their nostrils, and their hearts. Quoc, now wearing civilian clothes, watched as his mother's sensible act was replicated up and down the street. Piles of clothing were ablaze and weapons of all sorts – perhaps a hundred or more – were scattered in the street.

Quoc's mother intuitively knew that in the period between the South's defeat and the arrival of Communist forces, there would be no rule-of-law. She recognized that Communist sympathizers would be out for revenge. She scoffed at Minh's announcement. There was now no government and no power, she said, only people bent on looting, revenge, or both.

Some individuals in the street had criminal intent. Paradoxically, many were just giddy with victory. Throughout the area, Quoc and his family heard endless pistol and rifle shots, aimed into the air by people who clearly did not understand or care that gravity would bring the bullets back down. People flooded the streets and became engulfed in crowds, engaging in mayhem that ranged from firing the abandoned weapons to looting unoccupied houses or businesses.

Some celebrated, others were just curious. Most seemed to follow the crowd.

Quoc's family remained in the home, behind the locked door. They occasionally peeked through the blinds and observed the frenetic activity in their own neighborhood, imagining similar chaos in the rest of the city. A feeling of doom hung over the family.

Late that afternoon they heard a lone jeep driving down the street. It was an American M151A1 jeep, the mainstay of the U.S. Army throughout the war. Only this jeep was not occupied by soldiers, just a driver and a young woman in the black pajama-like uniform of the Viet Cong. She was standing on a seat, holding an AK-47 in her arms, aiming it at the sky and firing in every direction. She had an idyllic smile on her lips, and her hair streamed behind her as the jeep flew down the street. It could have been a propaganda poster. But it wasn't. It was the afternoon of April 30, 1975. The Communists had arrived at their doorstep.

6

WHY DIDN'T YOU ESCAPE?

"Life was not the same after 1975. Having taken over the country, the communists confiscated our belongings, forced us out of our homes and deprived all of us children of the chance to attend school."

Tran Dinh Thuc
Quoted in *Boat People*

MAY 1, 1975

Kim-Cuong stood there yelling at him.

"You are so stupid, Quoc. Why didn't you leave when you had a chance! Don't you know what will happen to you?"

"I did it for you. I did it for us. I did it for my family."

"How could you do this, Quoc? We had a plan. Now what do you think will happen?"

"But aren't you happy I'm here? Don't you love me?"

"I would be happier if you were safe, my love. Now I'm afraid for you."

Early that day, Kim-Cuong had pedaled up to the house with Ngan. Quoc knew it was his wife before the door opened; he could feel her presence. When she entered the house, she was shocked. Quoc was supposed to be on his way out of the country.

Quoc hugged Ngan and then tried to hug Kim-Cuong, to no avail. Ever respectful as a wife, she was nonetheless at once cold and angry. Her harsh words stung.

Quoc had created his own reality and written his own story during their days apart. He had come to believe – fervently so – that he had decided to remain in South Vietnam for Kim-Cuong's sake, for his children's sake, and for his extended family.

His words and thoughts rang hollow with Kim-Cuong. She pointed out what he knew to be the truth. He hadn't allowed himself to think about the future and Kim-Cuong was forcing that future on him now. He paused for a moment, then asked himself, "How could I have made such a decision?"

The night that South Vietnam fell was mostly silent, but sometimes alive with sporadic celebrations in the streets.

Still, there was turmoil in the hearts of the men, women, and children of the country. And now it was a former country. South Vietnam no longer existed as a political or military entity.

The defeat of any nation is usually greeted by the victors with relief that the shooting war is over. That is often followed with a realization that they are unprepared for the peace that follows. The precipitous fall of South Vietnam occurred rapidly as the political will of a nation collapsed and its American ally seemed to turn its back on the people of the country.

Nations and cultures are living creatures that do not cease to exist merely because they have lost a war. They must transition – either through order or varying degrees of chaos – to another existence and another reality. Few conquering military forces in history have been able to smooth that transition. Alexander the Great and most of the early Roman consuls and emperors accomplished it through a strategy of sustaining and nurturing the local culture, and embracing its political, religious, and organizational structure. Communist societies have not been so inclined.

Twentieth century wars varied in such transitions. At the end of World War I, the Western Allies failed mightily in the postwar world by imposing a harsh peace at Versailles. They also failed to assist the citizenry in basic survival as well as political, and economic organization. During World War II, Nazi Germany demonstrated great organizational and military strength, but their own brutality after conquest fostered underground movements, which helped ensure their eventual fall.

The Americans and their allies were able to win the war in 1945 but struggled with directing the peace. The Marshall Plan ultimately succeeded, but came three years after the war's end. And sadly, the failure of the Western Allies to successfully put an end to colonialism in Indochina facilitated the quixotic attempts by the French to reestablish their hegemony over what became North and South Vietnam. Their actions helped precipitate the rise of Ho Chi Minh and his Nationalist movement, under the Communist banner.

The fall of Dien Bien Phu in 1954, with strong Communist Chinese support, itself laid the foundation for the American entry into the war in less than a decade.

On April 30, 1975, North Vietnam was in the enviable position of having won a war and in the unenviable one of building a peace. The victims became the South Vietnamese people. It seemed as if the Communists were intent on imposing a Soviet-style economy and dismantling the economic framework of the country in the process. They also wanted to install strict authoritarian rule, but it became apparent that not all of the details had been considered. Nor had the leaders fully anticipated all of the consequences.

What Quoc, his family, and so many others in the South faced was genuine uncertainty at all levels. Sadly, they didn't know the harsh fate that awaited them. That was something the Communists did not tell anyone.

The reunion between Kim-Cuong and Quoc could not remain acrimonious. What Quoc had decided, Kim-Cuong would support. Dwelling on the decisions of the past served no purpose for a family that now had to focus on the future.

Quoc and Kim-Cuong quickly packed a few belongings and headed off on a cyclo to their apartment. As they were pedaled towards their home, they witnessed the results of the night of terror and furtively asked the driver to accelerate their pace. The scene at the apartment house, largely occupied by former South Vietnamese military officers, was much the same as at his parents' home. At the apartment house, they saw familiar faces and unfamiliar looks. Gone was the certainty of military might in the eyes of the officers. It had been replaced with an apprehension that bordered on fear.

In the apartment, Kim-Cuong attempted to put the house in order for an extended stay. They didn't dare to venture far. They didn't know how long they might be there. Though the apartment complex still housed mostly military and governmental personnel, they hoped their ranks and positions would remain unknown to the Communists.

That afternoon, Kim Cuong's uncle, Ut Duc – the man Quoc had learned was a spy for the North – paid a surprise visit to the apartment. After a few pleasantries were exchanged, he looked into Quoc's eyes and said, "You will be a prisoner. Don't expect to come home until you have grandchildren."

Quoc was bowled over by the sudden comment. "What do you mean by that, uncle?"

"Just what I said."

His uncle's words would remain in Quoc's conscious mind for years and in his subconscious forever.

At that moment, Quoc thought about Pol Pot in Cambodia, who, it was believed, was committing genocide on a countrywide level. He reputedly targeted anyone with an education. Indeed, Pol Pot and his followers presumed anyone who wore glasses to be educated. They were all targeted for elimination.

Briefly, Quoc thought the unthinkable: a bullet to his head might be the best option. He immediately dismissed that thought. He had to convince himself he would have a future of some kind in an independent nation.

Quoc had never considered incarceration. Now he was staring dumbfounded at Ut Duc, contemplating the concept with a mixture of curiosity, anger, and denial. "What am I being imprisoned for?"

"For your crimes against your country, Quoc. You were an officer fighting against Ho Chi Minh's principles and for that you must pay."

As Ut Duc spoke the word "principles," he made a sign with his fingers indicating quotation marks.

In his mind, Quoc was still trying to transition from an identity as a naval officer to being just a former officer of a country that had lost the war to its Communist neighbor. Nothing in his mind warranted the idea or the reality of becoming a prisoner. None of his contemporaries felt that way either. Each thought about past wars in history, from the American Civil War to World War I, where officers and men of the losing countries laid down their arms and began the awkward and painful process of rebuilding their communities and their lives, with the victors according them a certain level of dignity and respect. Quoc plaintively asked, "The war is over, Uncle. Why can't we just live our lives?"

"Quoc, it doesn't work that way. You know I like you as a person. But I'm afraid you will have to pay."

Kim-Cuong could only cry as she heard Quoc and her Uncle speak.

As he considered the words, Quoc recalled the tragic stories of

German prisoners interned by the Soviets at the end of World II. Just a handful of those prisoners returned. For the lucky ones, it still took years. Many never came home. So too, when China fell to the Communists. Officers from Chiang Kai-shek's army were thought to have remained prisoners for more than 25 years.

Quoc contemplated the words again. "Until you have grandchildren." Grandchildren? He and his wife only had young children now – just two children – and they were only 3 years old and a newborn. "Until you have grandchildren." Quoc sat and thought, "How long would that be? How could it be an accurate prediction?" To a 29-year-old, the years ahead to a time when he would see his children's children seemed forever. The words fostered a new sense of uncertainty in Quoc and his fellow officers.

Kim Cuong's uncle spoke with certainty, but not detail. He alluded to the Chinese Communists but could not give Quoc any specifics, simply because he had heard none. He had deep affection for Quoc, but he also had to represent the views of the Communist Party.

Ut Duc had positioned himself to benefit from the Communist leaders after the fall of the South. He was now a respected leader among the Communists. He carried clout and prestige in a new society he felt would form in the chaos ensuing the fall of South Vietnam. Despite his role in the party, Ut Duc was still family and as a result, respected. As an elder family member, his words carried significant meaning. Moreover, Ut Duc's chilling words were counterbalanced with what Quoc had begun to hear from the propaganda that spewed from loudspeakers in the streets. A short period of reeducation for former military personnel was going to be required.

7

ORDERS TO REPORT FOR REEDUCATION

"The reconciliation clock stopped in 1975," said Thai.
"Even 40 years later, I still search for real reconciliation."

Thomas Maresca
Special for USA TODAY
April 30, 2015

MAY OF 1975

The loudspeakers had appeared out of almost nowhere. Their sound was harsh, the message aimed directly at the people of the South who were now under Communist rule. To Quoc, the words spoke directly to him.

Suddenly, every block of Saigon and its many suburbs appeared to have sprouted speaker horns, flared at the ends and painted the muted green of the North Vietnamese forces. The waterproof speakers – some mounted on trucks – blared for hours at a time, sending a message designed to ensure order and set the stage for a transition to a Communist society. A speaker had been attached to a pole less than a hundred feet from Quoc Pham's apartment.

Ho Chi Minh had called the people who manned loudspeakers "Armed Propaganda Teams." They were military units, carrying minimal conventional weaponry, but powerful weapons of societal control. The units had been used extensively during the long war years, serving as an instrument of reeducation for liberated hamlets and other areas that had been taken over by the North. The South Vietnamese Army had even recognized their power and used the same concept.

The Communists used the loudspeakers in lieu of radio. While some might think such communication to be rudimentary and unsophisticated, the speakers served as a powerful tool of fear. They were also impervious to eavesdropping by the outside world. Although the BBC news continued to report on events in Vietnam as best as they could, the Communists strictly controlled the flow of information and only released what they wanted to the outside world. Compounding the problem, when discovered, personal radios were routinely confiscated.

The population became slaves to loudspeakers, controlled by the Communist Party leadership, who were all too adept at maintaining control and fostering the concept of reeducation. It was as if a huge tin can had been placed over the country, with the cacophony of the loudspeakers reverberating through the land. Only faint, muted echoes were able to reach the outside world.

Quoc, Kim-Cuong, and the two children remained in their apartment, as if they were under house arrest. For the first time since they settled there, they began to meet and know their neighbors. The first to introduce himself was Toan, a former Air Force officer who was five years older than Quoc. He was tall, with a look of quiet confidence and a bearing that commanded respect. Within a day of the family's return, Toan was speaking with Quoc like a brother. "Quoc, if the army comes after us, we need to figure out how to defend this place."

The men of the apartment complex quickly accepted Toan, with his wisdom and his courage, as their leader. He organized them into a platoon, assigning them fighting positions on the roof, with plans to use the weapons available to them. Toan also led the men through the mental exercises of resistance or, if necessary, compliance, whichever was necessary in dealing with the Communists.

Vong was another former Air Force officer. Tall, likable, and described as "100 percent South Vietnamese," by his friends, Vong got along with everyone. He was a man who knew how to nurture friendships and build deep bonds with others.

Quoc, Toan and Vong met regularly in each other's apartments to share any news and to strategize. They wanted to ensure that their families would look after each other during any absence they might experience, however long it might be. The family stockpiled some supplies of food and rationed it as best they could. But the small amount of money they had on hand was quickly devalued. As a result, bartering of valuables became a necessity, but met with limited success.

The Communists began sending food supplies and technology to the North, which slowly strangled the capitalist economy of the South. The North was in control and seemed intent on teaching the people of the South this harsh lesson by quickly converting the economy to Communism.

The family had limited ability to communicate with their neighbors. Soldiers stood guard outside of the entrances to the apartment complex. They regularly insulted Quoc and his fellow veterans, calling them traitors, and other more harsh and vulgar insults. Often, soldiers would enter Quoc's home, with rifles, prepared to shoot.

Local Communist militia was posted on each street. Anyone on a motorbike was stopped and the vehicle confiscated. The Communist soldiers were envious of the possessions that the South had garnered. They were happy to take those goods for themselves.

Quoc and Kim-Cuong had always thought of themselves as poor, but, compared to the NVA and Viet Cong soldiers, they must have appeared wealthy.

The family wanted to raise cash by bartering valuables, including their watches, bikes, and jewelry. The NVA viewed these as souvenirs of victory and paid a pittance for them. As a last resort, Kim-Cuong bartered for food with her wedding ring. She received barely enough money for one meal.

Lacking the competency to build infrastructure and administrative oversight, the Communists were ill prepared for the monumental task they were undertaking.

The transition of the country's financial system to one that incorporated Communist practices and principles was rapid and ruthless. An emotional and economic depression settled over the land.

The loudspeakers came on for two to three hours in the morning and messages were repeated in the afternoon. These messages began to specifically target those who had served in the Vietnamese military services. Within weeks of the fall, Quoc heard the loudspeaker announcements telling all former enlisted men to be prepared to attend three days of meetings. He also learned that high-ranking officers – which he presumed to be naval lieutenant commanders and army or air force majors and above – should gather food and supplies and be prepared to be away for a month. Quoc and so many others were considered junior officers. He was informed that his group should have enough supplies for a ten-day stay away from home.

Conversations among the men at the apartment complex were guarded:

"Ten days. Just ten days?"

"They must have something up their sleeves. They're going to trick us and then keep us in jail"

"But it would be stupid to send all the educated men away longer than ten days."

Quoc, his family and fellow veterans were suspicious, but they had no other choice than to stay hopeful that the Communists would be true to their word.

The departure of the enlisted men occurred in early May. As promised, thousands of men left and virtually all of them returned three days later. They came back seemingly unchanged, though Quoc heard a number of them say how they had been forced to admit their so-called crimes against the North. From what Quoc and his family observed, most of the men returned safe and apparently no worse for their experience. They appeared healthy and untouched.

A slight glimmer of hope arose in Quoc and Kim-Cuong as they watched these events unfold. Perhaps it would be relatively straightforward and over quickly for the junior officers. After all, the Communists had not lied about the enlisted men. The senior officers were only set to spend a month away.

As they held each other every night, Quoc would stare into Kim-Cuong's eyes engulfed in her love, seeking strength. Late one night, Kim-Cuong held Quoc more tightly than she ever had and told him something no one else yet knew. "Quoc," she whispered, "when you were home at the Navy training school in March, do you remember that we made love?"

"Yes, I do," he smiled back.

"Well, I'm pregnant, Quoc. We're having another child."

Quoc smiled, yet tears formed in his eyes as he spoke. He thought of another child and the uncertainty of the times they lived in. He thought of the camps. He looked at Kim-Cuong and hopefully asked, "Just how bad can the camp be?"

Kim-Cuong looked at him thoughtfully, her words carefully chosen, "It might not be bad, my love. But we never know."

8

THE REPORTING CENTER

"The notice to report for reeducation was from the Military Management Committee... It gave former high ranking government officials, like me and former middle to high ranking military officers thirty days ... to report ... I was eager to go for re-education to get it over with."

Minh Fullerton
Thank You America

END OF MAY 1975

Saying goodbye to Kim-Cuong and the children a second time was heartbreaking. Kim-Cuong attempted to be strong. She held Quoc tight, kissed him, and looked up in his eyes. "I know we will see each other again. And until we do, you will remain in my heart. Try your best. I will pray for you."

Quoc choked back a reply, "Thank you. I love you."

"And I love you. I know you must leave, but I can't let go of you."

"I don't want to leave, but I have to. You know that."

"I do."

They hugged again, moved slightly apart to look into each other's eyes and then squeezed each other tightly. Kim-Cuong looked up, choked back tears and could only get out one word, "Goodbye." Her eyes belied her uncertainty. The finality of the word goodbye sounded more like a requiem to Quoc. It chilled him as he walked down the street. He looked back, saw Kim-Cuong once more, then fumbled and struggled with the duffel bag, utilizing the straps that made it double as a backpack.

At the end of the month, Quoc had received word that junior officers should be prepared to turn themselves in, equipped with food, clothing, and supplies for a stay of ten days. Little else was said. The men quickly learned through their own internal channels that reporting centers had already been established. All junior officers like Quoc were to report to these centers during specified three-day windows.

Unknown to their future Communist captors, Vong, Toan, and Quoc made a commitment to stay together as a team. They arranged to report to a center at the same time and to strive to quietly remain in each other's group. Their friendship and unique bond would be tested long after they left their homes.

Quoc had carefully collected a small bag of clothing and equipment designed to keep him healthy and sheltered from the weather. He had been fortunate enough to obtain a U.S. Army poncho, which was durable and strong. He felt lucky to have been given a pair of U.S. sneakers – Nikes – that were durable and able to handle the heat, humidity, and rain. And he had a small hammock with netting for sleeping, a special gift from his mother-in-law.

Combined with a small knife, medicine, sewing kit, utensils, matches, and other camping gear, he was well prepared for a stay of up to 30 days. The only food he carried was some dried meat; he had been told that the Communists would supply rice. His friends were similarly equipped. All of these supplies fit into a U.S. duffel bag. The Vietnamese called the bag a "Submarine," due to its elongated cigar-shape. Quoc hid some money in his clothing and carried two cartons of French cigarettes, called Bastos, manufactured in Saigon.

JUNE 28, 1975

The week to enter the Reeducation Camp arrived, and Quoc, Toan, and Vong planned to report on day two, June 28, at around noon. The reporting center was a school about a mile from the home of his parents.

The three had taken cyclos to Quoc's parents' home that morning so he could bid farewell to them. Toan and Vong waited respectfully outside as Quoc met with his family. The parting with his parents was tearful, as neither Xuong nor Vo believed that the camp would last just ten days:

"Take good care, my boy."

"I'll do my best. It can't be that bad, can it?" Quoc attempted a weak smile.

"Of course not," said Xuong, looking away.

Both parents knew they were lying but gave the same answer nonetheless. Quoc looked at the two of them, tired and worn down, with circles under their eyes and a sadness he had never seen. He prayed that they would remain safe and healthy until he saw them again. As he looked at them the last time, though, he felt a premonition that he quickly cast aside.

Loc, ever steadfast in his love and support for Quoc, walked with him most of the way to the reporting center. Neither man spoke, but having Loc with him served as both support and shield for Quoc. Toan and Vong lead the way ahead of them toward an unknown future.

Loc bid farewell to his brother a block from the entrance. First, he provided a firm handshake, then a strong, brotherly hug. Loc admonished Quoc to take care of himself. Then Loc was gone.

The reporting center was a former high school – Chu Van An. The school was a tan-colored, five-story building designed for education, not housing. It sat adjacent to a large, triangular-shaped courtyard behind a high wrought-iron fence. Across the street was a Catholic church silently standing sentinel over a swelling crowd of former officers that joined Quoc and his two friends. They stood in line for hours. There was no formal check-in process and little in the way organization. It almost seemed casual to Quoc.

As they inched forward in line, the men eventually just elected to walk into the building. Guards motioned them to various classrooms. Perhaps 100 men crowded into each room. Quoc, Toan and Vong stayed together. The men estimated that nearly 2,000 officers were occupying the building by nightfall. While they knew they were captives, oddly, there were no guards in the rooms. The camp cadre was just posted in the hallways and at the building entrance.

As the three sat there, they heard a man in the crowd speak. "Be careful, boys. Don't buy anything these people say."

The words came from a man named Minh. They quickly learned he was a Marine. He had a hard edge to him and had obviously seen combat. He was three years younger than Quoc, but looked older. He seemed worthy of respect and trust. Quoc looked at Toan, whose eyes flickered the same conclusion. Minh was a man that other men naturally looked to for strength and support.

There was another man in the room, named Son. An army officer the same age as Quoc, he started a conversation with Quoc and the other two, offering perspective on their situation as well as support. He said, "We need to stick together to survive. They don't need to know that we know each other." Son had been an intelligence officer and was almost clairvoyant in his predictions of actions by their captors. His rich knowledge of history and the Communist regime helped provide both insight and perspective.

The five men conversed for hours, exchanging backgrounds and thoughts about the situation. They speculated about the camps endlessly. It might have been intuitive good luck or situational good fortune, but by evening, the initial threesome had morphed into a team of five that quietly swore allegiance to each other. Quoc knew he was fortunate to be with these men.

There were no adequate toilet facilities in the school. Sanitation quickly became an issue. While the men strove to maintain a healthy environment, the toilets soon backed up and the stench became overpowering.

The men huddled in their classrooms, barely able to stretch out. At around 5:00 p.m., a lone guard came in and demanded money from each individual, enough he said, for three days' worth of food. The price was 500 *dong* per meal.

Minh looked at Toan, who knew what he was thinking. Minh rolled his eyes and then, glancing towards Son, Vong, and Quoc, chuckled sardonically, "Here we go, men. Pay as you go!" The other men looked at him quizzically, but he seemed to know what he was talking about.

There were no mess facilities. Instead, the Communists ordered massive amounts of food from a Chinese restaurant close to the school.

Quoc and the others wondered at the strange juxtaposition of events. They were captives in their own country, about to eat take-out food from a local restaurant. Quoc laughed ruefully to himself, but his companions only saw a thin-lipped smile. They shared knowing glances with him: This almost seemed like a silly game.

That evening, the guards escorted each roomful of men to the schoolyard outside. Quoc's group was last. The men carried their own chopsticks, spoon, fork, and bowl to the food line, but the detainees from Quoc's group were met with empty containers and no food.

An older officer from Quoc's classroom – he was perhaps 35 years old – spoke up, "We have no food!"

A Communist officer ran up to him, stood within inches of his face, and shouted, "Shut up, and sit down. You are traitors. You don't deserve to eat."

The older officer held his ground, "But we didn't eat, and we paid for it, brother!"

"Shut up, or I'll shoot you!" As he yelled, the guard removed his pistol from its holster, brandishing it in front of the man, and again shouted his orders. They all froze in place.

The Chinese restaurant workers heard the exchange. A few minutes later they supplied some stale bread to the men. It was all they had left in their kitchen.

That night, Quoc and his friends slept on the concrete floor. For the first time they felt a gnawing hunger. They wondered if it would be the only time. They feared it wouldn't. Fear filled their guts instead of food. It inhibited their sleep as they contemplated a future that was no longer a silly game. The night was interspersed with whispered conversations among the five friends:

"They're dropping their façade."

"Look, it's best not to confront them at all. That older guy almost got decked by that officer."

"Yeah, not the smartest move."

"I can't believe how disorganized these guys are."

"Do they have any real plan?"

"Who knows, just go along and get along."

Talk inevitably turned to what they could expect, not only about what the camp conditions would be like, but the length of incarceration. Quoc repeated the words he had heard from Kim-Cuong's uncle. Others said they had heard similar things, but they hadn't dwelt on it. They hoped it wasn't true.

One man in the corner quietly asked, "But what if it is?"

JUNE 29, 1975

The next morning, Quoc's group was the first to eat takeout food from the local restaurant. The Communist guard who had brandished his weapon appeared chastened, attempting to soften his actions and threat of violence of the night before. I was as if he were under orders to appear benevolent. The men saw it as a façade, but did not yet know why.

After breakfast, the men in Quoc's group returned to their room, with a guard posted outside the door. A North Vietnamese officer appeared and spoke in a business-like manner to all the former South Vietnamese officers. It was almost a congenial conversation.

"We very much appreciate you coming in. I'd like to take your name, former rank, and address for our records."

It took more than an hour. He diligently recorded all the information in a small green notebook, and then carefully placed it back into his uniform pocket.

That day dragged on with continued speculative conversation interspersed with naps. The classroom was stifling. The men ate in the schoolyard that night. There were only two meals each day. They lay down again on the floor: Sheer exhaustion led them to sleep.

JUNE 30, 1975

The third morning, after another takeout breakfast in the school-yard, the same North Vietnamese officer appeared, with the same conciliatory and professional tone.

"Now we need everyone to write a biography of themselves and their families, a history going back at least three generations."

Paper and pencils were handed out. The men were given the morning to complete the task. After the officer left, whispered conversation between the five friends ensued:

"What the hell do they think we're going to write down?"

"Make sure it's accurate but not too accurate"

"Don't incriminate anyone in your family."

"This is ridiculous."

"We have no choice," warned Toan.

The others could only nod agreement.

Quoc, who had worked for the U.S. Air Force prior to his entry into the South Vietnamese Navy, wondered if he should report that. The consensus from his team was that he should not, so he did his best to gloss over that period in his life. He described himself as a "Translator in Saigon."

He minimized what he wrote, omitting every important post he held during his military career. He described his last assignment in Phu Quoc as a junior support officer in a refugee camp for the dislocated South Vietnamese during the war. As he scribbled down his family history, Quoc did not relate that his father once served under the Viet Minh and was jailed, or that he had later deserted to Saigon.

After they turned in their personal histories, the officer reappeared.

"Now, I want you each to provide me with a written list of officers who should have reported to a center but did not."

The task was as easy for Quoc as it was for his four friends. They listed people they knew who had been able to escape the country prior to its fall. In Quoc's case it was about a dozen men that he knew for certain who had steamed out of the river the night of April 29. Quoc did know one man in his apartment complex who had decided not to report to a detention center but did not disclose the man to his captors. Nor did Vong or Toan.

On the third day, after the evening meal, Quoc and the rest of the men in the classroom sensed something ominous might happen. Vehicular movement had increased on the street, and they could hear more guards on the grounds. Minh, with a sixth sense borne from jungle fighting, looked out the window and observed, "Okay, guys, now we're going to take a little ride."

At around 9:00 p.m., they heard and then observed a row of Russian-made Molotov trucks, GAZ51 models, with stakes and canvas coverings over the cargo area. Next to the trucks, Quoc saw a row of guards, all carrying weapons, mostly AK-47s. The men were told to line up and to count off, a common military technique to divide the groups into set numbers. Quoc and his four friends positioned themselves in the group so they were able to count off and still end up in the same truck. The GAZ51 had been designed to carry 20 Russian soldiers sitting on wooden seats facing each other. Perhaps 30 smaller Vietnamese men might fit inside. But now, 60 men were forced into each vehicle.

There was only room to kneel. Breathing was difficult and Quoc panicked, as the rear canvas was tied shut, with no ventilation or light for the men. Just before the curtains were drawn, he saw four guards on the outside of the truck, two in the front and two in the back.

One of his fellow captors sadly said, "Pray for your life."

Minh whispered, "If they try something, fight back, guys, because this could be the last night of your lives."

Toan disagreed and quietly ordered, "Now is not that time."

It took the Communist guards nearly three hours to force all the men housed in the school into the GAZ51s. At around midnight, the gears of the Russian-made transmission on Quoc's truck made a grinding sound. The vehicle jerked into motion. Cornering threw men from side to side and at least one man immediately vomited on his fellow travelers, perhaps from motion sickness but more likely from fear. Over time, there was more vomiting and a heightened feeling of claustrophobia.

The convoy was long. Quoc and the others had no idea how many trucks there were or where they were headed. He just heard dozens of diesel engines and the shifting of gears in large trucks. He realized then the reason they had departed after 12:00 a.m. The martial-law curfew set by the Communists became effective at midnight. No one would be allowed to follow them, and their whereabouts would not be known.

The trucks moved slowly, 10 to 15 miles an hour. Any convoy of vehicles takes a long time to reach what is termed "March Speed," with appropriate spacing and no gaps between vehicles. It is a maxim in any army that once a convoy gets to speed, it doesn't make many stops, because then time is wasted slowly accelerating the dozens of trucks back to a march speed. With 2,000 men, the convoy would have been at least 40 trucks, which would have been difficult to control and manage.

Only one stop was allowed.

The entire convoy came to a halt at around 3:00 a.m. The occupants were given five minutes to relieve themselves and to stand up and attempt to straighten their twisted bodies as they walked. A quick glance around into darkness, combined with the smell of vegetation, told Quoc that they were in the countryside. He didn't know where.

The men were forced at gunpoint back into the trucks, and the convoy began to jerk into motion again. Fifteen minutes later, a sudden stop threw them forward towards the front of the truck bed and into one another. They heard the sound of brakes and metal bending and twisting. Screams of pain and cries for help could be heard in the distance. They figured that one of the trucks had flipped over. One of the guards parted the side curtains on Quoc's truck and said evenly, "Well that's too bad – these things happen – glad that it happened to traitors."

The trucks ground back into gear, and the screams diminished in volume as the convoy put distance between itself and the accident. There appeared to be no effort to rescue or aid the victims. The men could not see anything through the drawn curtains; they assumed that those in the wreck had been left to die. With this assumption, a panic began to take root. Quoc had difficulty calming himself. So too did his friends; except Minh, who silently took it all in.

July 1, 1975

Two more hours slowly passed in the cramped and dark truck. Then the men began to see glimmers of light through the canvas. Dawn was breaking after a sleepless night. The truck came to a slow stop and diesel engines made clanking sounds as they shut down. The men were ordered to assemble outside the trucks.

The prisoners were bleary-eyed and exhausted. Astonishingly, they saw something incomprehensible. Stretched out before them, covering the runways and the fields were at least 10,000 people. There were no signs of buildings or infrastructure to support them. They were at an old American air base in Tay Ninh.

Four days had passed. They realized then that reeducation would not be limited to ten days. Quoc looked down at the ground and then at each of his friends. Their despair looked back at him.

9

BEYOND 10 DAYS

"A day in prison is longer than a thousand years at large."

Vietnamese Proverb

JULY 1975

Life is not a holding pattern for most humans. It moves forward and sideways and up and down and somehow gets to a place and time we call the future. It often moves at a pace which is swifter than one anticipates and sometimes slower than one desires.

But at Tay Ninh, life came to a stop.

At Tay Ninh, there was no movement, no action, and no hope, only the waiting and anticipation of what would occur next. The 10 days the Communists had promised for the reeducation of the junior officers of the South Vietnamese armed forces came and went at Tay Ninh and stretched to over a month. With it came a realization that the lives of its occupants would be on a new course as rocky and perilous as the future of their country.

The crowds that Quoc and his friends initially estimated at 10,000 turned out to be closer to 20,000. The old American base had a paved runway just over 4,000 feet long. It had served as an auxiliary base for smaller aircraft and the C-130s capable of landing on short and unimproved airstrips. The base was about ten miles from the Cambodian border. The width of the clearing might have been two thousand feet, with the perimeter disappearing into brush and trees. A rudimentary fence line still existed at the field.

Groups of about 50 to 60 men were crowded into small areas where they were managed by guards. The men dug very basic latrines to try to maintain some degree of sanitation. However, the latrines quickly became inadequate for their needs. The continuous monsoon rains further exacerbated the unsanitary conditions and resultant misery in the camp.

Within the larger groups, five to 12-person squads emerged. The units used the same organizational scheme they had used in their former South Vietnamese military units. Quoc's five-man group remained intact as a squad. There were no ranks used in the groups, as virtually everyone was a junior officer, ranging from second lieutenant to captain for the army and air force and ensign to lieutenant for naval officers.

The men did little else except to stay in their designated areas. They spent their days either walking the perimeter of the camp or resting in what westerners call the *Asian Squat*, squatting with feet flat on the ground and spread knees, the posterior setting on the ankles – a comfortable position to spend a lengthy amount of time.

Quoc and his four friends remained inconspicuous during their stay at Tay Ninh. They and the others in their platoon slept on the ground, using whatever ground cloths and U.S. shelter halves – two waterproof cloths snapped together to create a pup tent – they possessed in order to stay dry from the rain and the ensuing mud.

The men came to understand that they would be treated like animals. They also understood that those who argued, or even disagreed, with their captors would be beaten and subject to more privation.

The ground was hard and sanitation unsuitable. Food was scarce and the supplies the men brought with them quickly ran out. Some had brought dried meat and rice, others, U.S. C-Rations containing cans of such delicacies as "beans with meatballs." Though nutritious, U.S. soldiers viewed "C-Rats" with disdain. The Vietnamese liked them even less. C-rations could cause severe constipation. However, prisoners at Tay Ninh did not suffer constipation. Cases of dysentery were rampant.

After their own small supply of rations ran out, the Communist captors provided only minimal amounts of food to the prisoners. The meals were nondescript and might consist of a piece of a yam, barely cooked, or a small serving of corn. Only on occasion, were the men given rice. Servings were less than a handful per person.

If they were fortunate, the men received food twice a day. One or two men from each platoon would be told to report to a mess line. They would bring back a meager quantity of food to equitably distribute among their platoon members. Most, like Quoc's group, were respectful of the equal division of food because they knew they had to work together to survive, for the short and long-term.

At Tay Ninh, survival was paramount, and survival meant food. Ever-present and gnawing hunger was, literally, gut wrenching. The prisoners obsessed about food during their waking hours. With enough food and water, higher-level reasoning, desires, memories and emotions are intact. Without adequate nutrition – without this necessary fuel – higher-level functionality is stripped from the brain's workload, and the overwhelming and constant preoccupation with food is the only thing a person knows.

The days were surreal and inward-focused. One man, squatting among the others, would spontaneously begin talking about a meal, even describing how it was prepared and cooked. Others would listen intently and then add spices and other delicacies. The vicarious talk of delicious food itself seemed to provide sustenance. Such storytelling about food became a pastime and a method of survival in its own right.

Some of Quoc's friends had experienced privation in their youth. They knew that the first few days of hunger were the hardest. The stomach, used to normal amounts of food each day, begins to shrink before the hunger pangs subside. But hunger never really goes away. It just changes in feeling and intensity. As the lack of nutrition continues, the body begins to consume not just excess fat in the body but muscle as well. Quoc and his fellow prisoners began to look small in their clothes with their belts cinched up. Often a prisoner's pants would fall down when he stood up and his shirt would flap in the breeze.

Besides barbaric toilet facilities, running water was unavailable for either drinking or washing. The men carried containers to capture drinking water from the afternoon rains. Standing outside in the rain, if they had packed soap, they would wash and rinse themselves, leaving their clothes on. If they were lucky, they would then drip dry in the heat of the afternoon. If they weren't, they would sleep wet and shivering.

Even with evening temperatures of 65 to 75 degrees Fahrenheit, their depleted bodies were cold throughout the night. Often men would lay together in groups to conserve body heat, ignoring their own and their fellow prisoners' odors.

There were no military formations at the camp. Instead, daily reeducation meetings were held, where each group of fifty was assigned a Communist leader to teach them. The rest of the time the guards largely ignored them.

Quoc had grown up with schoolmates who had come from the North; his language and accent had been shaped by his peers. He thus escaped some of the scrutiny by guards, probably because his dialect and inflection seemed more normal to the NVA soldiers who were assigned guard duty. But while his linguistics may have prevented extra scrutiny, he escaped none of the hardships experienced by the rest of the prisoners.

At the reeducation meetings, a NVA soldier would march in and demand of the small group, "Tell me your crimes!" The officers, who had honorably served South Vietnam, knew the only crime they had committed was to be on the losing side of the war, but that explanation would not suffice for their captors.

Initially, the men refused to admit to any crimes. Many chose silence as an answer. Some cited the Geneva Convention but were shouted down by the guards. They asserted, "Criminals and traitors are not protected by the Geneva Convention."

One physician who had served with the South Vietnamese Army stood up and challenged his captors, "I don't know what you are talking about. I saved lives every day in the field. I committed no crimes. My role as a doctor is clear. It is to heal the sick and attend to those wounded. I did this for soldiers from either side."

The guard cut him off mid-sentence, shouting, "You ignorant fool! Shut up! You committed more crimes than anyone here. You saved lives so that your soldiers could kill more of their brethren from the North. You are a disgrace to our country and its leaders."

The physician stopped speaking, with a look of firm resolve. He was educated and knew he was dealing with captors bent on a mission to demand confessions and inflict retribution.

The men soon realized there was no arguing. Their only means of survival was to create a story that was acceptable to the Communists but also palatable to themselves.

The men quickly adopted a storytelling exercise each time there was a lesson. Eventually everyone was admitting to crimes in order to survive. They all knew there would be no medals for heroes who remained silent. Their only reward would be survival, living through the ordeal, and seeing their families again.

Toan's sage advice and maturity helped steer Quoc and his friends. He would quietly tell them, "Survive, guys. Just survive. Tell them what they want to hear and never worry about it. If they want you to sing at the moon and praise Ho Chi Minh then sing at the moon and do it. Just remember – your families are waiting for you."

Toan took on the role of block leader for Quoc's platoon at Tay Ninh. He helped them cope, ensured that their perspective remained intact, and that they all supported each other.

Minh taught them about survival and specifically the art of scrounging for food and foraging in the forest. He encouraged them, "If it moves, you can eat it! Don't worry about how disgusting it is. It's all in your mind. Your stomach will be happy to have it."

Minh was always the first to volunteer for mess hall duty. He quickly grabbed any scraps that others might have thrown away, be they chicken guts or the heads of fish. "You can always make a soup, boys, remember that," he would smile and wink.

The reeducation classes were sporadic and poorly organized. The Communists seemed ill prepared for the task of handling the numbers of prisoners in the camp. There was little evident preparation of the camp facilities and the day-to-day logistics required to house and manage them. There was no obvious concern for what the Communists considered traitors and criminals. Propaganda had shaped the guards' opinion of the South Vietnamese Armed Forces and its officers.

Even though they were from the same region of the world and spoke the same language, the Communists effectively dehumanized the South Vietnamese officers at Tay Ninh and at dozens of other camps around the country. There was no evidence of a mutual respect that the men had fought honorably. They had opposed the Communists and lost the war, period. As a result, the Communists thought of them as less than human and saw them as criminals who must be punished.

Minimal conversation occurred between prisoners and guards. No routine greetings passed between them. Acknowledging any sort of humanity would not serve the purposes of the Communists. The prisoners understood this immediately. Life was no longer about human decency and discourse. It was about something else: survival.

Many of the guards were less than twenty years old. Since the men did not know their names, they nicknamed them behind their backs with monikers like Skinny, or Fatso, or even Loud Mouth.

While the men suffered privation from poor sanitation and limited food, they were initially sustained at Tay Ninh by the health they had brought with them. Over time, sicknesses in the form of dysentery, colds, and outbreaks of skin disease grew common. In the beginning, the downward spiral of poor health did not often progress to death at Tay Ninh. That would come later.

Only one thing grew stronger at Tay Ninh: The reality that this incarceration would last into an indeterminate future. If the men asked a guard how long they would be in the camp, his terse reply, "We don't know."

There was no word from the outside, only the incessant loudspeakers that would daily broadcast Communist propaganda. Escape for the men was not seen as an option, even though there was only the rudimentary barbed wire fence around the perimeter and very few guards. They were just miles from the Cambodian border, but the regime of Pol Pot would not have accepted the men. And their fate would have been even less certain there.

There was tragic evidence that the camp was chipping away at the only thing that sustained each of them: Hope. One day a young South Vietnamese Army physician was able to somehow find a grenade. No one knew how or where. Without telling the others of his plan, he quietly walked out into an open area, held the device close to his chest, and pulled the pin.

Quoc felt the effects of the blast and then saw the remnants of the explosion and the remains of the body. As time passed, there were other suicides, each a grim reminder of their situation.

The stay at Tay Ninh ended abruptly. The men were assembled one night and forced into trucks. They left after midnight, again with the curtains drawn. They traveled for about five hours. The trucks labored up long stretches of hills as the elevation increased.

When the men eventually dismounted the trucks, they noticed that the soil was different. It was almost a burnt sienna color – less dark and more distinct than Tay Ninh's soil. Then a few came to recognize the place as Long Khanh, the headquarters of one of the last South Vietnamese battalions to fight heroically against the NVA.

Now it was just one more prison.

10

SAIGON

"Living under the new regime demands that you know how to behave."

Tran Tri Vu
Lost Years

JUNE-DECEMBER 1975

Cuu Pham was 19 years old. His high school final exams had been cancelled when the North's army began its final march on Saigon in the spring.

Cuu – or Nine in Vietnamese, signifying his birth order – lived at home with his parents and six of the nine children in the family. He was now one of the primary breadwinners since Quoc had left for the Reeducation Camp.

The night Quoc reported to the school, the entire family went to bed wondering just how long he would be in jail. They wondered, "Was he safe? How long would he be imprisoned? Where would he be kept?"

Three restless nights later, they were awakened with a hurried pounding at their door. It was one of their friends. He informed them the prisoners had been herded into trucks and driven away, to where, no one knew.

The days stretched to weeks and then to months. The family settled into an uneasy rhythm of daily life. They didn't dare to venture far from the house. The home was wall-to-wall with family, who slept anywhere they could find a place. They all woke up at about the same time, then stood in line for the use of the one bathroom. One or two of the women would then leave to go to the market, doing their best to purchase or barter for food, then rush back to their small home to cook. The men contemplated what could be done to make money in the new Communist environment.

Every day they knew they were waiting for something more to happen in the country; they were uncertain what that would be or how it would affect them. It seemed as if each day some new ruling or decree would be announced from the ever-present speakers in the streets, which began at 6:00 a.m., effectively awakening everyone. Normal conversation with individuals on the street was limited, largely due to the inability to speak openly for fear of Communist spies or authorities who punished any attempt at free speech.

There had been a level of martial law in the South during the most difficult times of the war, but it was nothing like what they now experienced under the Communists.

No one protested to the government, for they feared physical beatings by Communist soldiers. Few people argued. Some of the older men – many over 70 – would verbally fight back with the soldiers. Cultural respect sometimes protected them from abuse for these courageous acts of defiance; other times, they were beaten. Policemen and militia members created new laws and administered a justice they defined themselves, sometimes on a whim.

Groups made up of more than three people were banned by the Communists, who regularly dispersed even two men talking on a street corner. Additionally, if people wore stylish western clothes – like bell-bottom pants – policemen would cut the pant legs off.

The United States and the support it could have offered the people of the South had disappeared. Emotions ran high among family members and their friends as they discussed the way the superpower had turned its back on them. There was no hope of rescue by their former allies. The family's only option was to quietly consider the future possibility of escape from Vietnam. But right then escape did not seem like a possibility.

The family felt powerless. Cuu's father had saved money throughout his career as a merchant mariner. They took comfort that they could draw on that savings to provide sustenance for the family. That ended one day in late June when the loudspeakers announced the devaluation of the currency. Five hundred old South Vietnamese *dong* would now be worth one new Communist *dong*. In one bureaucratic stroke, their lifeline to survival was virtually eliminated. They would have to be frugal with their spending and wait until they were allowed to work in the new Communist system. If they were allowed to work at all.

Sadly, some weeks later, the final economic straw was pulled from their frail and failing financial structure. All personal bank accounts in South Vietnam were confiscated and turned over to the country's treasury. The family, which had had some limited ability to survive with its prudent savings, was now penniless.

None of them had jobs and, as former South Vietnamese citizens, were not allowed to work in any capacity in the new economy of the combined countries called Vietnam. They were now economic outcasts in their own city.

Cuu watched his mother and father receive the news about their bank accounts. Although just 19, he understood the economic impact. What he did not fully appreciate was the fear in the hearts of his parents as they watched a lifetime of work destroyed by the

Communist bureaucrats. In Cuu's estimation, the punitive actions of the Communists against their former adversaries demonstrated intentional retribution.

The Communists, it seemed, were bent on exacting pain and humiliation on a proud people who had fought against them. The Communists knew that no one – no country, no entity – would come to the aid of the South Vietnamese people. As far as the rest of the world was concerned, the people of South Vietnam did not exist.

Cuu's parents were aging before his eyes, and he began to observe a distinct decline in his father's health. A two-tiered system for healthcare became the norm in the country. Those who had formerly been South Vietnamese citizens were not allowed ready access to healthcare. If a person became ill, he or she could try to hire a doctor and pay him under the table. Access to a hospital was seldom possible. Xuong, who suffered from lifelong diabetes, was not allowed regular doctor's visits. His health declined quickly.

The family continued to be affected by ongoing change. Cuu himself was challenged by the Communists for failing to report to a reeducation center. One morning Communist soldiers banged on the door and demanded to see Cuu. "Why didn't you report for reeducation?" they demanded.

"I'm just a high school student. I never served in the military!" Cuu replied.

"You were trained as a soldier. You even fired an M1."

"That was just one short training session. I just fired five bullets and was considered qualified."

"You're a soldier, report to the reeducation site tomorrow!"

Cuu's parents and the rest of the family were terrified. There was no legal recourse. Any level of due process in the law had been replaced with Ho Chi Minh's Law: The interpretation of any action by someone in authority at any time against a former citizen of the South. Cuu's only choice was to comply.

Cuu reported to the center, located at an old South Vietnamese Army barracks not far away. He lived there for a week. Each morning the men were awakened and required to report for four hours of class. The topic was Ho Chi Minh – his beliefs, his attributes, and his accomplishments. If anyone said a word or moved during the training, he was summarily kicked in the back or on his side. Four more hours of class were held in the afternoon. There, they were required to recite back what they had learned about Ho in the morning. If they answered a question wrong, they were subject to more physical abuse by the guards.

At dinnertime, the men received a small bowl of rice with a few meat bones in it. Cuu would hungrily devour the bowl of food, licking each finger of his hand and carefully sucking the marrow from the bones. He was constantly hungry.

After dinner, two more hours of class were held. Again, the subject was Ho Chi Minh. The men would then curl up on the floor and try to sleep. It was a fitful sleep, filled with the uncertainty of what would happen to them. Most were teenagers like Cuu, who had not served in the military. They hadn't known the privations of such service and were not accustomed to living with strangers.

After a week of ten hour days, with little food and minimal sleep, the men were brought to the school's gymnasium. As they sat huddled together, a guard announced, "Some of you will be allowed to leave here tomorrow, but only those whose family members attend the graduation ceremony at 2:00 p.m. If no one comes for you, we will ship you to a camp."

Cuu was not sophisticated, yet he recognized that the Communists were again toying with the lives of people. Cuu desperately wished he could tell the guards, to "Go to hell," but he knew that the guards were bullies who took pleasure in putting pressure of any kind on anyone. He had no choice but to play their game and hope for the best.

Cuu drafted a note to his parents. After scribbling the letter, he went to the fence line outside the barracks. Knowing that the post office would never deliver a letter to his parents, he gambled on asking a stranger for help. At the fence, he motioned for a man to come over to him. The man warily approached. Cuu whispered, "Will you please deliver this to my parents? I need them to be here tomorrow, or else I won't be able to leave the reeducation center. They will pay you when you give the message to them."

The man looked at Cuu and looked at the old building, which now served as one of many reeducation centers in the city. He looked grimly at the place, then more softly towards Cuu, silently telegraphing his understanding of Cuu's situation and his own distress at what was occurring in the country. He asked, "Where do they live?" Cuu told him and thanked him, praying that the message would be received.

The next day, promptly at 2:00 p.m., the men were assembled for a short ceremony in the school's gymnasium. The ceremony consisted of yet another round of education about the venerable Ho Chi Minh and what wonders he had brought to Vietnam. The speeches lasted more than an hour. Throughout the entire time, Cuu didn't know if his family had received the message or even if his parents were in the gym. He sat mutely in his seat, wondering about his fate.

When the ceremony ended, a list of those who would be released was read out loud. Nearly all of the prisoners were on it, including Cuu. The fear and consternation of those who were not on the list was palpable.

At the end of the ceremony, the Communist announcer said, "Take these lessons home about our hero, Ho Chi Minh. You are all fortunate to be part of his country now. You will never be forgiven for what you did to our country. You will spend the rest of your lives making it up to us. Now go to your homes and think about your sins."

With that, Cuu turned around and saw his sister Lan standing in the back of the gymnasium. They ran to each other and hugged, tears flowing down their cheeks. Then they made their way back to the family home, where Cuu's homecoming was celebrated with the meager foodstuff they had. They commiserated about the Communists, knowing full well that their feelings couldn't leave the confines of their home.

Even within the home, though, there was conflict. Cuu's brother, Phuc, would sit quietly and listen to his parents and other siblings talk about what was going on in their country as they complained about the Communists. Eventually, Phuc spoke up. "What have the Communists done wrong? They are trying to bring peace to our country and are doing the best they can."

Xuong tried to reason with his son, pointing out the level of retribution that the South was undergoing, but the young man argued nonetheless.

"Phuc, they are bringing economic ruin to everyone in this country. Don't you know that a free market system is better?"

"Father, you will see – they know what they are doing – just give them time."

"You will listen to me son. I know better!"

It became a regular debate, always bordering on argument. And it always ended in a stalemate.

Without a bank account and with the establishment of the new Communist *dong,* the family was poor. It was a new feeling and one that did not fit with how they had lived previously. Though never wealthy, they always had enough to eat and to buy clothes. They had never had to think about their next meal. That was all changed now.

The Communists instituted a ration system. Each family was issued a ration book with coupons for the number of individuals living under a roof. With the coupons, the families were allowed to purchase a limited amount of food one day a month. Cuu's mother and sisters would leave for the market before dawn on a designated day each month, coupon book in hand. At the government-controlled supermarket, they were allowed to purchase only one pound of meat, dried beans, and broken rice noodles. No rice was sold, despite the fact that South Vietnam had been – and probably still was – one of the largest producers of rice in the world.

The end of a war in any country has huge economic downsides, but trying to cope with them by instituting a Soviet economic model proved to be catastrophic for Vietnam.

JANUARY-JUNE 1976

Even the name of their city changed. In 1976, the government abruptly changed Saigon to Ho Chi Minh City. But to the members of the family and the rest of the South Vietnamese, it would always be Saigon.

As the weeks and months dragged by, the family continually struggled with nutrition and their health. The situation was made even more challenging when Kim-Cuong asked them to take five-year-old Hung to live with them. Kim-Cuong and her family had experienced many of the same issues faced by Cuu's family, and Lan had volunteered to take Hung to care for him. Hung stayed with the family nearly a year.

A new disease erupted in the country. Called Liberation Disease, and thought to be scabies, it was highly contagious and spread like wildfire through the civilian and Reeducation Camp populations. It affected the skin, causing a deep and painful rash that was difficult to treat. The family bathed Hung in a purple-colored medicine, which too often failed to work.

At mealtime, the family struggled to ensure adequate food for Hung. He was painfully skinny. They gave him first choice at every meal and gladly gave up their own meager shares of food. Hung repaid the family in joy and laughter. He was a joy to his grandfather and spent hours on Xuong's lap, hearing stories about the old days in Vietnam and laughing at jokes and sea stories. Hung's presence in the home kept their thoughts away from the present and lent an air of hope to the future.

The official government food markets did not have the capacity to serve the needs of the people in Saigon. When those markets closed each day, small back-alley black markets opened. There, the family was able to buy limited amounts of rice, sweet potatoes and yams, and occasionally some meat and fish. With these, the women in the family cooked makeshift meals, often consisting of beans, yucca root, and broken noodles, all mixed together in a semblance of a stew.

Portions were limited. Each night the family went to bed hungry. Constant hunger and continued uncertainty hung over them and consistently robbed them of sleep.

In order to buy food and other basic commodities, the family needed money. Xuong held family meetings and devised strategies for survival. The house was owned outright, but they needed to pay for electricity, water, and propane for cooking. They could not afford any clothes, and toys for the children were out of the question.

The family took stock of what they had. Cuu's mother had some jewelry that could be sold on the black market, primarily to North Vietnamese soldiers who wanted to take home souvenirs to their wives and mothers. They also had tables, chairs, mirrors, a television, a transistor radio, a few extra pots and pans, and other items that could be exchanged for the new *dong*. Xuong, in his travels as a merchant mariner, had accumulated an extensive collection of liquors from ports around the world. More than 100 bottles of cognac, whiskey, and other easily sold liquors were in his cabinet. The Communists had not made any moves to confiscate liquor; and the family made sure that no one knew how much they had or where it was stored.

One thing that was almost universal in Vietnam at the time was smoking. Most men and many women smoked and the desire for American-made cigarettes was well known. No one liked the Russian-made cigarettes sold by the government so cottage industries of cigarette vendors had sprung up around the city. The family decided to join the market.

With a small amount of extra *dong* procured from selling some family belongings, Cuu and his brother purchased two cartons of cigarettes on the black market. They included American Lucky Strikes, and some Vietnamese cigarettes. The men would take turns on street corners selling one cigarette at a time, using a small table Xuong built out of scrap lumber.

At the end of the day, the men may have sold 100 cigarettes and reaped a profit of just two *dong*. It was enough to keep cash flow for the family, and somehow they subsisted that way for more than a year.

In addition to the efforts of daily survival, the new government required each family to supply one person per week for government projects. Termed community service, individuals would report to a nearby center and be transported by truck to some government "make-work" project. They might spend a day using old rusted tools to dig an irrigation ditch, or worse, they would be sent to the Cambodian border, where tensions were rising. Cuu was sent across the Cambodian border for several days where he cooked, did menial labor, and even spent time guarding Cambodian prisoners.

July 1976

In mid-1976, Cuu and his older brother, Hoang, chose to accept governmental jobs on a collective farm near Long An, in the Binh Chanh District, where they worked in the rice fields. The work was backbreaking, but the brothers were able to get enough food to eat and to provide for their loved ones. It was the family's first experience with the New Economic Zone, where individuals worked on collective farms. They were required to give up to 60 percent of their crops to the Communist government as a form of taxation.

Periodically, Cuu was allowed to bring back 44 pounds of rice to support his family in Saigon. He did not have enough money for bus fare. He used his own rusty bicycle and struggled with the huge bag of rice, pedaling 25 miles one way to deliver the badly needed food. Visits were brief, since once he made the decision to work the fields, he was not allowed to remain in Saigon.

In 1978, Cuu was given a choice by the government. He could remain in the fields, enlist in the army, or join a singing group dedicated to celebrating Ho Chi Minh. Cuu knew how to play the guitar and had a good voice so he volunteered to join the musical group. He diligently practiced and then performed what he knew to be falsehoods about the generosity and kindness of Ho Chi Minh. Like everyone else he knew from the old South Vietnam, he was living a lie. But he was alive.

As the family struggled, it was Xuong who first drew the conclusion in family discussions that, "The goal of the Communists is to keep us so focused on survival that we won't have time to protest or to rebel. They send the trained military men to camps, and then starve the rest of us. But they can't kill our spirit. We have to get out of this country, where we do nothing but survive. We need to live our lives once again."

Then he added, "We need to be free."

11

DIAMOND

"Anh yeu em" I love you.
"Nhieu lam" I love you so much.

Vietnamese Expressions of Love

As she lay awake wondering about the future, Kim-Cuong's thoughts were always about her children first and then – sometimes – about Quoc. Her emotions were erratic, from anger to hopelessness and then to resentment against everyone and everything. As she struggled to sleep, she would think, "Why didn't he just leave the country with Hung when he had the chance? He could have made his way to safety and perhaps been able to send money back to support us." She often would conclude, "Men are so stupid. Why, oh why, did he have to try to be so brave? He will die. Our children will have no father!"

Finally, the tears would come, and she would guiltily answer her own question: Quoc had decided to stay to be with both their extended families. Sometimes Kim-Cuong would lose her tenuous grasp on hope in the dark night, only to find it again as she saw the daybreak through sleepless eyes.

Today she awoke at dawn, lifting her head from the sleeping mat, reflexively reaching over to touch Hung and Ngan. The night had been better than most. The children had only awakened three of four times that night, crying from lack of food. Kim-Cuong had given them milk supplemented with water. That quieted them, fooling their bellies into thinking something substantive had entered their systems. But the quiet was short-lived and she hugged them until they fell asleep exhausted. She lay there, quietly weeping and feeling her own hunger pangs, holding her stomach, protecting the unborn baby in her womb.

She walked downstairs to the bathroom. Although at least ten family members now occupied the house, there was no line. After relieving herself, she stood at the tiny sink and mirror, splashing water on her face and staring at the emaciated figure that stood before her. A tap came on the bathroom door, and she left.

She took with her the mental image of the person she had seen in the mirror. It was not Kim-Cuong. It was a body she couldn't recognize. All her ribs showed, with only skin covering the bones. Her breasts were shrunken. Her stomach was distended, and it wasn't from the pregnancy but from the lack of nutrition. She looked more like a starving woman than a pregnant one. Her hair had lost its luster. Her eyes were sunken and lined with worry about the children, both born and unborn.

Kim-Cuong had to shake off that image. She quickly put on her clothes and got ready for work. Tot, her mother, made some coffee; and she gave her daughter a small bowl of pho. Kim-Cuong gratefully slurped the soup and appreciated the few noodles floating in it. Then she kissed the babies goodbye and pushed her bicycle out of the entranceway into the street. The ride along the busy Saigon streets was 10 miles, but she didn't mind. She was happy to have a job as an accounting clerk. Her sister, Dong had arranged for it, through her connections in the government. The pay wasn't much, but it provided a small income for a family that had few breadwinners left.

As she pedaled, she thought guiltily that Quoc had not yet entered her mind that day. She hoped he would understand. The family itself was in the middle of a struggle for survival. The economic aftermath of the war and the confiscation of bank accounts had turned their lives into a subsistence-based existence, which sapped their energy and afforded little time for reflection.

Even though Kim-Cuong was always hungry, the priority for food went to the children. She felt guilty that she used water to fill their stomachs, but it could sometimes calm their crying. More wet diapers were the result; however, a shortage of detergent meant fewer washings, which resulted in diaper rash and infections.

It was a cycle of shortage and hunger and crying, a sadness that came over each adult in the family as they looked at the emaciated, sickly expressions on the children's faces. It broke Kim-Cuong's heart to see her children suffer. It gave her no solace when she recognized in her son Hung a stoicism that was much like his father's.

When she had said goodbye to Quoc in June, Kim-Cuong had no idea how long their separation would be. The Communists had promised 10 days in the Reeducation Camps. But no one trusted promises any more. They only wished them to be true. Like so many other things happening at the time, no one had any points of reference and could not anticipate or plan.

Kim-Cuong often remembered her uncle's admonition that Quoc would be a prisoner "until your children have children." Most family members chose not to believe this statement, but Kim-Cuong could not shake the feeling that there was a kernel of truth in what he said. That thought also contributed to her sleepless nights as she lay close to her babies.

Her full name was Kim-Cuong Thi Duong. She used the hyphenated "Kim-Cuong." Her name remained the same after she married Quoc Pham. Women in Vietnam always kept their maiden names.

In Vietnamese, Kim-Cuong's name meant *Diamond*. She shone like one, especially in Quoc's heart. She was almost as tall as her husband, about 4' 10" to his 5' 1." She had long, pitch-black hair. When it wasn't pulled up onto her head, it fell to her shoulders with a soft wave on either side. Kim-Cuong's eyes were a deep brown color, almost black to the non-discerning eye. In a culture of attractive women, she was considered exceptionally beautiful, with high cheekbones, a soulful expression, and eyes that transmitted confidence and caring. People often thought she looked like Phuong Hoai Tam, a popular singer in Vietnam at the time. Hung would sometimes call out, "That's Mommy!" when he saw a photo of Tam.

JUNE – JULY 1975

Kim-Cuong had kissed Quoc and held him for a long moment that day in June when she said goodbye. After a time that seemed far too short for either of them, Quoc reluctantly broke the embrace. Kim-Cuong felt emptiness in her stomach as she held back tears and watched him pick up each of their children. He lovingly embraced Hung and then Ngan.

Quoc lingered with each hug and soft kiss, pausing to take a long look at each of the children. He was trying to impress into his mind what they looked like, what their voices sounded like, even how they smelled. Kim-Cuong knew what Quoc was thinking. They had been married five years and it was impossible for him to hide his feelings. He too had no idea how long the separation would be.

Although she knew he was being torn apart inside, Quoc was too strong a man to show any external emotions. Quoc didn't want to frighten the children by breaking down into tears. His role was to be strong. He would be that way until he was out of sight. Kim-Cuong knew that.

Quoc turned back to Kim-Cuong. He looked into her eyes, and she saw them mist over. Her heart ached. She was saying goodbye to her life's love, not knowing what the future would be for him or for their family. A thousand thoughts coalesced into just one, a love for this man that translated into a prayer that he be kept safe however long he was away from her.

They kissed again. He held back his emotion and huskily said, "I must go."

She was unable to speak, barely whispering "Goodbye." He began to turn away, but she held his hand a second longer, squeezing it one last time, looking into his eyes and his soul. Then Quoc abruptly turned and walked down the street carrying his pack. He paused to adjust the straps on the pack, glanced back at her and then walked off. He didn't look back again. Tears rolled down Kim-Cuong's cheeks.

She slowly composed herself as she walked back into the house in which Quoc had grown up. The tiny row house might have been reasonably comfortable for four people, but today there were nine members of Quoc's family crowded into the place in addition to Kim-Cuong and her two children. Kim-Cuong planned to return to the apartment that she and Quoc owned. There she would be among other military officers' wives, where they would wait out the time their husbands were in the camps.

Kim-Cuong spent some time that day with Quoc's family. She had always felt a deep affection for all of them. Throughout her childhood, she and Quoc's families had often socialized. Indeed, Quoc and Kim-Cuong had been friends all their lives.

When Quoc was drafted into the Navy, his mother sat him down and pragmatically said, "You're going into the military now, Quoc.

It's time that you get married so you can have children who can carry on the Pham name in case you get killed."

"Now, Mother, don't push me."

"Kim-Cuong is a perfect girl for you. She's beautiful, smart, and comes from a good family."

Kim-Cuong had experienced a similar situation. Her mother had mentioned almost casually one day, "We've found someone for you, Kim-Cuong."

"Mother, I don't want just anyone."

"This isn't just anyone. You know his family and you know him. It's Quoc Pham."

Days of emotional discussion had ensued, with a considerable amount of tears. Kim-Cuong's family considered Quoc, with his college education, a good catch. They had seen him grow up and mature during the war years and saw in him a man who would take care of their daughter and be a partner through whatever the future held.

Kim-Cuong liked Quoc, but she was young and hadn't expected to marry right then. Her mother, though, was quietly insistent and eventually prevailed. While Quoc was given no choice, Kim-Cuong eventually came to the realization that the match was good for both families and for her.

Quoc and Kim-Cuong later learned that their parents had seen something in each child and in a relationship that would bloom and endure. Quoc especially realized his parents knew more than he did about this young woman with the beautiful eyes and uncommon strength of character.

As a result, an arranged marriage of sorts materialized in 1970. In the intervening years, the young girl with whom he had grown up had become the woman Quoc loved more than any other person in the world.

Kim-Cuong was especially close to Quoc's younger sister, Lan, who was two years younger than she was. The two girls had known each other as children and had formed a deep friendship when Quoc and Kim-Cuong were married. The relationship was a friendship akin to birth sisters. They shared thoughts and concerns with each other and often confided their perceptions of what the war had visited upon their families. Originally, their common interest had been Quoc and their love for him, but that had broadened over the years as their children were born. There was nothing now they did not share.

They knew they would continue to need each other, however long Quoc was away. Lan tried to comfort Kim-Cuong, assuring her that Quoc's incarceration would be for a short time. Kim-Cuong needed a counterbalance to her own fears and readily accepted Lan's optimistic outlook, though she knew it was mostly hope.

The day Quoc left, Kim-Cuong stayed at his family's home until well into the evening, and then decided to spend the night. They all knew that Quoc and his fellow officers had reported to a school a short distance away, but didn't know any details of what happened there. If they could get information about Quoc tonight, they would all receive it together.

A few friends stopped by the house during the evening and laughingly related that there had been a long line at the school where Quoc had reported and that the Communists had appeared extremely disorganized. This came as no surprise to Kim-Cuong or to Quoc's family, but since they didn't know the political allegiances of these friends, their conversations were muted and soon ended.

The family had already heard about beatings from Communist soldiers and newly appointed policemen. They had learned quickly that to respond negatively might subject them to retribution by their new Communist rulers. Thoughts about the new Communist regime would need to stay within the family and confined to late night whispers.

Kim-Cuong awoke the next morning, and fed the two children from the family's meager food supplies. She hugged each family member, deferentially spending more time with Quoc's mother and father. She noticed then that the past few months had visibly aged each of them. Lines of concern etched their faces, and she thought she discerned more gray hairs. It was no surprise. They had already lost a daughter in the past month and now the Communists had incarcerated three of their sons. Quoc's mother, Vo, asked, "What will become of our family?"

Kim-Cuong didn't know the answer and mouthed a nearly silent, "I don't know. I can only pray." Vo sadly nodded her head in agreement.

Kim-Cuong wished with all her heart that someone did know. But this was a world where there were no answers. There was now nothing but uncertainty with the defeat of the South by the North. That uncertainty was like a crumpled map whose course had no visible starting or ending point.

Lan followed Kim-Cuong out the door and hugged her once again. "I'll try to get word to you if I hear something about Quoc."

"Thank you, sister. We will pray he is all right. I will be at our apartment or you can contact the rest of my family if you hear anything. And I'll send word if news comes our way as well."

"Don't worry, Kim-Cuong. It will be all right. I love you."

"I love you too."

There were no phones. Word-of-mouth and messages from friends would have to suffice as their means of communication.

Kim-Cuong went back with Hung and Ngan to their small apartment. Her sister, Dong, came every day to visit. Like Lan, the two had become more than sisters. They were confidantes and friends. That relationship had grown deeper when they learned that Quoc would be sent to the Reeducation Camps.

But the women did not focus on Quoc. They did not know what was in store for him in the camps, and they could not worry about what they did not know. The heart cannot carry two burdens simultaneously. It can only focus on what is necessary, not of what might be. What was necessary was the care of two young children, Ngan and Hung, and another yet to be born.

Dong, like Kim-Cuong, was a strong woman, strengthened even more by war. She was the primary source of strength for Kim-Cuong as the days, then weeks, and then months, went by with no word from Quoc.

Dong was now an employee of the Vietnamese Communist government. Up until April, she had been a junior at Saigon Law University. Joining the Communist government was her way of providing some level of safety for the family.

Dong had no particular affinity for the Communists, but she was smart and realized that the best way to navigate treacherous waters was to align herself with the most powerful fish. Over time, Dong's relationship in the government would prove invaluable for each member of the family. And it would be especially important to Quoc in the years ahead, often in small nuanced ways, and at other times, in momentous ways that would affect all of their futures.

AUGUST- SEPTEMBER 1975

The promised 10 days in the camps for Quoc and the others came and went. No word came from Quoc or anyone else.

Dong was the first to recognize that the Reeducation Camps were prisons and that the goal of Communist leadership was to marginalize anyone who had held any rank in the government or armed forces of the South. Dong also realized earlier than the other family members that there was no specific timeline for the incarceration.

Additionally, it appeared there wasn't even a plan for housing or logistics. This was confirmed when Dong began to hear stories of men sent into the jungle and forced to survive on their own. Dong did not tell Kim-Cuong all of the stories she heard. She only told her the minimum of what might be happening to the men. Telling Kim-Cuong more or repeating unfounded rumors would be neither caring nor productive.

Dong had no children of her own, but as an aunt she was devoted to Hung and to young Ngan, doting on them in every way possible. In turn, the children adored Dong.

As weeks went by, Kim-Cuong spent hours telling Dong about her anger, and her concerns and fears for the future. One day, Kim-Cuong and Dong sat drinking tea and talking. They heard hammering on the wall outside Kim-Cuong's apartment. They crept to the door, cracked it open, and saw Vietnamese soldiers hanging a sign. When the soldiers left, the women entered the hallway to read the sign, which read, *Property of the Socialist Republic of Vietnam.*

Like the family's bank accounts, their home had been confiscated by the government.

Later that afternoon, Kim-Cuong and Dong heard pounding on the front door. Two armed men stood there and demanded, "You and anyone who lives here must vacate this apartment now!"

Kim-Cuong begged, "But I have young children; I must find a place for them to stay. Please give me some time. A week, a month, whatever you can do!"

"You have 24 hours." One of the soldiers said the last remark with a trace of a smirk on his face. Then they walked to the next unit, intent on evicting more "criminals" from apartments now owned by the state.

Leaning against the doorjamb for support, Kim-Cuong stood there in shock. She closed her eyes, saw darkness, and for the first time felt hopeless. She teared up and stood silently for several minutes until her own sobbing merged with cries from Ngan, jolting Kim-Cuong back to the present. Dong moved to her sister and held her tight. Kim-Cuong sobbed, "What will the future hold for my children?" Dong's answer was a tighter hug and a whisper, "Whatever happens, we will raise them together."

Later that day, Cuu and two other men helped Kim-Cuong move her few possessions from the apartment into her parents' home. Like Quoc's family home, the house was full.

Kim-Cuong's oldest sister, Nga, had left her two children in the house. Nga had worked as a clerk for the South Vietnamese government. She had already been ordered to move to the countryside south of Saigon to a collective farm in the New Economic Zone. Nga was not allowed to bring her two children with her to the zone. There was not enough food and shelter for them.

Besides Nga's children, Dong, Kim-Cuong, Hung and Ngan and two other sisters lived in the house. It might have comfortably held four to six people. Now there were 10 under one roof. Tot, Kim-Cuong's mother, did her best to make everyone comfortable though she herself suffered from continual pain and fatigue.

The family knew that she was struggling but Tot hadn't been able to get medical attention. No one knew at the time, but Tot was suffering from early stage breast cancer. Once the family learned the diagnosis several months later, they couldn't afford proper medical care.

Quoc's unknown situation was always on Kim-Cuong's mind; however, the difficulties and demands of her immediate family were redirecting her attention and draining her energy. Until one day when she received the first news about Quoc through one of Dong's Communist connections: Quoc was gravely ill and he needed her help.

12

ALL THAT WE ARE

"All that we are is the result of what we have thought."

Buddha

September 1975

"I can't move."

"Is this a dream?"

"Am I dead?"

He had been at Long Khanh for two months, living the daily privations of the Reeducation Camp. This morning he could not move.

He looked at the rough-hewn thatched roof above, commanding his body to roll over and rise from the fitful night's sleep, but his muscles would not react. His brain sent repeated signals through the neural pathways leading to the hundreds of muscles in his body, but he lay there with only his eyes blinking. He was paralyzed, and he was terrified. He felt like he was dying, but finally recognized he was still alive.

While he could still breathe, only a weak moan came from his lips when he tried to speak. He mouthed words, but little more than a whisper came out. He watched a mosquito fly over his body and land on the skin of his arm. He ached to swat the pest, to kill it before it was able to bite him. He saw it put its needle into his skin and fill itself with his blood, as he lay there motionless and helpless. Engorged, the creature lazily lifted off and flew away. He wasn't even able to scratch where it had done its damage.

Quoc had been feeling weak for some time, dragging himself from the barracks to the field and to the latrine when necessary. There were no specific duties at the camp, but the reeducation classes required his presence and participation each day. Those days became increasingly more difficult, something Quoc attributed to his continuing weight loss and malnutrition. Sitting on his sleeping platform or standing up on both feet were a struggle and shuffling down the hall or the stairs took a Herculean effort.

All that ended that morning. Quoc Pham was no longer just a captive of the Communists; he was a prisoner in his own body.

Quoc and his fellow prisoners occupied small rooms in a barracks with a raised wooden floor that served as a bed for twelve men. They slept side-by-side on the wood, covered with whatever mosquito nets they owned.

Long Khanh was surrounded by a chain-link fence and bordered by rice paddies and a wide stream. The stream served as a communal bath for the men, but the guards only allowed them to use it after the cows and water buffalo had spent time in it first. That left a putrid-smelling brown pool that only partially cleansed, but nonetheless cooled the prisoners.

Adjacent to most of the buildings in the camp, just outside the fence line, was a large wooden structure with no windows. It looked like a depot of some kind, though the men were never told its purpose.

Quoc's five-man team had remained intact at Long Khanh. Their solidarity and caring for each other had strengthened, even as their bodies became weaker. No one looked the same as he did when he entered the Reeducation Camps in July. Four months had passed. All looked haggard and emaciated, their clothes hanging from their bodies as if they had been made for someone much heavier. Some men had seen their pants disintegrate in the humid climate and had begun wrapping old sandbags around themselves like skirts.

Signs of age and stress were evident in each of the men, though none of them had a reference point other than the faces of their peers. There were no mirrors. Each might have imagined that he looked just as he was when the entered the camp.

In actuality, their eyes bulged out of their sockets; their cheeks were hollow and their abdomens were swollen from the lack of food and the resultant malnutrition. Each had medical issues – some with skin conditions, others with dysentery and still others with their gums bleeding continuously and their teeth falling out. A few had lost hair in bunches. More than a few gray hairs had begun to show in their beards and on their heads.

None of the prisoners was affected as seriously as Quoc.

Quoc's friends were dumbfounded by his condition. Knowing that there were no doctors available in the Communist cadre – and that you could not trust them if you did find one – Toan, ever the leader, quickly located one of the South Vietnamese Army physicians in the camp. He arrived in short order, gently and professionally examined Quoc, manipulated his legs and arms, and palpated his neck. He carefully examined Quoc's tongue and throat.

The doctor recognized the symptoms and knew from experience that they reflected severely lowered potassium levels in Quoc's body, which worsened the muscular effects he was experiencing. With time, and under normal conditions, Quoc would likely recover, with potassium levels slowly rising naturally in his body, allowing the proper flow of ions to the muscles and restoring normal control over the skeletal muscles. Administration of potassium would accelerate that recovery and help prevent permanent damage or death. But the doctor had no means of ordering or procuring any medications for Quoc or his other patients.

Given his potassium deficiency and his debilitated condition, combined with skin disease, periodic dysentery and malnutrition, there was now a real likelihood that Quoc would die. The doctor did not say it outright, but his friends intuitively knew it to be true. So did Quoc.

Quoc was afflicted with the disease known as Hypokalemic Periodic Paralysis or HypoKPP. It has been recognized by medical science for more than 50 years as a condition that afflicts some people through heredity, affecting the voluntary muscles of the body, which are primarily located in the skeletal system.

Clinicians describe it as, "Genetic mutations, which affect some of the ion channels located in the skeletal muscles. Skeletal muscles are sometimes called voluntary muscles because they are the muscles we have control over. They are the muscles which move us from place to place, throw a ball, pick up a glass of water, maintain posture, chew, speak, etc."

Symptoms occur periodically in those afflicted and can be precipitated by the very nutritional privations Quoc was experiencing. Ordinarily, the condition might not manifest itself. But Quoc's stress and lack of nutrition likely triggered it and its harsh advance on his body.

There are times when events in a person's life are affected inexplicably. It was as if it were written somewhere that Quoc was not meant to die in Long Khanh. Some call it divine intervention. Quoc was not outwardly religious, but he believed that life was in the hands of a higher power than his own. Whatever or whomever that was, something changed that very week, when the prisoners were allowed to write letters home. Even more fortuitously, the guards said that each prisoner could also ask for one package to be sent by their family. Each would be allotted about two pounds per package.

The guards said it was to help celebrate Tet, the Vietnamese New Year.

In a barely audible whisper, Quoc dictated a short letter to Kim-Cuong through his friend, Vong. In it, he told her he was alive and relatively well, but a recent medical condition required the administration of potassium. In his normal understated tone, he assured her that he would be fine, but could he please impose upon her to send the mineral. As was typical with Quoc, he did not say that his life was in danger. He felt Kim-Cuong had too much to worry about already. He needed to be strong for her. It was an illusion that his loving wife would immediately see through when she read the letter.

Quoc's outright paralysis lasted about 36 hours. He remained in a weakened condition, with symptoms flaring at random over the next several weeks. His friends brought food to him whenever the Communists meted it out, and they gently carried him to the latrine as needed, several times a day. Though each member of Quoc's team was going through his own hell, they nursed Quoc in any way they could and ensured that whatever food was made available to the prisoners was also provided to him. Minh was able to scrounge fish heads from the mess hall and made soups for Quoc. The stews he made tasted vile, but the nutrition they provided his body helped him recover. Vong followed him around the camp, helping him exercise as much as possible.

The guards mostly ignored Quoc. They assumed he would die. That was on Quoc's mind, as he contemplated his condition and calculated how the Communists might view him as a liability.

There was no compassion from those guarding Quoc and his fellow prisoners – nor had there ever been any compassion in the months they had been held. The guards viewed any sickness or suffering on the prisoners' part as justice against traitors. It was easier to consign the prisoners to death as a means of justice than to consider them innocent – or indeed human – in any way.

At times Quoc could drag himself into a sitting position and occasionally stand, but the weakness in his muscles and near-paralysis did not markedly improve until he received a package one day.

In the package, Quoc found rice noodles and other foodstuff. There in the box, wrapped in newspaper, was a large bottle of potassium chloride tablets. A letter was attached, carefully worded and ending with, "Here is some Kali-Chlor. I hope this makes you feel better. Love, Kim-Cuong."

Quoc choked down one of the pills with some water the minute he opened the bottle. The South Vietnamese doctor had cautioned him that a metered dose of about two tablets a day would have the most beneficial results and that it would take some time to feel the effects. He also told Quoc to be patient; more than two tablets a day would have negative consequences.

The next day, Quoc dissolved two pills into water to help their absorption into his system. The following morning Quoc thought he felt a bit stronger. Each day thereafter he had more energy. And though he did not spring back to full mobility and health immediately, within two weeks he found he could walk reasonably well. It was more like the gait of an old man than someone in his early thirties, but still, he could walk. There was no real strength in his muscles and the doctor cautioned him that he could expect relapses. With the potassium, the relapses lessened from twice a week to barely twice a month, as he slowly recuperated.

He had mobility again. For that he was thankful. The love of his wife and family was something he always knew, but its manifestation in the form of those pills was a miracle for a man on the verge of death.

Except for the regular reeducation sessions, there were minimal duties for the captives in the camp at Long Khanh. The sessions were well-rehearsed recitations on the part of Quoc and his fellow prisoners.

The theme remained the same, with questions that included,

"Tell us how many Viet Cong and NVA you killed." And, "How many battles were you in?" as well as, "State your crimes. Confess your sins against your country. Admit you are a traitor. Tell us who served with you."

Quoc became adept at making statements with no real meaning. He succeeded in simultaneously meeting the requirements set by the guards and ensuring solidarity with his fellow prisoners. When required, he consistently wrote down that he had been drafted as an officer; that his specialty involved logistics and supply in the Navy; and that he had never been in any battles. Nor had he killed anyone.

Oddly, the guards did not routinely attend the reeducation sessions. However, many prisoners believed that there might be spies in their midst. For that reason, the men never stopped the charade of daily confessions and retribution for their allegedly traitorous acts. Quoc and his four friends also made sure that all the other prisoners heard the same story they wrote to their captors. Quoc only missed the sessions during his illness.

At Long Khanh there were some limited exchanges with the guards, usually with grim humor. A man would ask, "When can we expect to go home?"

The answer, "When you're good."

"Well, how do we know we've been good?"

"You'll be home."

The guards had only known war throughout their lives and it was obvious they had no sympathy for their former enemies.

LATE 1975

While the guards were untrained, some of their officers demonstrated psychological techniques that had an adverse affect on the morale of the prisoners. For example, in addition to the daily loudspeaker's propaganda, the men were repeatedly lectured that everyone had forgotten them. They were told that their wives had moved on with their lives, and that they would be in the camps until their children had children. The harangues would include, "The people of Vietnam have turned their backs on you. You no longer exist in anyone's mind. You are criminals. You are traitors. You will die, and no one will know where you are buried!"

Intellectually, the men knew the statements to be untrue. But that knowledge could not silence the doubts in their minds or the emotions in their hearts. What began as tiny uncertain voices in some prisoners' heads and hearts soon transformed into shouts that nagged continuously at their thoughts and influenced their dreams.

Quoc did not internalize what he heard. Nor did he allow his emotions to rule him. As the guards lectured, Quoc would picture Kim-Cuong, seeing her steadfast determination, her courage in the face of adversity, and her love for him in her heart. He would not betray himself as he pictured the love of his life. He would just feel her in his heart and know a love that transcended time and distance.

Others could not muster such images, leaving them in despair. Despair casts a shadow over hope. Such despair can lead to desperate actions, like the first escape attempts at Long Khanh. As there was no apparent end game for the camp, a few prisoners decided their best and only choice for survival was to escape its confines, and return to the real world and then escape from the country.

The first attempt occurred late one night after the guards had largely departed the compound, leaving minimal security at key points on the perimeter of the fence. A former army officer schooled in survival skills planned his escape for weeks, timing the guard's movements and tracking the phases of the moon. That night was moonless, with only a few stars visible. The army officer motioned with one finger to his lips, indicating quiet to his fellow inmates, then noiselessly departed the room, carrying a pack with whatever food and survival gear he could gather.

As the officer left the room, another man who was pretending to be asleep, noted his departure. He waited a short while and then left the room himself, supposedly to go to the latrine.

What the army officer did not know – nor did Quoc and his friends at that time – was that the camp had a number of Communist sympathizers who served as intelligence conduits for the camp guards. The man dutifully reported the escape to his superior only minutes after the officer slipped through the fence. The pursuit was easy for the Communists, though it still took them two days to finally find the officer.

He was brought back into the camp and displayed in front of an assemblage of the prisoners. Quoc stood there, at once admiring the man's courage and still fearful of what he considered to be imminent death for the brave army officer. However, the Communists had another plan. They brought out a small steel Conex container, one of thousands left by U.S. forces. It measured less than four feet by four feet and was barely three feet tall. Originally designed for shipping and storage, it had been modified with a small slit, ostensibly for air and minimal light to enter. Looking at it from even a short distance, one could not imagine a human being occupying its dimensions. Nor could one imagine the claustrophobia that would ensue from being locked within its confines.

The man was about 5' 4" tall, ruggedly built from years in the armed service. The guards dragged him to the Conex. A Vietnamese captain walked to the front of the formation and announced, "This traitor has tried to escape. Escape is impossible! You cannot escape from us. There is no hope for you to return to your loved ones. Criminals like this must be punished."

It took four men to force the officer into the Conex. They slammed and locked the door. He would remain there, unable to crouch, or to stand, or lie down for nearly 24-hours each day. The temperatures inside the container likely reached 130 degrees Fahrenheit at the peak of the afternoon sun. He was released for just 15 minutes a day, during which he would struggle to stand upright and try to manipulate his muscles. He remained in the container for days. When he was finally released, he was not able to walk upright for three days and suffered from dehydration, malnutrition, and joint pain that would linger for months. He had also been repeatedly bitten by mosquitoes and was doubtlessly exposed to malaria as a result. He was later transferred to another camp. His fate was never learned.

Despite the prisoner's punishment, other escape attempts continued. None were successful.

The men began to get a sense that their captors had inside intelligence and information that gave them the upper hand. It would take some time, but the prisoners eventually ferreted out those Communist spies who were sleeping in their ranks. They knew they had to stop them.

13

DAILY LIFE IN LONG KHANH

"A little food while hungry is like a lot of food while full."

Vietnamese Proverb

WINTER 1976

Pigs are like family pets. They are fondly cared for. Families grow attached to them, torn between affection they feel for the creature and the certainty that one day they will be eating them.

The camp pigs had been given to them by a Communist captain, the first person in a year to show any level of compassion for the prisoners. The officer had recognized the men's descent into near-starvation during the harsh winter in Long Khanh.

The captain had been in the mess hall one day as many of the prisoners stood in line, receiving the daily meal ration, which consisted of a few morsels of food for each man. A small amount of corn and two types of squash were plopped into some salty brine. One squash had a name that sounded vaguely like the Vietnamese word for *argument*. Another sounded like *stuck*. One man grimly said to his fellow prisoners, "I am definitely stuck between two arguments."

They all laughed quietly and sardonically. The captain, who

was relatively new to the camp, overheard the ironic humor. A few days later, the officer located three piglets somewhere in the central warehouses of Saigon. He delivered them to the prisoners the next day and announced, "These are yours to raise and eat."

Three of the prisoners who had grown up in rural areas were chosen to care for the pigs. Their job was to raise the pigs until they were ready to be butchered.

The men began to eagerly anticipate the day when the pork would be served. They enjoyed telling stories about their favorite pork recipes, regaling each other with vivid descriptions of the anticipated bounty. Each day the stories became more fantastic; the men could almost taste the spiced and fragrant food. This fantasizing about food reminded them of something that had been locked away in a corner of their minds and was now refreshingly familiar. It was like a breath of fresh air on a sultry day. Although, rationally, the men could quickly calculate the meager amount of pork that each of the 1,000 prisoners in the camp would be allotted, nonetheless, the pigs brought happiness to them.

The days passed at Long Khanh in a familiar routine: Morning classes with well-rehearsed confessions and lessons in Communist ideology, the normal harangue against traitors and criminals, and the silent internal rejection of propaganda by each prisoner.

There were no vocal challenges against the Communists anymore; each man practiced his disagreements in silence to maintain sanity. Some men would verbalize their confessions to the group, then silently refute each point in his own mind, establishing a dialogue that no one could hear.

Those prisoners experienced in the effectiveness of propaganda knew that absent rational discussion and true dialogue, perception could grow into reality, which could convince even the most educated person of something that was not true. No human is immune. The reinforcement of a prisoner's internal dialogue was a rudimentary mind game that could often effectively inoculate a man against the onslaught of the daily sessions and the incessant drone of the loudspeakers. That, combined with support from his peers, helped each man through the day.

Each man's internal mood varied. It ranged somewhere between despair and hopefulness. Some messages from the Communists were repeated endlessly: "Your friends and family have forgotten you, because you are traitors. Your wife left you. She has remarried. She hates you. Give up any hope, because you criminals are no longer part of our society. The Americans laugh at you. They used you, and they have now moved to other countries to wage war."

Some men couldn't keep themselves alive in the face of the continued onslaught of propaganda and privation. They died despite an outward appearance that did not indicate imminent death. There also continued to be suicides. Others chose to escape and often died as a result.

Occasionally, the men would get some news about the outside world, usually something that was overheard from a conversation between guards and clandestinely exchanged among prisoners. The prisoners held onto these snippets from the real world as though they were lifelines.

The men continued to suffer from skin diseases. Skin became almost unbearable to touch. At the peak of a breakout, men couldn't wear clothes anymore and resorted to loincloths or makeshift skirts.

Most people say that temperatures of 55 to 60 degrees Fahrenheit are relatively mild, but few have ever experienced those temperatures coupled with malnourishment and disease. As winter descended, the prisoners had been confined for more than eight months. At night, men shook uncontrollably as the temperature dropped. A few had malaria, which itself caused such involuntary shaking, but most were just so sick and had so little body fat that their bodies could not burn enough calories to maintain their core body temperature.

The few letters to the outside world that were allowed were rigidly censored. The challenges that the men described were crossed out, as were their own feelings about the camps. They could not tell their families their whereabouts. They were not even allowed to write that they missed their loved ones.

The men tried to put codes into their messages. Some worked; others didn't. Quoc tried, but was not successful, in relaying his location. In his letter to Kim-Cuong requesting medicine, he attempted a rudimentary code. The results were not what he would have expected. Knowing that Kim-Cuong was pregnant when he left for the camps, Quoc began the letter with the salutation "Dear Long." He hoped the guards censoring the mail would believe Long was either Kim-Cuong's nickname or some sort of endearment.

He hoped that Kim-Cuong would see Long and recognize that it was out of place. The only other word that was out of place would be in the letter's close. In the last few sentences, he asked Kim-Cuong to name their unborn child Khanh. He hoped that she would piece together the two seemingly incongruous words and figure out his location, Long Khanh.

Unfortunately, Kim-Cuong didn't decipher the code. She was too burdened with her own deprivations, with two small children and no place to call her own. Although their new daughter had been born in December and named Quyen, when Kim-Cuong received Quoc's letter in January she went straight to the public records office and changed the young child's name to Khanh.

While not a girl's name, it nonetheless became a name that Khanh would carry all her life, a reminder of her father's courage in overcoming the intense challenges of incarceration and her mother's love for her father.

As the cold winter transitioned to spring, Quoc's health continued to improve. He had a limited amount of potassium on hand. He took it once a week and calculated that it would last at least another few months – enough to continue his recovery and perhaps someday feel whole.

The pigs were a constant source of diversionary discussion for the prisoners at Long Khanh. They thought about caring for the pigs and imagining a morsel of pork to supplement their diets. The vivid discussions of rare delicacies took on an added dimension with the very real possibility of actual meat in their diet.

In the camp, however, hope created by something as simple as the pork from a pig can be lost in an instant.

14

DEATH COMES

"Where life is exhausted, death comes."

Vietnamese Proverb

APRIL 1976

Quoc likened the smell to tear gas. It was the first sign that something was wrong. It seemed to be coming from the large structure adjacent to, but outside the fence line. It was probably from gunpowder, or perhaps older ammunition that might have contained cordite.

Quoc had sought the shade outside of the stifling barracks. Some of his fellow platoon members remained inside, lying on the raised floor. No one ever thinks of the consequences of such simple actions. Yet, like so many other decisions, the move outside likely spelled the difference between life and death for Quoc.

That morning, he had spent time in deep thought. Quoc had been a prisoner for almost a year. He was away from the wife and family he loved and had an uncertain future, but he had survived. Others had not been so fortunate.

Even before he fully processed what was happening, Quoc instinctively decided to move. The smell and the acrid smoke in his eyes were precursors to something else. He subconsciously knew explosions would follow. And they did.

Though still partially handicapped, Quoc retained his military instincts. He half-walked and half-jogged out across the yard, away from where he sensed the smoke. Then he heard the first explosion. It was about 2:00 p.m. Quoc recognized heavy ordinance, shrapnel, and individual bullet rounds, but the sounds were neither coordinated nor continuous. They were random and uncontrolled.

Bullets fired from a rifle or from pistols have a distinct sound and texture to them. Combine a firecracker with a whip. That's what a bullet sounds and feels like as it leaves the tip of the gun barrel and heads to its destination at a thousand feet per second. It is not just one distinct sound. It is a combination of sounds and sensations that differ depending upon the location of an individual experiencing them. For the person firing a rifle, for instance, the sound is loud, but the feeling is visceral, as the stock drives back into the shooter's shoulder and the recoil moves the muzzle higher with each shot. For the bystander, there is a loud sound and then a crack of sorts that is distinct but varying, based on the angle and distance away from the firearm.

For those on the receiving end of a bullet, there is less of a crack or explosion and more of a muted firecracker sound created by the bullet's initial muzzle departure. Depending upon velocity, the sound can come just before or after a sharp supersonic crackling – a whizzing or zipping sound – as it passes inches or feet away from the person who is downrange.

Much has been written about those hit by bullets. Sounds are probably less a part of the experience than the shock and agony of the projectile's entry, at least for those who remain conscious when it happens. That day there would be many who would experience bullets, shrapnel, or other munitions. Many would not survive.

The explosions Quoc heard built in intensity and were still

random. While many prisoners had been involved in firefights and artillery attacks in combat, none had experienced them lasting for hours on end. What Quoc heard almost all at once were tremendous booms, followed by multiple explosions, then cracks and supersonic whizzing sounds. It was a cacophony of explosive power with a texture, materiality, and sound that were unique in his experience.

The building must have been an ammunition depot that was located just a hundred feet from the prisoners' compound. It was on fire. Its deadly storehouse of materiel was in the process of cooking off: Like a pressure cooker, it spewed out in force, in this case, a deadly rain upon the camp.

Quoc wasn't inclined to investigate. He moved as quickly as he could away from the explosions. Escape was constrained by the ever-present chain-link perimeter fence.

Other prisoners scrambled, too. Many ran to the fence, attempting to push it down. But the proximity to the depot put one in jeopardy of dying from the blasts that repeatedly burst through the building's walls.

Quoc moved instead through the vegetable garden and by the pigpen. His instincts took him towards the mess hall, a well-built structure that might provide better shelter. It was also the building furthest from the blasts. A few dozen other men made the same choice.

Quoc moved quickly into the hall. Along with several others, he knelt down beside a wall in the direction of the blasts. He and his compatriots pulled one of the heavy tables sideways and aimed it towards the wall. The table, constructed of heavy wood planking of the sort found on a picnic table, was about six feet long and two to three feet wide. It offered a secondary obstacle and protection as the explosions continued unabated. Quoc and about nine or 10 other men jumped behind the table, hugging the floor.

Quoc was at one end of the table, with his back slightly exposed towards the direction of the depot. The men hunkered together and prayed. With racing heartbeats and dripping with sweat, they hugged each other tight. As one, they flinched with each successive blast. Some screamed; others made no sound. It was impossible to know who did either. It was not even possible for a man to know if he himself was making a sound. The concussive waves literally tore the breath out of each man's lungs. Besides prayer, Quoc could think of nothing more than to somehow try to make himself smaller than he already was.

In their intensity, the explosions sounded like the grand finale of a fireworks display. Those displays, in the moment, seem to last forever but then finally stop. The fire and explosions that day did not. More ordnance exploded and more shrapnel and projectiles cooked off in the extreme heat of the firestorm. Like a mythical dragon spewing fire and death, no one wanted to confront it.

Quoc heard and felt the hits to the table in front of him. The ceiling and parts of the beam structure fell. The walls disintegrated under the withering explosions. The tin roof collapsed onto the floor around the men. Quoc thought he recognized the sound of some of the projectiles – including mortar rounds – as they passed through the walls.

Though it was daylight, it seemed as if a primal fire, flickering brighter at times than the sun, illuminated the camp. The brilliance penetrated even closed eyelids.

As the explosions continued, a man suddenly ran into the hall, forcing himself behind Quoc and pushing Quoc further into the group. The man's back – not Quoc's – was suddenly exposed at the end of the table.

Quoc closed his eyes and prayed. He implored, "If you want to take me, just do it now!" These words reverberated in his mind for what seemed to be hours. At some point he passed out. Later he thought he might have been in a sort of Zen state, where time stopped around him. Hours or minutes might have passed. When

Quoc awoke, his clothes were soaked with a warm, viscous liquid. He was covered in blood. He slowly moved his hands up and down his body to see where he had been hit. As he did, he heard raspy breathing from the man behind him. The breathing was labored, with the sound of lungs filling with fluid. Quoc slowly realized it was not his own, but the other man's blood that covered him.

He looked at the dying man, who stared, eyes wide open, seeming to look at something far in the distance. A large piece of shrapnel had passed through his back, entering his chest and exiting sideways through a lung. The metal piece left a fairly clean hole at its entry point in his back but a tangle of flesh, blood, sputum, and bone where his chest had been. Quoc felt an uncontrollable urge to vomit, but only bitter bile filled his mouth with the taste of stomach acid. Fear and despair consumed him.

Quoc and the surviving men had no choice but to stay behind the table. They heard more explosions, though the sounds eventually began to diminish and the cook-off seemed to slow. Periodically, a projectile would still strike what was left of the mess hall, and the heavy table took more hits.

At around midnight, more than ten hours after the first explosions, a semblance of silence descended upon the camp. Fires continued to burn. Moaning and the screams of wounded men replaced the sounds of explosions.

In the darkness, Quoc pulled himself out of the pile of men and gently rolled the dead man away from him. He took one last look at the man's face, wondering how it was that God had chosen to save Quoc and not this fellow prisoner. The man's face was untouched and the eyes continued to look out, unblinking and unseeing. Quoc tried to close the man's eyes, but rigor mortis had set in and the eyes just reopened. It seemed as if the man did not want to stop seeing the world he had just departed.

Quoc shuffled to his feet and made his way through the wreckage of the mess hall. He slid on the blood of the dozen or so bodies lying on the floor. He staggered to the prison yard. What he saw in the moonlit night was virtual desolation, as if an apocalypse had descended on the ordered life of the prisoners. None of the structures were intact. They were just remnants of wood, with fires smoldering. Men wandered aimlessly. No guards were present.

Quoc returned to his barracks. He found a hovel. There was no roof, only remnants of charred bullet-torn walls. Those prisoners who were in his barracks when the explosions started lay dead in the rubble. Those who had survived milled around the area, uncertain what to do.

Minh, ever the pragmatic combat leader and Toan, the block leader, took a roll call of the men who were housed in what used to be their barracks. None of Quoc's group of five was seriously injured. As they looked at Quoc, their attention was drawn to the blood covering him. Quoc said nothing, just shook his head, mournfully looking down as he did so.

Toan, Vong, and Minh remained unscathed, though they all looked shell-shocked. Son had a minor wound on his left knee, but he chose not to report it to anyone. Minh bound up the wound with a spare shirt, and they all squatted there, mostly silent, with a few speculating on what had just occurred

No one ever knew what had started the fire. The guards blamed the prisoners, though none of them – even privately and years later – took responsibility for the blast. Later, the Communists claimed that it was just a minor fire.

Out of 1,000 prisoners, about 300 were estimated to have been killed that day. Several hundred more were injured. Most had their wounds dressed by fellow prisoners and hoped they would heal. Those who were taken away from the camp for treatment by the Communists never returned.

During the previous full year of captivity, a few dozen men had died. In one day that had changed and hundreds had died. The fire

alone was not the only cause. In a tragic attempt to escape the confla-
gration, some of the prisoners had pushed the chain-link fence down
on the opposite side of the camp. But, as they had surged out of the
camp, they were felled from blasts of the guards' by the Chinese
Type 88 machine guns. Many of those men died immediately. At
least a hundred were wounded. Many lingered painfully for days,
finally dying in the heat of the sun.

The Conex container, previously used for punishment, held a sad
fate. One of the prisoners had spied the steel box, and assumed it
would be a safe refuge. He crawled into the container. He was found
later the next day, long after the explosions ended, lying peacefully in
what was now a metal coffin. Shrapnel had pierced the metal, torn
into his rib cage, and killed him instantly.

One round injured two guards. It probably did not explode, or
it would have killed them. Other guards may have been injured or
killed, but the men never heard of any other Communist casualties.

The Communists chose to erase the memory of the event. No
one was allowed to speak about or acknowledge the tragedy. Even
though the sounds were heard 60 miles away in Saigon, the explosions were officially expunged from the collective recall of those
present. Anyone mentioning it was punished.

The guards were adamant.

"It never happened."

"If the news of this explosion gets out, you will be severely
punished."

The prisoners just whispered among themselves, exchanging
rumors as to the cause of the explosions.

Food and water were even more limited following the explosions. Wounded men suffered and died. Quoc had stabilized from
his paralysis and could at least move, even if his recovery stalled
somewhat.

The initial cleanup at Long Khanh took two weeks. The guards didn't do the dangerous work. Instead, they ordered surviving prisoners who had South Vietnamese Army explosive ordinance disposal (EOD) experience to clear the camp of unexploded ammunition.

The majority of the surviving prisoners were confined to what was left of their barracks while the explosives experts set about their tasks. As the EOD personnel searched the area, they repeatedly found scorched or horribly burned bodies and body parts which were littered throughout the camp.

The remains were placed in an area outside the fence line. The Communists said they would be buried, but suspicions remained that the bodies were thrown into an open pit and covered with a few inches of dirt. Within a few days, most areas within the compound were accessible, but the camp was no longer a livable place.

And the pigs? The pigs, which had given comfort to the men of Long Khanh for so many weeks?

During the day of explosions, one of the pig's caretakers hid behind the gentle creatures. Each, by then, had grown to more than 300 pounds. The pigs lay there, sheltering the man from the successive blasts, a bulwark against the assault, living fortresses protecting their masters. The man hugged each pig as he would a lover. He never moved from their rough skin, burying himself in the mud behind the animals' backs, shielding himself from likely death.

As the explosions began to die down, the caretaker took stock of the pigs.

The animals they had cared for so many weeks – the pigs that had given hope to a campful of men, were all dead. They were mutilated beyond recognition.

For Quoc something fundamental had happened, though. His one prayer had been answered in the mess hall: He had survived. He knew it was a higher power that had been responsible. Hope had sustained him through his time in the camps. Now faith had saved him and would be his North Star from thereon.

15

THE BOTTOM OF THE WELL

"A frog living at the bottom of the well thinks that the sky is as small as a cooking pot lid."

Vietnamese Proverb

JUNE 1976

Long Khanh was no longer habitable. For a week, the men slept on the ground amid the ruins of the barracks. There was no food. They ate whatever they could catch – rodents, lizards – just to survive.

A line of trucks arrived one morning. The guards did not wait for nightfall; the men were ordered into the trucks right away. The curtains were quickly drawn, the gears began grinding, and the lumbering vehicles made their way along bumpy roads for two hours.

When they dismounted the trucks, Minh immediately recognized the camp as an old abandoned military base in Long Giao.

The Communists again demonstrated their lack of planning by moving the men into another long-abandoned camp with no suitable housing or usable facilities. The camp didn't even have water.

The majority of prisoners were assigned to rebuild the barracks. The rest were given the task of digging a well. None had done such work before. Still recovering from paralysis, Quoc was unable to dig. However, he was able to carry dirt brought up by buckets from the bottom of the hole, some three feet wide.

The first day, a total of 10 men, alternating in teams of two, were able to dig about 12 feet into the earth. Bucket loads of earth were sent up to Quoc and the others, who emptied the contents onto a pile nearby and then sent the container back below. The depth exceeded 25 feet the second day and nearly 40 feet the next.

Quoc noticed that the workers who were spending time in the well, when pulled up by rope, had an ashen pallor and appeared to have difficulty breathing. In minutes, they would recover. They typically continued to work in teams of two, relieving each other every hour.

On the fourth day, the rhythm of well digging and bucket emptying had become routine. A bucket would be lowered and about five minutes later a tug on the rope would signal that it should be pulled up. The men above would hoist it up. As they worked that day, the pace seemed somewhat slower. Longer and longer periods of time elapsed from when the bucket was dropped until a yank on the rope indicated that it should be pulled up.

Then a bucket was lowered. No tug came in return. The men at the top yelled down to the diggers below. They received no reply. Repeatedly, they yelled more loudly and became increasingly concerned.

One of the diggers topside volunteered to be lowered into the well. The men lowered him into hole, by now some 55 feet deep. As the rope went slack, the men at the top heard screaming, "Pull it up! Pull it up!"

The men hoisted the line. An unmoving body with a horrible pasty color emerged. A few of the prisoners laid the man onto the ground and tried to revive him, while the others pulled up another body, also inert and still. Then they pulled up the rescuer, now nearly comatose himself.

The first two men who had been pulled to the surface were dead. They had succumbed to asphyxiation. Unknown to the men, it was not uncommon in hand-dug wells. None of the men had ever dug a well before and did not know the dangers or the precautions necessary.

The physics were simple once the men analyzed it. The warm air at the top of the well had created an inversion layer, effectively blocking circulation of the colder air from the bottom with ambient air above. As a result, a build-up of carbon dioxide and a precipitous drop in oxygen had doomed the men as they struggled to dig. A fan to circulate air might have saved them.

The Communist guards displayed no emotion. As the rescuers initially tried to revive the two victims – and then paused to grieve over their dead bodies – one of the guards said, "Get these bodies out of here, and get back to work."

Shouts went up from the prisoners, "You bastards. These men just died! You sons of bitches."

Several of the men advanced towards the guards with seething anger; they were met with the stock ends of rifles butted into their heads. Others who wanted to fight the guards were held back by fellow prisoners. Such inhumanity to other men was inconceivable to Quoc. He watched with a darkening sadness, knowing that still two more men would not return to their families.

The next day digging commenced again; this time with men spending no more than 15 minutes at the bottom of the well, and other men taking time between shifts to fan the air below using palm leaves. Though less effective than an electric fan, this helped the workers survive as they dug the last few meters of the well.

When the well was complete, enough water filled it to supply the men in the camp, but the price for this necessary commodity had been paid in lives.

The daytime move to Long Giao gave the men something they hadn't had in a year, a view to the outside world. And it gave them something else: visibility. Family members who had established a network in search of their loved ones quickly received word that a movement of prisoners had taken place. Dozens of family members went to Long Giao. They surrounded the fence line, clamoring to see if this was where a husband, a father, a brother, or an uncle was held. Quoc did not see Kim-Cuong, but he knew that if the others had found this place then she would eventually learn of it too.

During what would become a three-month stay at Long Giao, there would always be a handful of family members near the camp. The men learned various techniques to send word out through those on the outside. A prisoner would approach the fence line, each time saying his name quietly, while looking away from the faces outside. The visitors intuitively knew that they should not acknowledge the prisoner. Quoc and the others sensed that their names would be remembered: Somehow word would be relayed back to their families.

JULY 1976

Once the basic necessities were set up in Long Giao, the Communist captors left the men to themselves, struggling with their near starvation and continued confinement. Reeducation classes weren't even held. The days were spent in trying to conserve one's strength and passing the time in a constant state of hunger. Food supplied by the camp was nearly non-existent. If anything, a tiny ration of yam and corn or rice and salt was supplied to the men once a day. There was no meat or fish.

Each day, abdomens swelled, gums bled, and men felt weak and dizzy. Hunger continually gnawed at their stomachs. It felt like a knife being thrust into one's gut, and included joint and muscle pain, as the body continued to consume its own muscle tissue to survive. It evolved into hollowness and an overwhelming fatigue and loss of focus. Most men hallucinated.

Such were the signs of starvation in the time they spent at Long Giao.

Quoc and his friends returned to a technique, which helped their psychological survival: They spent hours telling stories about imaginary cookbooks, which were filled with recipes, including how to cook traditional pork, stew or sour fish soup. The long hours were filled with imaginary culinary journeys, helping the men survive an ordeal with which only the power of the mind could cope.

During their time at Long Giao, the men learned that the Communists were deciding where each prisoner would eventually be sent. Those considered to have committed the worst crimes would be sent to the North. The men who committed the least traitorous acts were to be released from the camps to another type of confinement, the Soviet-style collective farms in the New Economic Zone.

Those who were considered to be moderate traitors would remain in captivity in the South, at least for a while. Quoc thought that he was regarded as one of those in the middle, with not too many marks against him, though enough to ensure continued captivity.

Meanwhile, the guards continued to insist to the prisoners that their countrymen had abandoned them. "They have forgotten you. Everyone in the country has accepted Communism. They all know you are criminals and traitors. Your wife is sleeping with someone else. You're as good as dead."

And then the prisoners were moved again, this time to a place called Katum.

16

DESCENT INTO DESPAIR

"The Communists used political techniques involving rumors to govern southern Vietnam after the war ended in 1975. They used these techniques to get former South Vietnamese officers into what they euphemistically called "reeducation camps," but which were actually labor camps."

Le Huu Tri
Prisoner of the Word – A Memoir of the Vietnamese Reeducation Camps

AUGUST 1976

Each prisoner who survived Katum would always remember it. No one could recall it without tears.

The men had been abruptly relocated from Long Giao. For hours they were driven deep into the forest to Katum. It was just six miles from the Cambodian border and a hundred miles from Saigon.

Quoc's five-man team had been together for more than a year. Their luck could not have held out forever.

The team, still unidentified by the Communists as an organized group, was broken apart in the move to Katum. It was both disorienting and depressing to experience the separation. Each had been a support for the others, bolstering confidence and ensuring that the others' needs were met. Most importantly, they together had thwarted the Communist propaganda's effects, each telling their friends that their families still loved them and that the country had not forgotten. The team's pledge of mutual support had been there for an entire year. Each had been loyal to his word.

Quoc now found himself with a new group of men. He had no friends, no allies and no one he could trust.

There were no barracks, no facilities, and no camp. There were merely a few existing huts that had been haphazardly built. There was no fence. Ironically, there was no need for one. Where would a man go? The men quickly realized any escape would be to Cambodia, a place of unrest and continued warfare. Open conflict between the two countries was expected any day. There would be no sanctuary in the forests and hills of that country.

There were only about 300 prisoners in Katum when Quoc's group arrived. The men learned later that smaller groups were interspersed every several miles throughout the area. Thousands would eventually be held prisoner in Katum.

A few small shallow wells provided dirty but somewhat potable water for the men. Those like Quoc, lucky to still possess hammocks, were able to string them up between trees. The vast majority of the men dropped wearily to the ground beneath the trees, suffering innumerable insect bites, never knowing if they would be attacked by a wild boar or bitten by a snake. Those who were ill or injured suffered in silence.

During the first few weeks, the men were not provided with food. They ate insects, mice, and any other animal they could catch. They collected bamboo and greedily ate the small, young shoots. More mature trees could not be consumed.

If the men were able to build fires, they roasted any game they could find. However, it was common to eat animals raw.

Shortly after their arrival, the officer in charge held a formation, where the men were lined up block by block. He told the men, "It's up to you to build shelters for yourselves. I need huts built that will sleep 30 men."

The men were divided into work teams. Quoc was assigned the daily routine of foraging in the forest, looking for mature trees or bamboo that was strong enough to make frames. They searched for plants to use as twine to bind the parts together. The enormous leaves of lemon grass served as roofing and walls. The harvested wood initially lacked the strength to support the structures. Men from rural backgrounds taught the others that bamboo readily hardened in a campfire, giving it a strength far surpassing other wood.

They also built raised sleeping platforms from the bamboo, so they could elevate themselves above the forest floor's dangers and discomforts.

The second day in Katum, Quoc encountered another naval officer. The man told Quoc that he had commanded about a hundred men in the South Vietnamese Navy. He said he had been in Katum for more than a year. Quoc was eager to find a friend and confidante.

Quoc and the man, Thai, seemed to share a number of common experiences and readily fell into conversation. Thai invited Quoc to his makeshift hut where they talked at length. Finding a fellow naval officer and what seemed to be a kindred spirit, Quoc spent hours answering the man's questions about where he had served and his experiences in the previous camps. Thai was surprised to hear about the explosions at Long Khanh and pressed Quoc for details. He encouraged him to continue talking into the night. Only after midnight, after a long evening of discussion, did the men fall asleep.

The next morning Quoc was assigned a foraging detail. Around noon, a guard singled him out. Forcing him at rifle point, the guard demanded that Quoc follow him to the guard shack. There he met the officer in charge and two other soldiers. The officer angrily ordered Quoc to sit down and then approached him with his hand made into a fist. "What lies have you been spreading, Pham?" he screamed. "You are spreading blasphemy about an explosion at one of the camps. You will be punished severely if this continues."

"Nothing, I have said nothing."

"Yes, you have. You will pay for this."

Quoc sat there motionless, not knowing what would befall him. He suddenly realized his new friend was actually a Communist spy who had passed on the details of their conversation. Quoc was punched repeatedly, all while receiving threats of more severe punishment. Before they released him, the guards elicited a pledge on Quoc's part that he would never spread what they called, "lies and blasphemies," in the future.

Quoc never spoke to Thai again. He also quietly ensured that his fellow prisoners became aware of the man's duplicity. Over time, other Communist spies would also be identified. The circumstances were much the same as those encountered by Quoc. About 20 men would eventually be befriended by the Communist snitches, and then later brought into the guard shack to be confronted with their lies.

The prisoners learned that the informants were rewarded with extra portions of meat and candy for the information they provided.

The prisoners were amazed by the ineptitude and disorganization of the Communists. Quoc's military experience informed him that obtaining continuing intelligence from prisoners presumed withholding identities of those who snitched. To do so, it was important to wait several days or weeks before confronting those prisoners who shared the compromising information. However, the Communist guards reacted to such information immediately, by confronting the prisoners, which in turn quickly signaled who the informants had been. These spies quickly became pariahs throughout the camp, ignored by their fellow prisoners and treated disdainfully by the camp guards. This would not, however, eventually be the only justice meted out for their actions.

It took a month to build enough shelters for three hundred men. As the men worked, they became expert in construction techniques using the most basic of tools, native bamboo, and hardwoods. By the time the men finished the 12 to 15 shelters, three acres had been cleared. It looked, though, more like the remnants of a logging camp rather than a military facility.

Next, the men had to build fences, which required more bamboo than the huts. To get materials, the men ventured further and further into the forest. Each trip into the thick forest affirmed the futility of contemplating escape. Where would they run, and how would they survive? There was no easy avenue of escape from Katum.

After several more weeks the fence line was complete. One more task remained.

OCTOBER 1976

The prisoners were assembled and issued instructions to build a hall big enough for several hundred people. It had to be at least 100 feet by 30 feet, with a roof at least 30 feet tall.

The construction teams, using the material supplied by the daily lumber-collection, erected the walls. That took 10 days. Then they did their best to frame roof trusses, which were long expanses of wood tied together by cord. At least 20 or more men struggled to hoist the trusses into position and then tied them together with the cords.

From all appearances, the construction technique was strong and substantial enough to support the lemongrass leaves and other tropical plants that served as roofing material and shingles for what came to be known as the Great Hall.

The men foraged daily for materials. Huge piles were created near the skeleton of the Great Hall.

A team of a dozen men began the arduous process of positioning and tying in the leaves to create the walls and roof. The hall began to take shape. The men took some satisfaction that with little architectural knowledge or engineering training they had actually created such a massive structure.

As each successive course of leaves was placed on the roof, the trusses appeared to hold. Throughout a long hot week, men worked inside, handing the leaves through openings to the men above, who positioned the branches and secured them.

One afternoon, Quoc returned from foraging for leaves. As he walked towards the Great Hall, he noticed that the men on the roof appeared to be swaying. It looked as though a strong breeze was blowing the structure, but there was no breeze. Before Quoc's brain could resolve what he saw, the swaying suddenly stopped and a sound like a soaked towel slamming into a cement floor filled his ears. The roof disappeared into the walls of the structure, and men on and around the structure scrambled to avoid the falling pieces. A fine powder-like dust that looked like smoke arose as screams began.

Workers immediately became rescuers.

They struggled to move the heavy trusses and mountain of debris from inside the structure. As he helped, Quoc saw blood and recognized a face. He cringed at the sight of the crushed body. The man was dead. Other bodies were quickly removed. There was only one doctor among the prisoners, and he quickly performed triage to identify the dead, dying and those who could be saved. Two men had been killed instantaneously by the roof collapse; and at least ten others had injuries varying from broken bones to severe gashes and wounds.

Several men broke arms. One broke a leg. The guards dragged the seriously injured away, pulling them from the care of the South Vietnamese doctor. Some of the prisoners attempted to pull them back but were struck by the butts of rifles or forced away at gunpoint. A few of those less severely injured who could walk or run melted into the group of prisoners. They were treated by their compatriots with whatever basic herbs or medical equipment they had.

The Communist guards forced the rescuers to return to their work clearing the debris and then start construction anew. The prisoners struggled for days to redesign and engineer the Great Hall. In three weeks, a new structure was erected, sturdier and stronger than before. The construction materials were the same. This time the new design had been written in blood.

17

THE DAILY ROUTINE IN THE CAMPS

"All human unhappiness comes from not facing reality squarely, exactly as it is."

Buddha

Eyes closed, Quoc listened intently to the words, "Remember, the first noble truth tells us that life is suffering. The second noble truth involves modifying your wanting. Wanting deprives each of us from contentment and happiness."

Each night, long after their daily routine and many chores, devout Buddhists in their ranks would lead a session in Zen Buddhism. It centered Quoc to hear the words and the wisdom taught by Buddha being recited by men who embraced and embodied the religion.

That wisdom was as powerful as anything they would hear. The compassion they received and shared with each other provided a bulwark against the daily pain in the camps. It also helped manage their anger and desire for vengeance. Even hard-nosed officers would admonish, "The best revenge you can get is to survive. Beat one man's brains in, and you won't survive a day. Just bow and scrape and know you will see your families again."

The Buddhists among them would add, "We are no longer fighting a war. We are meant to survive this ordeal, not win it. Remember that, my friends."

The words helped the men bear the daily routine.

Every workday's schedule was set out the night before. Each block leader – many who were known or thought to be Communist sympathizers or spies – reported to camp headquarters and received the next day's assignments. The work was specific, like building the Great Hall or a roadway. Generally the orders centered on quotas related to the specialties to which each man had been assigned. Some were on teams meant for tree cutting and clearing, others carpentry, blacksmith work, gardening, and mess hall duty. Some men were naturally inclined towards specific assignments due to their previous experience or expertise. The block meetings occurred anytime after 9:00 p.m. and sometimes as late as 10:00 p.m.

The next morning at 5:00 a.m., block leaders woke the men from their wooden sleeping platforms. Dozens of men shared the platforms, which were placed a few feet above the floor of the barracks, at the eye level of watchful guards outside, who could observe the men through openings as they slept.

The men were led outside where they did daily calisthenics and stretching exercises. To the prisoners it was bitterly ironic, considering the daunting physical demands placed on them every day. Most figured they were awakened that early just to inflict misery.

At around 5:30 a.m., the men were allowed to use the latrines, which were just deep trenches located adjacent to the barracks. The stench was overpowering. The men fanned away thousands of flies and saw rats scampering through the human waste and garbage.

At 6:00 a.m., the men reported to their assigned mess hall. There they would find out if there was any food available. If there was food, it would usually be just a small yam per person and hardly ever any rice. Most of the time, there was no food. The men always left hungry.

There were plenty of reasons to hate the Communists. Each morning, for instance, the guards would line up as the men hiked to work. The prisoners were expected to acknowledge each guard not by name, but with a salute and greeting, "Chào anh" – "Good morning, brother!" If a prisoner failed to acknowledge the guards – including the exact terminology – he would be beaten, often to the point of unconsciousness.

Most of the men worked in the forest. They set out single file in 20-man teams, armed with axes and saws, and makeshift packs and ropes. They would hike up the long hills in Katum, through thickly forested areas to their individual work sites. Along the way, they would pick up bamboo shoots for nourishment, and if they were lucky, find a grub or other insect to consume as they walked.

Clearly, the most challenging of the duties was working in the forest clearing trees and then hauling the wood back to the camp. Smaller trees, four to six inches in diameter, could be cut down with the primitive tools shaped in the blacksmith shop, trimmed into three foot lengths, and stacked on a man's back. The larger trees, which could be several feet in diameter, had to be hauled using other trees as rollers. Shouldering ropes slung beneath the trees, as many as a hundred men struggled for days in the deep underbrush transporting the heavy logs.

Quoc was usually a team leader. His training and inherent navigational skills always helped the group find their worksite and return safely before nightfall each day. Some teams were not so lucky and occasionally found themselves sleeping in the forest.

The one-way trip was normally six to seven miles. Often it was longer. It would take over an hour to get to the worksite in the morning and at least two hours to return, as the men struggled with heavy loads of wood.

The rolling terrain was a much higher elevation than Saigon. It was mostly forest filled with large deciduous trees, some as high as a hundred feet. There were areas with smaller trees, which were also cut and cleared.

As Quoc trudged through the heavy underbrush, he often daydreamed about Saigon. He pictured his beautiful Kim-Cuong, holding their children, smiling and laughing as they played. He smelled her perfume, touched her hair, and held her in a warm embrace. They smiled and laughed. This was his private time with his wife and his family. Then it was gone.

The men arrived on-site about 9:00 a.m., and worked until 4:00 p.m. depending on the time of the year. They typically did not arrive back until 6:00 p.m.

At the worksites, the 20-man teams split-up into squads of five. There were relatively few armed guards with each team. Typically the men worked alone and were checked by their overseers only about twice an hour. As a result, four of the five men would work diligently on the work assignments while the fifth man foraged for food, looking for any insect or animal protein and every edible item the forest had to offer. This, in turn, he would share with his team. Each team would also return to camp with some food to share with those prisoners who had remained in the camp working on assignments there.

Once the men arrived back in camp, exhausted from 15 or more miles of trekking and laboring in the forest, they hit the mess halls once again. Availability of food was erratic, but it was at least meagerly supplemented with food gathered in the wild. No one ever had enough food, but almost all the men shared equally whatever they had.

One day, a forest work detail came across an unexpected supply of meat. As they began trimming a tree, the men were surprised to see a set of orange eyes with vertical pupils. The creature was camouflaged against the large tree, with a zigzag pattern of white, yellow-brown and dark brown patches. It was a reticulated python about 30 feet long. The men quickly killed the snake by slicing its head off with an axe. It took 20 men to carry the long reptile back. The snake quickly became the news of the camp.

When they brought the python back, the guards confiscated most of the meat, leaving remnants to the prisoners. A few men ate pieces of the flesh raw; others cooked pieces over a fire until it was charred, and some lucky few grabbed a piece to throw into some rice.

Each evening, from 7:00 to 9:00 p.m., the men sat in their barracks and recited lessons they had learned in the reeducation classes. Since they weren't always supervised, they would often break into favorite Vietnamese or Western songs while one man kept a lookout for guards. If one approached, a simple signal changed the key, the volume, and the song in an instant to a patriotic refrain praising Ho Chi Minh.

They also related stories about what happened during the day and told tales and recreated movies on-demand. That was Quoc's specialty. He could recall details of any movie he had ever seen and even improvise stories for some he had only heard about. He would carry on for hours about the same movie, enthralling the other prisoners and taking their mind off of their plight. His was a gift of storytelling that helped the prisoners' morale each evening when they were supposed to be regurgitating the lessons of reeducation.

But, most important to everyone were the Buddhist teachings and the pep talks they gave each other, throughout the day and at night:

"Stay healthy, brother."

"Don't kiss their asses, but don't kick them either."

"Support each other."

Prisoners did not routinely report to the Communists for medical attention. They knew too many men who were taken for medical care and never returned. The few men who survived Communist medical treatment reported that their already tiny ration of food was immediately reduced by at least a third in the medical hut. Additionally, they were given herbs in a powder format that generally seemed to have no medical benefits.

Disease was rampant in the camp. Malaria was by far the most common jungle malady, and there were no medications like quinine available. Quoc had befriended a prisoner who was a pharmacist. He had collected and hidden a number of herbal remedies during his incarceration. Though limited, the herbs were effective in healing wounds and reducing the fevers and shakes that occurred with the onset of malaria. Fortunately for Quoc, his hammock's netting shielded from him the mosquitoes carrying the disease.

With the onset of malaria, a prisoner was reduced to alternating periods of fever and chills and he was confined to his hammock or bedding, where he sweated through whatever clothes he had. A number of men died, not necessarily as a direct result of the disease. However, when it was combined with malnutrition, bug bites, dysentery, and poor sanitation, malaria caused weakened bodies to no longer be able to sustain life.

Persistent skin maladies were rampant, and it was not uncommon to see men with oozing sores covering their bodies as a result of these infections.

Reeducation classes did not occur every day. They were concentrated into weeklong sessions, and hard labor was suspended. The men spent twelve to fifteen hours per day being lectured and harangued.

The prisoners only knew 30 or 40 men in their particular area of the barracks or work details. Quoc's group, while not as supportive as his initial five-man team, was nonetheless helpful towards each other and caring in their approach to each other's needs. There wasn't time to socialize with men from other groups, with the exception of rare volleyball games that were occasionally staged during the weeks of reeducation. However, even then, the men were intent, for self-preservation, on allowing teams of guards to win the contests. There was no extra time to get to know the other prisoners.

One man named Hoang, Quoc later learned, was a quiet man who seldom talked to the others in his barracks. He was targeted by the Communists for a demonstration in a camp-wide formation, held during a week of reeducation classes. Everyone had to show up for those formations. The men were lined up in military fashion, block by block, and those who did not come out of their barracks suffered the severest punishment.

When the whole camp was in formation, the Communists could be especially cruel, using any tool to inflict psychological pain. Hoang had received a letter from his wife, which the guards reviewed and withheld from him. At one particular formation, Hoang was called to the front of the assembled prisoners.

One of the guards, with a look of seriousness, used the camp loudspeaker system and announced, "We have told you men for a long time that the people of our country have turned their backs on you. Your families no longer want you. They know you to be traitors, and they never expect you to return. Listen to this letter. Here is what Hoang's wife just wrote to him."

Hoang looked surprised and shocked, his jaw slack and his eyes wide as the words were read aloud, "I know how difficult it must be for you in the camps, but it is even more difficult for me at home. I have struggled with this for a long time, but I must write you today that I have met another man, who I have grown to love. I hope you will understand and forgive me, but I cannot go on living with the hope that you will ever return."

As the letter was read, tears rolled down Hoang's cheeks. His shoulders shook. He sobbed. At one point he fell to the ground, but two guards abruptly lifted him to his feet and yelled, "Stand like a man!"

Each prisoner in formation at first cringed, then ached, as he heard the contents of the letter and saw Hoang break down. Some men cried. Everyone had struggled with his own demons. They knew the years in captivity – the starvation, privations, and continued indignities, as well as the uncertainty of their futures – affected each in their own way. More than a few were already depressed. No amount of positive energy or optimistic outlook could change that.

The formation broke up. Hoang fell down once again, sobbing uncontrollably, his face buried in the dirt. A few of his friends came to his side to console him. He made a weak motion with his hand as if to push them away. In time, he pulled himself to his feet and half-walked and half-crawled back to his hut.

The next morning, Hoang was found hanging from a tall tree, a vine wrapped around his neck.

He had taken his own life.

18

EVEN TO LIVE

"Sometimes even to live is an act of courage."

Seneca

SEPTEMBER 1976

The overall look of a scorpion is already foreign – maybe exotic or disgusting – even before picking it up, tearing off its stinger, and putting it into the mouth. First, there is the furry texture skittering on the tongue and then, the unique crunch when the teeth crack its hard exterior. Those who have eaten insects remark on just how loud the sound is when the exoskeleton is cracked. Mentally, though, such sensations are set aside because the stomach still needs to accept this protein, however unappetizing it may look. Some compare the taste to a bitter lobster or crab. But those, even eaten raw, are often served with a spicy sauce. A man without access to heat, cooking tools, oil, or spices, eats a raw scorpion without garnishment – and would gladly eat more.

When a man is starving, he doesn't consider what others might see as disgusting. It isn't something he thinks about. A man in a prison camp who has not eaten solid food for three days has no qualms about picking up any insect, and chewing and swallowing it. He only knows that anything edible brings a welcome response to a stomach that has done nothing but growl for days. The scorpion is filled with protein. So are crickets and maggots, which are especially rich. The reasoning mind is the only obstacle to their consumption and it becomes easier to set aside as hunger mounts.

Such hunger and its companion misery continued unabated at Katum throughout 1976. Food was scarce, disease rampant, and death all too common.

Men eventually tried to escape – knowing that their chances of survival on their own were low – but recognizing that their chances in the camp might be equally slim. Those that succeeded in escaping were never heard from again. Those who failed encouraged an endless chain of retaliation from the guards against the men, of agonizingly slow death in confinement or the brutality of instant death by gunshot.

The guards were no doubt punished by their superiors for the continued escapes at the camps and for the decreased lumber production from the prisoners, whose physical condition continued to deteriorate each day. Some years later, Quoc learned that the unit assigned to guard the men in Katum eventually were massacred in a battle with the Khmer Rouge forces in 1979. Those that remembered them at Katum bore no grief when they learned the news.

The reeducation classes and guard statements continued to emphasize how relatives and friends had turned their backs on the prisoners. Quoc stood impassively as he heard, "Your families, your friends, your country. The whole world despises you." All the while, he held himself within the circle of Kim-Cuong's love. This was his sanctuary and bulwark against the constant verbal onslaught.

Even with their limited physical strength and declining morale, all of the prisoners did their best to withstand the brainwashing. Resisting authority in whatever way possible seemed to create energy in the men. For some, resistance might manifest itself in lower quotas of lumber delivery or less forest clearing. For others, it might be a deep-felt private rebellion or a growing need for retribution against the Communist spies among them. Tears, anger and depression were constants in most prisoners' lives.

OCTOBER 1976

In October the men were ordered into formation. The loudspeakers blared out, "We will have a visit next week by television journalists from around the world. In the next days you will prepare the camp for that visit, and make yourselves look presentable."

The next day in the reeducation classes, the guards told the men they were allowed to only speak Vietnamese with the journalists. Not English, not French – just Vietnamese. Guards would interpret.

The men were issued a new set of clothes similar to the uniform worn by North Vietnamese soldiers during the war: long sleeve khaki shirts and dark green pants. The men speculated, "Maybe this means better treatment for us!"

"Yeah, but I doubt it."

"This is a show by the Communists, plain and simple."

A work detail erected a sign at the entrance to the camp that read, "Agricultural University of Katum."

The day of the visit came. All work details were cancelled, and the men were instructed to walk freely around the camp. The reporters and photojournalists arrived in a small convoy of jeeps and trucks. They set up cameras and took still photos and videos, occasionally stopping to question one of the guards or prisoners.

One of the reporters, who Quoc assumed was a Frenchman, approached him, "Parlez-vous Francais?" (Do you speak French?)

"Je ne sais pas Francais." (No, I don't speak French)

A nearby guard immediately barked at Quoc in Vietnamese, "What did you say?"

"Nothing, I said nothing," Quoc insisted.

The guard, who obviously did not speak French, looked at Quoc with suspicion. He never left Quoc out of sight the rest of the day.

The journalists at first seemed less interested in conversing and more interested in observing. A Communist officer whom the prisoners did not recognize created a narrative at each stop throughout the camp, explaining that the men were learning new skills in agriculture and agronomy that would help transition them to civilian careers. The men at Katum had been specifically selected, he said, for their intelligence and leadership. They would serve as the initial cadre in the New Economic Zone being created by Vietnam.

This was the first time that Quoc heard about the New Economic Zone. It would not be the last. He had nearly missed this reference because of his incredulity at the lies being generated by the Communist officer, who was obviously well schooled in propaganda.

The journalists began questioning the officer and engaging the prisoners, who were called students by the officer and guards. A journalist would ask in French, "How do you like it here?" which was translated by the guard as, "Tell him you like it here!"

The prisoner would glance at the guard then at the journalist and slowly reply, "It is a good camp, well constructed. We are learning a lot, but we miss our families and don't know when we will see them."

The guard would translate, "This is an opportunity for me to learn new skills so that I can better support my country and family."

One prisoner, hopeful that the journalists understood Vietnamese, blurted out, "We are prisoners and have not seen our families in almost two years."

The guard calmly translated, "He says it is worth being away from his family right now."

That man was beaten senseless after the journalists departed.

The sham of the visit ended late that day as the convoy pulled out of the camp just as quickly as it had arrived. The men were called into formation and ordered to disrobe. They were ushered single file into one of the camp's administrative structures and ordered to neatly fold and pile all of their new clothes.

They walked out naked. And they walked out alone. The outside world had beckoned for a brief moment. And, like sunshine on a cloudy day, it disappeared into darkness.

The men never heard the results of the visit or ever saw any articles, photos, or video footage. In the dark that night they speculated about the meaning of the journalist's questions and why they had come to Katum. Some felt that the American CIA had undertaken the mission for intelligence gathering. This was quickly dismissed by those who had long replaced hope of U.S. assistance with anger at what they saw as American betrayal. Perhaps, others said, the United Nations (UN) had sent an undercover team to the camp to determine where prisoners were held and under what conditions they lived.

The men never knew if or how the information was relayed back through various channels to the UN, but it likely was. The journalists were skilled observers. Despite being told to walk freely about the camp, a prisoner cannot act free. His gait, his look, his demeanor – all indicated incarceration and deprivation. A skilled journalist, like an experienced police officer, recognizes such things intuitively. They also noticed that the uniforms worn by the men were new and still creased from storage. They observed the gaunt figures and hollow, sunken eyes. The conditions of the camp were filthy and the facilities obviously not able to supply enough food and medical assistance to the men inside.

The observations and conclusions made by those observers did not take long to get back through formal and informal channels to the United Nations. Unofficial discussions by a number of countries began to put quiet pressure on the Vietnamese leadership and their Chinese and Russian allies to make change. But change would not occur for months and, in some cases, years.

The Communist plan to display Quoc and his fellow prisoners as model students at an agricultural school ultimately backfired, and it no doubt saved lives.

NOVEMBER – DECEMBER 1976

One of the prisoners at Katum who served as a ready intelligence conduit to the Communists was nicknamed "The Snitch." Quoc had met him the first day and had avoided him ever since. All the men had stopped talking to him, but he walked around the camp smugly, with a look of superiority that never failed to incite a burning but quiet anger. The prisoners hated him. Some began to make a plan to deal with him. His name was Thai.

19

MURDER IN THE FOREST

"Revenge is a confession of pain."

Latin saying

JANUARY 1977

The tree fell and accelerated quickly. It fell with a groan and loud crack, then an inevitable rush of wind and loud cushioned "foomph!" when the tons of wood and leaves hit the floor of the triple-canopy forest.

It was a huge tree, standing more than a hundred feet high, about five feet in diameter, with wide and thick leaves. The men had worked all morning to fell it as part of their regular assignment of clearing the forest and harvesting lumber for the massive construction projects underway in Katum.

The crash of the tree was a normal sound for the 10 men working in the area that day. Dozens of trees fell daily, immediately followed by axes chopping and the routine sawing that began the process of dismembering the tree in just hours that the work of nature had taken decades to create.

This time the tree felling wasn't followed by the sounds of tools.

At first, a silence that was as large as the forest fell over Katum. Then one agonizing scream was heard, followed by more eerie silence. Shouts began: Calls for medical assistance and for more men to help handle a dire emergency. The calls came only from the camp guards. The prisoners, to a man, remained silent. The guards thought something had gone terribly wrong. The prisoners knew otherwise.

It started as a normal day, with clear skies and a gentle breeze. There was a crispness in the air that early fall day. The dozens of ten-man teams assigned to the forest that day received their usual assignment to clear a thousand square feet of varying sizes of deciduous trees, many of them hardwoods several feet in diameter.

The prisoners tackled their work; never entirely confident that they could meet their quotas using the primitive tools assigned them by the Communists. They focused on their tasks: It wasn't easy for the men to distinguish between 900 or 9,000 square feet while surrounded by thick vegetation. Focus was always important because retribution from the guards for poor performance was always a possibility and sometimes even a certainty.

Humans speak with words but communicate even more effectively in other ways. During their years of captivity, the prisoners learned the nuances of nonverbal communication. A sideways glance or a slump of the shoulders meant something they should heed; a hurried stride and a quick comment could speak volumes.

The guards never wandered far from the compound, so the prisoners talked more and subtle body language decreased the further they ventured into the forest. The guards never monitored individual conversations as the teams dispersed to their worksites. As a result, every day men spoke freely about camp conditions and their desire to eat full meals.

It was also time when men could plan and work towards united goals.

Today would see one goal realized. Over the last several weeks, a small group of men had devised a plot that would address a long-standing grievance. The plan had been carefully formulated based on careful observation and analysis. It involved a subtle communication strategy that would help the plan work: Few prisoners knew the details and only a handful knew the day and time, but everyone knew something big was going to happen that could change things at the camp. A long-overdue punishment was about to unfold.

The focus of this retribution was on two men, Thai, and another prisoner named Thach. The prisoners had long identified Thai as an informant. Quoc and the other men hated him due to very personal experiences. More than a few men had been sentenced to time in the Conex containers because of him, and it had very often been a death sentence.

Thai's fellow informant and co-conspirator was Thach. He also ratted out any prisoner in exchange for special privileges, like more food and better quarters. Although they were former officers in the South Vietnamese armed forces, both Thai and Thach had demonstrated loyalty to the Communist cause and a disdain for their fellow prisoners.

The other prisoners carefully observed Thai's and Thach's daily routines.

Both snitches were always assigned to the same work teams. This varied noticeably from the assignments given to other prisoners, who often had different tasks on different teams throughout the week.

On a daily basis, Thai and Thach were met with a stony silence regardless of who they worked with. As snitches, Thai and Thach felt protected by the Communists and exempt from the authority of the work team leaders. Their lackadaisical attitudes about the work assignments were apparent. Inevitably the two men drifted off by themselves. It appeared to other prisoners that Thai and Thach smirked at them as they worked, as if to flaunt their status. Even if it wasn't true, this perception was widely held.

Thai and Thach's sessions together in the forest became predictable and notorious. Men motioned to the, "two old ladies talking" or commented that, "the rats are chatty today." If the two men heard them, they appeared indifferent and unfazed. They disregarded the work going on around them and left to find a place where they could talk.

The day of the accident, the work teams began working as usual. However, on this day, secret code words were cryptically exchanged – words of warning – and spread from team to team. The message: "Stay away from that area over there," followed by a quick gesture to the northwest quadrant, "And stay away from Thai! And no questions!"

The incessant sound of saws and axes filled the forest air. Occasionally a shout of "Timber!" would be heard, followed by the familiar sound of a tree falling. The cutting and clearing continued normally, with the sound of men struggling to drag trees away, then trimming branches and stacking brush. The men had established a rhythm to their work, and it would have taken a heightened degree of discernment to notice that there was something different going on in the northwest quadrant of the work area.

A team leader who was not associated with the team to which Thai and Thach were assigned brought his crew to an area 30 yards from where the two informants were engrossed in their usual morning conversation. The pair didn't seem to notice anything unusual. Sounds of men working had merged into the background noise of the forest.

The 10-man crew near Thai and Thach worked steadily on the largest tree they had tackled that day. They worked with a sharp focus as they notched the tree in the exact direction where the two informants were sitting. The men were experts in cutting down trees with a surgical precision, knowing within a few feet where they would land. They also knew exactly when the tree would be ready to fall.

Sometime during mid-morning, the team motioned to their leader that they were ready to move to the next phase of the felling process. The teams usually took a 15-minute break at this point to get some water. The timing for the final execution of the plan was now right. The team leader yelled for that break, and the refrain was picked up by the dozen other ten-man teams working in the area. The pace and intensity of the sawing and chopping began to subside as the teams stopped their work. It was a process that usually took a couple of minutes. Only then would the forest return to silence.

During the time it took for all the other teams to cease work, the team executing the plan made some last-minute axe swings and a final cut of the saw. The tree gave way to the pull of gravity and began its inexorable trip to the ground.

This time, there was no shout of warning, "Timber!" However, just milliseconds before it struck, someone noticed the fall and reflexively yelled, "Tree!"

No one would ever know whether Thach and Thai heard the belated warning or if they recognized that the tree had been precisely aimed at them. They were probably engrossed in conversation. The other prisoners always said they were plotting against their fellow officers until the very end, but they could have been talking about anything.

Those nearby did see what they thought to be shadows scurrying away from Thai and Thach's location. The men might have escaped the large tree, for it did not strike where they scurried. But its massive girth encapsulated another smaller tree, which fell a few degrees to the right of the first tree, precisely where Thach had moved to avoid the larger tree's trajectory.

The sound of both trees falling seemed amplified, perhaps because they were the only ones that fell during the work break.

An agonized scream was heard from under the branches, then dead silence.

Nobody moved. Nobody said a thing until one Communist officer and a guard rushed to the scene. Thai appeared from beneath the leaves of the second tree that had fallen. His face was pale, and he was shaking uncontrollably. He spoke in a trembling and halting voice, sobbing. The men in the area, including Quoc, understood that Thach wasn't as lucky as Thai.

A Communist officer ordered the men to move the fallen trees. At least 20 men lifted the first tree and dragged it several feet. They lifted and dragged away the second tree, which had covered a grim sight. A human body lay there, though it was very nearly flat. Thousands of tons of force had struck something that just minutes before had been a man named Thach. Now he was, as some of the prisoners later said, as "flat as rice paper."

A guard looked the body over and half-heartedly tried to find a pulse on what seemed to be the neck, knowing this was hopeless.

Quoc saw the body. Although he, like all the prisoners, harbored resentment towards Thai and Thach and the other informants, he took no joy in the sight of the disfigured body that had moments before been a living, breathing human.

Some men quietly nudged each other with a sign of victory, but Quoc's thoughts took him back to a war that had lasted most of his lifetime. It had torn families apart and sundered a nation. This death was no different than the thousands of deaths that had occurred in the many theatres of the war. North Vietnamese, South Vietnamese, Americans, French, Koreans and Australians. So many already died.

While the mind could justify the retribution against Thai and Thach, the heart scripted another story. Yet another mother's son, husband, father, brother, and uncle was no longer among the living. And, for what?

Briefly, Quoc thought of Kim-Cuong. Perhaps Thach had a love like his. Perhaps a beautiful young woman waited at home and would learn someday that she was now a widow.

Thach's body was put to rest in an unmarked grave in a field adjacent to the camp. Like so many others in Vietnam, his family would never have a place to visit or grieve and pay respects to an ancestor, and Thach's soul would have no place to rest.

The next day, three snitches were mysteriously transferred to another camp. One of them was Thai.

20

RETRIBUTION

"Intelligent men are cruel. Stupid men are monstrously cruel."

Jack London
The Star Rover

JANUARY 1977

For about three days after Thach's killing, the Communist guards almost withdrew from sight. No one knew why. The prisoners were allowed to smoke Thuoc Lao tobacco, sucking it through a bamboo tube. They also were allowed to play soccer. A few of the contests were held with prisoners from nearby camps.

Though debilitated and hungry, the opportunity to participate in sport after a year of captivity was like a gift from God. It also gave the men an opportunity to share information about the disposition of the camps and how their fellow prisoners were being treated. The other men reported the same treatment and cruelty by the their guards.

The few guards that did appear handed the men soccer balls and even allowed wrestling contests and some ping-pong games.

It was surreal. It provided a break from the routine of reeducation and the daily lumbering assignments. But after three days, it ended. Perhaps some higher headquarters eventually figured out that the prisoners had murdered Thach. Perhaps there was debate on how to handle the accident. Perhaps someone thought that the prisoners had been pushed too hard by the guards or not hard enough. Whatever it was, it all changed: The already difficult and deprived lives of the prisoners escalated to lives of daily survival. Brutal beatings and retribution at the hands of their Communist captors were commonplace. Malnutrition and resultant starvation accelerated.

FEBRUARY – APRIL 1977

One day, a man named Quang failed to report for reeducation class. The other thousand prisoners were brought into a large formation. Quang was hauled out of his barracks. Everyone heard him screaming. Without warning, the guards threw him to the ground and, using their rifles, began to shoot.

The prisoner was dead after the second round found its target, but that was not enough for the guards. They kept shooting, first his body, then his head, then his limbs. Hundreds of rounds tore away at the flesh of the dead man, making it unrecognizable. In seconds, a human being became a pile of flesh. The guards kicked what was left of his head around like a soccer ball as the prisoners looked on in horror and disgust. Then the guards gleefully turned their weapons menacingly towards the formation of men. Out of instinct, the prisoners dropped to the ground. The guards laughed, but did not fire.

Later that day, Quoc and his team tearfully made a rudimentary tombstone for Quang. They carefully gathered up what was left of his body and mournfully placed it into a grave. Quoc would later learn that Quang was a distant cousin of Kim-Cuong's.

The men were not being fed. They were dying of disease and brutality. Most felt they might never see their families again. Many believed that escape was their only option.

If they tried to escape and failed, they would die. If they remained and did not try to escape, they would still die. Quoc believed this, but his lingering illness following the paralysis was extremely limiting. For that reason, he could not seriously contemplate flight from the camp. However, many others did.

The men limited their Escape Committees to groups of no more than two or three men. No one ever knew when someone would attempt to leave the confines of the camp. At one point, a small group of Vietnamese naval officers asked Quoc to teach them the basics of celestial navigation. They felt that knowledge of the stars might help them set a course if and when they escaped. The men were of Chinese descent. From them, Quoc learned for the first time of the historic attempts of escape by sea in other countries. The officers said there had been a quiet but condoned exodus from mainland China after the Communists took over. The regime had allowed wealthy Chinese to build small boats to sail to Vietnam in 1949.

This information opened up thoughts of a potential escape opportunity for Quoc, which would utilize his expertise as an experienced mariner.

The camp was surrounded by a fence with guard towers. It was just six miles from the Cambodian border, but the men knew they would receive no protection from the Khmer Rouge if they escaped to that country. Their only hope was to go east or southeast, and attempt to make their way back to Saigon, where they would hopefully escape by sea.

Every day a few prisoners would be missing from camp. Those who were found in the forest would be brought back and summarily executed. The guards accepted as normal that a few men would fail to report for morning work details. One morning, though, roll call was conducted. About 60 men were missing from the compound. Retribution was swift, with beatings and shootings throughout the next two days. The Communists sought to strike fear into the remaining prisoners.

However, desperation overrides fear and escape attempts continued. Eventually, about 150 of the 1,000 prisoners left the confines of the camp. Quoc would never learn their fate, but he always hoped that they gained their freedom from the tyranny at the camp and the brutality of the guards.

Quoc in 1963 or 1964 in front of his family home

Pham Family photos

Quoc Pham in 1967, Studying for Maritime Exams

Pham Family photos

Quoc Pham and high school friends – Graduation 1965
Pham Family photos

Quoc Pham in 1970, prior to joining Navy
Pham Family photos

Quoc Pham in Saigon on his motorbike – 1967

Pham Family photos

Quoc Pham in Vung Tau on a break from
Merchant Marine duties – 1969

Pham Family photos

Kim-Cuong and Quoc's younger sister Lan – 1969

Pham Family photos

Quoc Pham in uniform for Navy Training, with his sister Lan
Pham Family photos

Kim-Cuong – 1970

Pham Family photos

Quoc Pham and Kim-Cuong (rear of picture) on their wedding day
Pham Family photos

The newly-married couple in 1970

Pham Family photos

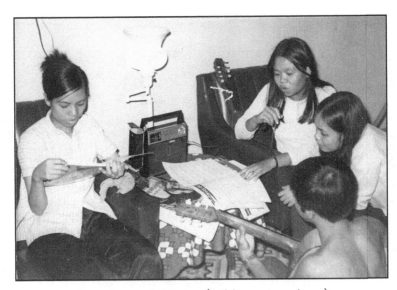

Kim-Cuong, left, Nga (holding microphone)
and two cousins in Quoc's family home
Pham Family photos

Kim-Cuong in 1971 at the Pham family home
Pham Family photos

Quoc and Kim-Cuong in 1971. Kim-Cuong is pregnant

Pham Family photos

Kim-Cuong, 1971 – latter stages of first pregnancy

Pham Family photos

Kim-Cuong and her infant son, Hung – 1972

Pham Family photos

Quoc's mother Vo, Kim-Cuong and Hung – 1972

Pham Family photos

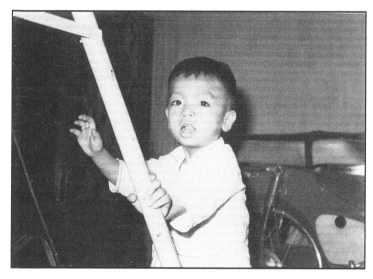

Hung – 1972

Pham Family photos

Quoc's brother Cuu, 1974, age 17 or 18

Pham Family photos

First escape boat – La Tu hired Quoc to refit – 1979

Pham Family photos

U.S.S. San Jose

Photo courtesy National Archives and Records Administration -
Records of the Office of the Secretary of Defense

*San Jose crewmen struggle to lift escapees from forward
hatch of Quoc's boat, January 20, 1980*

Photo courtesy National Archives and Records Administration -
Records of the Office of the Secretary of Defense

*San Jose crewman assists a female passenger up
the boarding ladder, January 20, 1980*

Photo courtesy National Archives and Records Administration -
Records of the Office of the Secretary of Defense

San Jose crewmen assist passengers through both
hatches of escape boat, January 20, 1960

Photo courtesy National Archives and Records Administration -
Records of the Office of the Secretary of Defense

Another view of the San Jose rescue of the
55 Refugees, January 20, 1980

Photo courtesy National Archives and Records Administration -
Records of the Office of the Secretary of Defense

*Chief Master-at-Arms James Brown talks to some of the 55
Vietnamese refugees rescued from the boat on January 20,
1980. Quoc is shown to Brown's right, wearing the sailor cap*

Photo courtesy National Archives and Records Administration -
Records of the Office of the Secretary of Defense

*Chief Master-at-Arms James Brown, front row kneeling, poses
for a photo with many of those rescued from Quoc's boat*

Photo courtesy National Archives and Records Administration -
Records of the Office of the Secretary of Defense

Petty Officer 1ST Class Tupola stands with escapees from Quoc's boat.
Bottom right, the boy being hugged by the taller boy is Quoc's son Hung

Photo courtesy National Archives and Records Administration -
Records of the Office of the Secretary of Defense

Quoc's identification card at Hawkins Road, Singapore (front)

Quoc's identification card at Hawkins Road, Singapore (back)

Pham family photos

MiddlesexN

VOL. 18 ● NO. 225 ● 44 PAGES   THURSDAY, MARCH 16, 1989

PHOTO BY JULIA A. SHAPIRO

Quoc Tan Pham is all smiles last night after being reunited with his wife, Kim Cuong Thi Duong, after nine years of separation.

After 9 years, a family once again

By John Nogowski
and Ellen Ishkanian
NEWS STAFF WRITERS
BOSTON — "I feel bad," Quoc Tan

DON'T MISS INSIDE

MARLBORO:

■ Digital plans big move into Franklin.
PAGE 8A

■ Gotham Ink begins

Pham said through a giant smile, his left arm tightly clutching 9-year-old son Cuong. "I didn't recognize them. They spotted me and came over. They called me 'Dad.'"

It was something he'd been waiting nine years to hear.

Pham, who works at Encore Computers in Marlboro, last saw his wife, two daughters and son nine years ago, when he and eldest son Hund left Saigon in a 30-foot boat. The others were too weak to make the dangerous boat trip, according to Pham.

"I would never have left had I known it would be nine years before we would be together again,"

> "I would never have left had I known it would be nine years before we would be together again."
> QUOC TAN PHAM

he said.

Pham's family obtained exit visas from Vietnam with the help of U.S. Rep. Chester C. Atkins, D-5th, who was armed with letters and petitions signed by thousands of local residents.

"I'm so grateful to have so much support," Pham said. "It is overwhelming."

Pham spent yesterday repainting the family room of his Methuen home, trying to stay busy and "get my mind off the matter
FAMILY, NEXT PAGE

*Quoc Pham and his wife Kim-Cuong on the
family's arrival, March 15, 1989*

Courtesy: The MetroWest Daily News (formerly the Middlesex
News) and GateHouse Media, March 16, 1989

After 9 years, a family once again

Wife, 3 children rejoin husband, dad in Boston

FAMILY, FROM 1A

until they get here," he said.

He also cooked a pot of pho — Vietnamese noodle soup — as a special surprise for his wife.

"I do it myself," he said. "I never knew how to cook before. It is going to give my wife a shock."

A little after 9:30 p.m., the diminutive Pham moved underneath the horde of television cameras, photographers and interested spectators and stood at the far left of Gate 19, just inside the red cloth rope. It was the best unobstructed view he could get.

Cuong and youngest daughter Khanh Kim, 13, were the first to spot him, his son extended both arms and hugged the father. His daughter clutched him tightly before spotting her aunt and reaching for her.

His oldest daughter, Ngan Kim Thi Pham, 14, was next. Her hug was interrupted to make way for the first embrace between Quoc Tan Pham and wife Kim Cuong Thi Duong in nearly a decade.

She let out a cry and her husband looked up and reached for her. Her eyes were red and wet and they embraced quickly, barely long enough for the cameras to record it. Then, arm in arm, they hustled through the crowd to pick up their luggage.

Pham, who had no contact with his wife other than through letters, said he had seen a photo of her "three or four years ago."

"But that was a photo I didn't show to anyone," he said. "There was a lot of strain on her, raising three children in that kind of life. I am happy now that I can take over."

"Now she looks great," Pham added, as he made his way through the photographers and reporters. "Beautiful. She was beautiful when I met her and she's beautiful now. She has changed a lot, but she's still beautiful."

"I'm so happy to be here together," Kim Cuong, who does not speak English, said through her husband. "It's been a long, long time."

The Pham family was welcomed by Pham's brother, Tikim Cuong Duong, and her sister Dong Duong. They stayed huddled together, hugging, crying and talking. There was much to catch up on, and it looked as if the family would have a long night.

"None of us have slept at all for at least 24 hours. Most of a week, really," Tikim Cuong said. "And we won't be sleeping for a while. But I am so happy for everybody."

Though he barely stopped smiling for a second, Pham remained frank about trying to resume a normal family life.

"I want to get to know my children," he said. "And I want them to know me. And my wife and I had something before that I hope we can have again. I love her so much.

"But this," he said, hugging his son closer, "It seems natural. Like I saw them only yesterday."

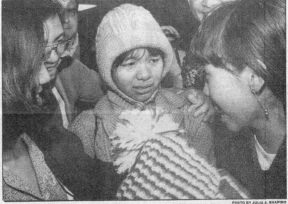

Khanh Kim Thi Pham, center, shares tears of joy with sister Ngan, right, upon their arrival last night in Boston. Their mother, Kim Cuong Thi Duong, looks on at left along with their brother Hund.

---

than resign

on a Health Board issue.

Steere has spent much of the past few weeks studying 19 years of town property tax and farm records which he requested through the federal Freedom of Information Act. On Tuesday he paid the town clerk's office $14.80 for a copy of the 148-page recall petition against him.

Steere did not say what he hopes to glean from the documents.

"We know what we're going to do but I won't say," he said.

Sculptor carves out a legend of hockey

ORR, FROM 1A

at the New England Sports Museum, joining another of LaMontagne's works — the figure of Larry Bird.

Montagne, who lives in North Scituate, R.I., has also sculpted

Quoc Pham stands at the front door to the apartment he and his family owned in 1975, and from which Kim-Cuong was later evicted

Dave Bushy photo collection

Quoc Pham and his second wife, Duong in Vietnam – 2016

Pham family photos

Quoc Pham and Dave Bushy, Phu Quoc, Vietnam, 2016

Dave Bushy photo collection

Quoc Pham (center) and his family, left to right,
Cuong, Khanh, Ngan and Hung. They are celebrating
Hung and Kimmy's wedding, May 11, 2014

Pham family photos

21

THE CURRICULUM OF REEDUCATION

"At Katum, every prisoner could recite his crimes by heart. The memories were worn into each brain like the ruts on a dirt road."

Quoc Pham

Besides reciting crimes in the reeducation classes, there was a standard curriculum to which the men were subjected. It was repeated approximately every five months, roughly as follows:

One week of classes (five lessons)
Two months of hard labor
One week of classes (five more lessons)
Two months of hard labor
One week of classes (final five lessons)

The lessons were not part of a standardized curriculum created by educators. Instead, they more closely resembled a pernicious game of "telephone." Poorly educated guards from the North who had listened to stories and songs throughout the war tried to parrot the teaching they had received. Once they had given a lesson to the prisoners, they followed with surprise tests, administered late at night.

At any hour of the night, the prisoners were woken up, and ordered to come to attention and regurgitate what they had heard in class. Sadly, the man who heard the facts or story might not have heard them the way the guard thought he taught it. And, the guard who administered the lesson during the day might not necessarily be the person posing the question in the middle of the night. So despite their best efforts, the prisoners often unsatisfactorily answered the questions posed by the guards. They weren't sent back to school when they failed to answer correctly. They were beaten.

There was no easy way to pass the tests and there were a hundred ways to fail.

The classes always focused on the adoration of Ho Chi Minh and the vilification of the South Vietnamese criminals who had opposed him. It inevitably followed that each man was required to once again put on display his own sordid past related to what he had done to oppose Ho and those who supported him, the real heroes of Vietnam.

There were 15 different lessons that were administered to the prisoners by their Communist teachers. This could vary depending upon the camp and the guards.

The first lesson was the history of Vietnam and its proud independence from its neighbors, especially the Chinese. Stories of victories over their neighbor to the north were common, especially those involving Tran Hung Dao (1228-1300), the legendary general who soundly defeated the Chinese in a naval battle. All Vietnamese people, both North and South, considered these lessons substantially true.

However, from this point forward, the lessons – and the facts – diverged substantially. Historical facts weren't taught by the instructors, most of whom, Quoc guessed, had very limited educations, perhaps only the equivalent of third grade. The entire focus of the lessons was on the cult-driven history of one personality, Ho Chi Minh. The guards fervently believed that Vietnam had come into existence as the direct result of Ho's inspiration and leadership. They had been taught that so-called imperialists, namely the French and the Americans, had thwarted his work.

Ho, the guards told the prisoners, was an immortal saint who had brought peace and tranquility to the citizens of Vietnam. The men continually heard about a temple in Vinh Long that had been dedicated to Ho Chi Minh. They heard endlessly that his body had been housed in a mausoleum in Hanoi and preserved much like Lenin's body in Moscow. It was said that thousands viewed his remains every day. The small house in which Ho grew up was located in Hoang Tru in Nghe An Province, and was called the Worship House.

Ho had died in 1969. The guards said Ho had been confident that the North would win the war and that the Communist principles upon which he had devoted his life would prevail.

The prisoners were required to know all these so-called "facts," and be able to recite them verbatim when asked.

They also had to know and sing, with fervor and enthusiasm, a song that had been composed by Huy Thuc after Ho Chi Minh's death. It was entitled "Bác vẫn cùng chúng cháu hành quân." (You are still marching with us, Uncle Ho).

The North Vietnamese soldiers and many Viet Cong had routinely sung songs celebrating Ho and his life. Now, ironically, the prisoners of those who fought against them were forced to perform the songs as well. If they missed a word or failed to carry the tune in a convincing way, they were beaten by guards who always saw them, not as fellow citizens of one country, but as criminals who had sullied the name of Ho Chi Minh.

Quoc and many of the prisoners had benefited from a formal education, which included Vietnamese and world history courses. Quoc knew the history of Vietnam, including the regional conflicts that had occurred throughout the centuries. Battles between the people living in the North and the South had not been uncommon.

Unlike the North, which had virtually no free press and limited access to outside media broadcasts, South Vietnam had had countless printed and broadcast media outlets and access to U.S. and British news. As a result, the populace possessed a level of critical thinking that always made citizens wary of one-answer solutions. The prisoners concluded that the Communists had instilled no such thinking into the general education of their people.

Questioning and challenges to the status quo are encouraged in societies with open access to the media. Those without some freedom of speech, Quoc believed, developed a certainty and a jingoism that is powerful for unity and sense of purpose in war, but develops in its citizenry a rigidity that limits the thoughtfulness required to move societies and nations forward. In the camps, Quoc and his fellow prisoners had come face-to-face with a certainty built on dogma and a brutality based on the lessons they had been taught from that propaganda.

The history that Quoc and most of his fellow prisoners knew differed substantially from the stories promoted by the Communist guards. Ho Chi Minh, Quoc knew, had indeed been a leader in Vietnam and had worked against the Japanese occupation during World War II. Ho was as much a Communist as he was a patriot, however, who allied himself and his Viet Minh forces with the Soviets and the Chinese. He left the country in his early twenties, and involved himself in Communist causes throughout the world. He did not return to Vietnam until 30 years later.

Quoc knew many who had disagreed with Ho's approach to government and nation building. Quoc's father, Xuong, had been one. Ho had repressed those who opposed Communism, killing thousands in the process and enforcing law and discipline with the iron hand of a dictator. He had forbidden the free press, so that ordinary citizens could not hear divergent viewpoints and learn facts he did not want them to know.

After the defeat of the French at Dien Bien Phu, a peace accord was negotiated between the two countries in the 1954 Geneva Accords. The Viet Minh set up headquarters in the North. Hanoi was the capital. There they set up a single-party Communist state. Those who wished to escape Communism could move to the South. The guards who taught the prisoners did not know about a 300-day period when more than a million people abandoned the North. More might have followed, had Viet Minh forces not stopped them. The right to have their own country for those in the South was then denied by Ho Chi Minh, who began a military campaign to invade and conquer the region.

Quoc knew there had been corruption and failures on the part of successive South Vietnamese governments. He was also conflicted regarding the American role in the war. Were they there to defend a nation against an invader, as they said, or were they there for strategic gain in the Cold War? Quoc believed the latter. He was angry at the United States for its sudden departure and lack of support since the fall of South Vietnam. Nonetheless, he appreciated that America had spilled its own blood and expended enormous resources to defend South Vietnam. Quoc felt the North Vietnamese might have been stopped and an armistice agreed to, much like that agreed upon with Korea. However, the Tet Offensive – though ultimately a military victory for the Americans and the South Vietnamese – fundamentally changed world opinion and U.S. resolve.

The prisoners knew of an even earlier history, which they were certain the guards did not know. A millennial-long fight between the Chinese and Vietnam – then known as An Nam, had ended in

938 A.D., when a unified army under Ngo Quyen, King of An Nam (later Dai Viet), defeated the Chinese. The country experienced continued interference from foreign adversaries like the Songs, a Chinese Dynasty, as well as from the Mongols and the Chams. This was followed by the Ming empire's short occupation of the Red River Valley, near present-day Hanoi and Haiphong. There were also wars with the Machus. Throughout that time, there were continued internal conflicts and civil wars within the country now known as Vietnam.

Then the European invaders came. First the Dutch and then the French occupied the region, subjugating its people and using its natural resources for their own national gains.

When the Japanese lost in World War II, the French decided that they could once again establish hegemony over Indochina. Ho Chi Minh's forces fought against the occupation and eventually, in 1954, at a valley called Dien Bien Phu, French forces were finally defeated.

History is always told by victors. The history endlessly delivered by the guards in reeducation classes continued with its sole focus on Ho Chi Minh or as he was reverently known, "Uncle Ho." The brutality that resulted from missing class was always horrific and at times deadly.

Quoc's so-called crimes and military background, in his estimation, kept him from heavy scrutiny by the Communists. Former naval officers were not automatically treated in the same harsh way as Army and Marine officers, who the Communists felt had committed the most heinous crimes. Unfortunately his naval background was not destined to serve Quoc as well as he hoped it would.

22

VISITS

"Adversity is the Mother of Wisdom."

Vietnamese Saying

MID 1977

Family visits were going to be allowed. The prisoners couldn't understand such a dramatic shift. However, they didn't care about the Communists' motivations. They embraced the move as a genuine gift and longingly looked forward to the day they would see those who were dear to them.

The men were required to write letters to their families – the married men to their wives, the single men to parents or close siblings. They were instructed to indicate that they were healthy and desired to see their family. They couldn't provide their location, mention their health or actual physical condition, or their political views.

They were given paper and pens. Within an hour, most had written short letters. Each was addressed to the last known address of their loved one. The Communists indicated they would mail the letters and coordinate the visits. They followed through: The letters were delivered and visits coordinated. The prisoners were also given strict rules concerning food allowed and conversation permitted.

The men speculated endlessly. Perhaps the change had come about because of the 1976 visit by journalists. Perhaps the international community knew that former members of the South Vietnamese armed forces had been put to hard labor, and word about their treatment had leaked. Perhaps there had been a change in leadership in Vietnam.

The guards appeared angry that the edict for visits came from a higher authority. Nonetheless, they were forced to comply with the orders.

The level of organization for the visits amazed Quoc and his fellow prisoners. Never had the Communists been so well organized in the nearly two years the men had been prisoners.

A few weeks after the letters were sent, about 15 men were called away from their work details and instructed to follow guards. The men were distrustful and apprehensive. Some thought the walk out of the camp would be their last day alive. They had no idea this would be a day of reunion.

Late that night, the men returned. Each seemed changed. Most carried about 20 pounds of rice and other foodstuff. Some could barely carry the burden. Psychological weights appeared to have been lifted off their shoulders. Barely containing their joy, they shared their food with others in the barracks while relating their stories of reunions with loved ones.

Each day 10 to 20 men from the camp departed, and each night they returned, renewed in small ways.

One morning in December, Quoc was called along with 15 other men. Four guards were assigned to accompany them.

The prisoners, emaciated and disease-ridden, walked like old men. It was a long distance, about 10 miles away. Later they learned that about twenty men from each of the six 1,000-man camps would converge on the same location each day for the short reunions. Throughout the long hike, Quoc prayed he would see Kim-Cuong.

Quoc was brought into a courtyard with about a hundred other men, where he waited for more than an hour. Then his name was called. Quoc walked into a room arranged with tables, with a chair on one side and a single chair opposite it. A guard stood by each table, holding a rifle.

At a table he saw someone who instantaneously became the only person in the room.

It was Kim-Cuong.

He had dreamed so much about her in the past two years. His mental image of her seemed clear. Often it was a bigger-than-life picture of a smiling face on their wedding day; or a feeling of joy they both felt when Hung was born. Mostly, though, she remained a feeling – the safe place in his heart and the only certainty in his life.

But the woman before him differed from his memories. As she sat in the chair, she looked smaller than he remembered. She was emaciated. She appeared to be forcing herself to be even smaller and non-threatening than she was, perhaps to deflect attention. Her eyes looked careworn. He thought he saw a gray hair at her temple.

His heart ached as he saw the woman he loved in such a condition. In so many ways, her haggard and starved appearance mirrored his own. Yet she was still the woman he loved. She was still the person who was his rock and his foundation. She was still the woman who sustained him. His heart remembered what his eyes did not see. It beat more rapidly as he moved towards her.

Quoc noticed a flicker of unfamiliarity on Kim-Cuong's face. She quickly surveyed his face and body. He could not blame her. If he had seen himself in the mirror, he doubted he would recognize the person before him. His frame had always been slight, normally weighing just 115 pounds. He guessed now his weight was 80 pounds. He must have looked horrible, with sores on his skin and the pasty pallor of a man held prisoner for nearly two years.

In an instant, though, the old recognition came back. The love and the passion blossomed in her eyes.

The guard motioned for Quoc to sit down on his side of the table. Quoc wanted to rush to Kim-Cuong and embrace her and hold her to his body. Reluctantly, he sat down. From the other prisoners who had already visited, he learned that no whispering was allowed; no touching tolerated; and no codes or information could be passed between the two. He also knew that only a few minutes of visitation were permitted.

He looked intently at Kim-Cuong. She looked at him. They each held their gazes for a long moment. The pent-up fear, anger, and uncertainty came welling up in each of them. Tears flowed freely. He reached across the table to hold her hand, but the guard's look of warning, combined with the four feet of table in between them, precluded touching.

"How are your father and mother and the rest of your family?"

"They are all well, Quoc. So is your family."

"That's a relief."

"And how is our new daughter? Tell me all about her!"

"And how are the other children?"

Kim-Cuong smiled, "They are growing and being children. They are the best thing for both our families. They bring us so much joy."

Quoc smiled and felt a pang of pain, knowing that he wasn't able to be with his own children. Still, he took comfort in knowing that everyone was surviving.

He wanted desperately to ask about their home, about their financial straits, and what was happening in Saigon and the rest of the country, but the Communists forbade such conversations. In order to remain at the table, he dutifully followed the rules dictated by his captors. He and Kim-Cuong were forced to make small talk that seemed nonsensical, but nonetheless allowed them to hear each other's voice. Kim told him she had brought a package of food for him. The guards, she said, had told her they would inspect it before giving it to Quoc.

Towards the end of their short time together, Kim-Cuong looked at Quoc with deep love. She softly whispered one phrase. It was a command, a request, and warning all in one, "Make it home safely."

Quoc did not reply. He just nodded his head affirmatively as he looked into her eyes.

Quoc could tell Kim-Cuong was going through her own trials. Her eyes said it, and it humbled him to see her so willing to be his rock and his firmament. His eyes filled with tears again. She began to cry as well.

The guard motioned for Quoc to leave. He reluctantly stood up and gazed into Kim-Cuong's eyes one more time. His message was unspoken but powerful: Promising her with one last look that he would do what he could to make it back to her.

Quoc went back to the courtyard and squatted next to the other prisoners. None of them dared to speak before the guards, yet they all communicated through their motions and expressions. The guard called Quoc's name and handed him a sack full of rice and some dried shrimp. He was so emaciated from the starvation of the previous months that it was nearly too heavy for him to carry. Quoc learned later that to buy the rice and shrimp, the family had scraped together most of their limited resources.

That afternoon, the prisoners and their guards began the long trek back to Katum. Each man carried 10 to 20 pounds of food. Quoc often stumbled and fell with the heavy load. He held it tightly and eventually made it back to the camp. Like his compatriots before him, he shared some of the food and then ate as much of it as he could. With his shrunken stomach, it didn't take much to fill him. He reveled in the feeling of contentment despite the discomfort he felt in his stomach. It actually hurt from being so full. For the first time in more than a year, he fell asleep without the hollow feeling that had become part of who he was.

His heart was full as well. Full of hope, but also pain. He had seen Kim-Cuong and knew everyone was alive and surviving, but the family's struggle had been written on Kim-Cuong's face.

Each man, including Quoc, frugally rationed his food for nearly two weeks, gaining strength and health as a result. Their spirits also rose markedly, knowing that their loved ones had not forgotten them. The depression they all felt at Katum did not completely lift, but it felt lighter and more manageable. Each man could read it in the other's eyes.

MID 1977

One form of resistance by the prisoners was subtly malicious compliance in completing tasks demanded by uneducated officers and guards, who had limited ability to judge technical projects and other undertakings.

The camp at Katum, like so many others in the region, lacked road access to the populated areas of the country. In the monsoon season in the late spring and early summer, the dirt paths became virtually impassable. As a result, the leadership cadre at the camp received directions from their headquarters in Saigon to have the prisoners construct a 10-mile long roadway southeast out of the camp. It would provide an all-weather road to link the region to supply lines.

The project was not ordered for the benefit of the prisoners but to provide a means to resupply the army in its fight against Pol Pot's Khmer Rouge at the Cambodian border.

The men assembled into a formation, now numbering about 800

weary and malnourished men. The guards gave the order that the road must be constructed as quickly as possible. The men collectively shrugged as they contemplated the reserves of strength they would need to draw upon to complete the project.

One of the prisoners had served in the Army Corps of Engineers and was a trained civil engineer. He had specialized in the construction of roadways. He willingly accepted the assignment and could barely contain a spring in his step as he contemplated his plans for the road. Working with a few other senior prisoners, he devised a plan for construction of the new roadway.

Fortunately, much of the area was already clear and an existing pathway could be used as the foundation for the surface. The men would build a road not dissimilar to what the American settlers termed a "corduroy road," with crisscrossed logs to support vehicular traffic, the design thought to date back about 5,000 years.

The task took three months. Each day, dozens of teams of men dug out the sides of the pathway, to widen it. Other teams brought freshly cut logs from the forest that were carefully laid crossways into the roadway, following the design determined by the engineer. Each section of the roadway looked professionally done and appeared to be both strong and permanent.

What the prisoners barely knew and the guards did not recognize was a built-in design flaw. While it looked strong, each meter of road was only sufficient to carry a walking man or something no heavier than a jeep or motorbike. Any weight greater than 1,500 to 2,000 pounds would cause the roadway to collapse into a pile of timbers. If one succeeded in traversing part of the collapsed section, the next was ready to fail. It was a well-laid trap for anyone trying to drive heavy vehicles on it.

Once the 10 miles of roadway was complete, the engineer reported to his Communist supervisors, telling them it was ready for testing. As he assumed, they scoffed at a test and announced that it was now open for traffic and began allowing heavily laden vehicles to proceed down the full-length of the highway. Typically, the NVA routinely overloaded the Russian-made cargo trucks. Something the engineer knew and anticipated was that a vehicle designed for five tons could be loaded to a gross weight of twice that amount.

The first truck, moving slowly, began lumbering down the length of the new highway. It did not go far when the first timbers gave way. It became stuck in the mud and corduroy road. Another vehicle backed up and its driver hooked up a cable to the first truck, and attempted to pull it free. Then the towing truck fell through still another section of roadway. The guards looked puzzled and motioned for the engineer to come forward. He looked at them brazenly and said, "It's not the roadway – you overloaded the trucks." Prisoners observing the debacle laughed silently at the scene, and then later with vigor when they returned to the barracks.

Retribution that was expected for this roadway resistance never materialized. Another event would engage the guards and prisoners. This one involving yet another move.

23

REMEMBERED

"Never forget benefits done you, regardless how small."
Vietnamese Proverb

JUNE 1977

The heart is a lodestone for both hope and love. Contrarily, it also harbors life-altering suffering that can never be adequately described or even shared.

The prisoners experienced many feelings during the year they spent at Katum. Bitterness, anger, hunger, and despondency are some of the emotions that took up residence in their memories. Their experiences, like those memories, remain embedded in other parts of their bodies. Their stomachs know what pain feels like, for instance. Their skin feels the itching of scabies, even years later. Their vision sees images that transcend just sight. The men who lived through Katum carry it with them like unseen backpacks. They are heavy backpacks that will always be there, the burden weighing each man down. Others can't see or feel the weight. The burdens that haunt the men are unknowable to others.

The guards at Katum applied their pain strategy through

brutalizing work, starvation, and propaganda to extinguish hope. The men were told repeatedly that their country had forgotten them and had turned their backs on anyone who had fought against Ho Chi Minh and the heroes of North Vietnam.

The incessant loudspeakers, the reeducation classes, and the morning formations with violent deaths – all were intended to do their best to extinguish hope. Some men succumbed and died of broken bodies and hearts. Some took their own lives. Most of the men, however, somehow continued to nurture some hope in themselves despite what they experienced. Hope instructed their revenge against their Communist captors with the killing of Thach, and their resistance to the mandate requiring construction of the highway.

The visits with their family members and the life-sustaining food they brought provided further fuel propelling them into their uncertain future.

They realized that their hope was fragile. At times they had debates within themselves, particularly with the questions planted in their minds by the incessant propaganda targeting them. During dark nights and into the early morning when the calming effects of tobacco wore off, the men would sit passively, silently crying to themselves, questioning their own value, and wondering if they held any value to their families and to the world beyond.

Shortly after the debacle of the corduroy road – and before the Communists could avenge the duplicity of the design engineer and his work crews – the men were suddenly transferred to another camp. They were told to gather their belongings and report to an area just outside the camp's main gate. They were organized by their captors into groups and told to wait by the road.

After about an hour, the men heard the familiar sounds of trucks. Soon, they were engulfed in the familiar smell of diesel fumes; something so discernible that military men can identify which manufacturer produced the engine. Something about the fuel injector pumps or fuel-to-air ratio or engine displacement made a difference for each type of diesel, and it was as distinguishable to the men as a woman's perfume.

The men were boarded 60 to a truck. They were all so thin now that it was an easy fit. Something was markedly different than the previous times the men had been transported. This time, there was no top canvas on the trucks and no side curtains. The men were free to look at their surroundings and try to figure out their route, using their knowledge of geography, the direction of travel, and by observing the sun.

The men noted that the guards from Katum had been replaced. The new guards seemed exceptionally young and new to their roles. They regarded the prisoners with curiosity and, Quoc thought, some respect, although it could have been deference due to the age differences between themselves and their prisoners.

The guards didn't talk much, but when they did, they were even-tempered, instructing the men to dismount or board the trucks at rest breaks. Unlike the Katum guards, there was no maliciousness, or physical abuse. The guards appeared to enjoy the sunshine as much as the prisoners as the trucks jostled down the dirt roads. When clouds of dust inevitably rose, the guards quietly pulled up their scarves to cover their faces.

As the trucks lumbered along, the convoy came to what the men recognized as the market at Long Hoa, near Tay Ninh. It was market day, and the village of Long Hoa was crowded with shoppers at roadside stands. Vegetables, meats, and other foodstuff were for sale, along with prepared foods like bean cookies and drinks.

This was the first time in two years the men had seen anyone other than the guards or a close family member during that one short visit. It was a moment of fear for the prisoners. Would they feel scorn or anger from their fellow citizens? Would they feel shame as a result? Would the two years of propaganda that their countrymen hated them be proven true? Would their countrymen regard them as traitors? The men tried to shrink into the wood benches. Their gazes moved downwards into the bed of the truck. They feared the worst reaction from the people in the marketplace.

And then it began.

Slowly at first, a few shouts erupted. For a brief second, the prisoners feared some sort of retribution. Then reality registered: The entire crowd cheered as one. These were cheers of appreciation, of love, of respect. The villagers were cheering the prisoners as if they were returning heroes.

Food began to be handed and tossed to the prisoners, followed by money. Men and women alike cried as they saw the emaciated bodies of the prisoners.

The prisoners cried, too. For the first time in two years, they cried not out of fear or sadness, but out of gratitude.

The lies that the men had heard endlessly for the past two years melted away. Here were people that knew what the prisoners had done for them when they fought the Communists. Without fear of possible retribution, the people supplied them with food and money, and, most importantly a renewed sense of worth.

Spontaneously, the prisoners started to share the extra food with their guards. It was a transcendent act. Perhaps it reflected the validation of their own humanity. Or maybe it was a cathartic reflex necessary to push the experience of Katum behind them. The guards didn't expect it, but they readily accepted the humble act of sharing by the emaciated prisoners.

Humanity returned for a brief moment; and it was enough to tell Quoc that there were possibilities beyond the camps. Perhaps the rest of the country shared the same beliefs as these villagers.

The convoy continued on for more than two hours, traversing about 80 miles until it reached Dong Xoai and halted. The men thought it was one of the pre-planned breaks for the men to relieve themselves.

They were surprised: The truck happened to stop in front of a restaurant specializing in *Pho*, Vietnamese noodle soup. The officer in charge came to the back of the truck and said, "Go ahead and get yourselves a bowl of soup. You have money now from those people in the market."

The prisoners looked at each other, first with skepticism, then with an emotion that had been dormant for too long. The men actually felt a sort of nervous enthusiasm. Quoc and several others went into the restaurant. The customers stared at the emaciated, dirty, and disheveled prisoners. Then the proprietor said with a smile, "Hủ tíu or mì?" (What would you like?)

"*Pho Ga*, please. *Pho Ga*." (Chicken Noodle Soup)

"Sit down, please. I'll get it for you right away."

In minutes, each man had a steaming bowl of *Pho* in front of him. No meal ever tasted so good before or since. They ate quickly; not knowing how long their reprieve would last. Each piece of chicken and noodles and the savory broth felt like heaven.

When they finished, Quoc asked, "Please sir, how much?"

A sad and pensive look covered the owner's face. Tears were in his eyes as he shook his head from side to side,

"Don't worry about that, it's my gift to you."

Stunned, they walked to the door. As they did, a woman motioned for the group to follow her to the back of the restaurant. Then she handed each man some coins and bills. She sobbed as she spoke,

"My brother was in the camps, just like you. I just came from visiting him in Saigon, so I don't have much to give. This is all I have. Just promise me: Make it home to your families. God bless you"

Crying, she ran out the door. Quoc ran after her, gently touching her arm, "I will make it home safely. I promise. Thank you so much, and God bless you."

Quoc and his fellow prisoners cried. They cried for their fellow countryman who had been imprisoned. They cried for the kindness of the woman and the restaurateur. They cried because they had not been forgotten. They were remembered. They were loved. Each would carry those feelings forever.

The convoy took hours to pass through Tay Ninh province. The men continued to receive gifts and food and steady encouragement from the villagers. Most of the residents were part of the Cao Dai religious movement. Caodaiisim was a new religion, established in Tay Ninh in 1926. It was just 52 years old at the time the convoy passed. During the war, the villagers had taken up arms against the Communists as a way to preserve their religious freedom. The religion itself is one of the most eclectic in the world, combining elements of Buddhism, Christianity, Taoism, Confucianism, and Islam. The religion has its own pope, and to this day, the seat of power remains in Tay Ninh.

The men were thrilled, but two years of behavior designed for survival in the camps could and would not be so easily unlearned. They talked, but never spoke above a whisper for the remainder of the long trip.

"Did you see that? I always knew the Cao Dai people were genuine and caring. I knew they wouldn't fall for the Communist line."

"I hope the rest of the South Vietnamese feel the way the people of Tay Ninh do!"

"I'm sure of it," smiled another.

The exchanges were not loud enough for the guards to hear. If they caught some brief conversations between the prisoners, most of the guards seemed not to care. They carried out their functions professionally, without the zeal, dogma and brutality of the guards at Katum.

The experience in Long Hoa market and Dong Xoai became a beacon and enduring reminder for Quoc that helped him endure.

On that truck ride, the idea of escape suddenly crystallized for Quoc. Not as an idea or plan but as a feeling. The feeling made him breathe more rapidly and his heartbeat accelerate. The idea became a flame that flickered like a candle in his head and his heart. It stayed lit for the next three years, through the winds and rains and challenges he couldn't yet foresee.

The men were on the road for more than 10 hours that day. They stopped repeatedly. The constant bouncing and jostling of the trucks exhausted their emaciated bodies, but thanks to the people of Tay Ninh and Dong Xoai, their stomachs were full. They were even able to cat nap occasionally.

As they progressed further, they recognized the surroundings and region as Bu Gia Map, a province about 60 miles from Saigon, almost due north of the capital city.

They arrived at a clearing. There were some primitive structures. They knew their tasks would be similar to the jobs at Katum. Cut trees, haul them to a site, clear more land and build more buildings and more accommodations for the prisoners who would be housed here. That night, as the men found places to lay their sleeping mats and fall into an exhausted sleep, they didn't dwell on the tasks before them. They reflected on their ability to endure the first two years of their captivity.

Quoc lay there for a few minutes. He pictured Kim-Cuong and the children, all smiling at the stories he would tell them about this day. He visualized the gentle curve of Kim-Cuong's face, the sweet smile, and the dark intelligent eyes. And then he drifted off to sleep.

24

A CHANGE IN THE WIND

"Giving just a crumb to the hungry is worth more than giving lunch to the satisfied."

Vietnamese Proverb

JULY-SEPTEMBER 1977

At Bu Gia Map, things were markedly different. Katum had been a living hell for the men. The brutality and the deprivation had made them believe the Communists were bent on destroying their spirits and their lives. The men had never been able to comprehend why, but the evidence had been real, and most of the men had come to believe they were not meant to survive.

However, the mood from the very beginning of the truck convoy leaving Katum was different, through the wondrous experience in the village of Tay Ninh, to their arrival at the sparse camp in the forest at Bu Gia Map – all of it was like a different world, a different feeling, a different environment.

The men were still prisoners, but the focus on retribution had been replaced with a feeling the men could not fully define. It was powerful. It manifested itself in the renewed ability to smile and to make eye contact with one another. It was as if an invisible prison of shame and pain had been lifted from the men. They were captives still, but they were no longer under an unspoken death sentence.

None of them trusted the feeling they were experiencing; and they continually lapsed into denying that things were actually changing for them. Men who have experienced such brutality have a limited amount of optimism, and it is continually offset with cynicism. Skepticism, based on first-hand knowledge and experience, had been seared into their memories.

The routine at this camp was much the same as it was at the other ones. The number of camps and the moves to and from each of them was a blur. After two years, the men often lost track of where they had been and exactly what happened where. Administrative details, after all, were quite similar in every camp.

At Bu Gia Map, men were confined as usual, and they were, as was the norm, afforded sparse or no quarters. However, they received a bit more food. And, after years in the camps, there were no surprises with either the reeducation classes or the inevitable work details. Stories and confessions were now well rehearsed, and they readily parroted what their guards required and expected.

The prisoners now knew who specialized in certain work details. Some men were better at building, at jungle clearing, doing roadwork, or working in the blacksmith shop. Some were good at scrounging for food and preparing it. Each prisoner now gravitated toward certain work details and accepted assignments from the guards.

Quoc was in a group of 60 in a camp that held several thousand prisoners. The men were surprised to learn that among these prisoners were former South Vietnamese soldiers who had been in captivity since well before the end of the war. Some said they had been prisoners for a decade.

The camp was located along a wide dirt road covered with red dust. The road was the main route from Bu Gia Map to the center of Phuoc Long, a small city about a hundred miles north of Saigon. The road was frequently traveled by local buses, as well as military trucks.

Quoc and a number of other teams were assigned a unique challenge – to build a visitor center and visitor quarters in a secluded grove of trees about five hundred feet outside the official confines of the camp. They labored for more than a month to finish the construction, which included ten small huts. To the men, the main visitor area was a further indication of change.

The small huts the men built were close together, usually in rows. The structures were tiny, with just enough room for a bed, table, and chairs. The men would soon realize that the huts would serve as places for wives to stay overnight.

The Communists hoped these visits would motivate couples to stay in the New Economic Zone to populate the collective farms. The program was making less progress than the government had hoped.

As the huts were completed, the men received permission to send another letter to their families with instructions for a visit. They were allowed to ask for food but could receive no publications, books, or even photos of the outside world. The word spread rapidly.

The guards didn't indicate how long family members could stay, but they told the men to tell their loved ones to be prepared for overnight stays after the long trip from Saigon.

In a matter of weeks, it seemed that every man in the camp was receiving regular visits by their wives. This continued for as long as Quoc and the other men were held at Bu Gia Map.

There was now no doubt that the men were happier. They were able to spend time with their loved ones and were able to engage in the physical act of love for the first time in years.

Quoc hadn't received confirmation from Kim-Cuong that she received his letter. He thought of their reunion often and daydreamed about their meeting. He wanted so desperately to hold her and to thank her for her love, which had so sustained him.

He had been assigned to work in another camp several miles away one day and was returning late one night, at about 8:00 p.m. As he dismounted the truck, he noticed that the visitor center was already crowded with people. A guard motioned for him to enter. As Quoc walked in, he noticed about a half dozen young women sitting on a bench, along with several children.

He immediately recognized one woman, even though her face was partially turned away. It might have been the curve of her cheek or the way she held her head. His beautiful Kim-Cuong sat before him for only the second time in two years. Their first meeting had been across a table for just 15 minutes.

His heart pounded, realizing he would be able to hold her, kiss her, and to talk with her and once again be part of the world she occupied.

Quoc walked over to Kim-Cuong and gently placed his hand on her shoulder. He felt a slight tremble in her body and then a calm of silent recognition. She turned and smiled, a tear gently running down her cheek. Quoc kissed her and held her closely. The embrace lasted for minutes. Then he kissed her again, a long kiss, remembering those lips and their love.

Instead of treating Kim-Cuong and Quoc's reunion like a family visit to an inmate in prison, the guards stood back a respectful distance. They gave the two the opportunity to hold each other for long minutes without pause.

Quoc did not know how long the visit would be allowed, but then the captain in charge of the camp yelled, "Hey you! Are you out of your mind or what? Why don't you take this lovely lady to your quarters to rest?"

As the officer spoke the word "rest," he grinned and made a thrusting motion with his pelvis.

Quoc looked at him, confused. Was it a joke the officer was playing on him? He had never seen other guests allowed to visit the prisoner's quarters.

Then a young guard with a rifle motioned to Quoc to follow him. Kim-Cuong and Quoc walked behind. They looked at each other, confused and worried. After the short walk into the prisoners' camp the guard ordered the group leader to clear the kitchen of one of the huts. He declared it would be closed to everyone until the next morning. A makeshift bed was quickly prepared with help from fellow prisoners.

Once they were alone, Quoc and Kim-Cuong quietly sat there on the bed. They held each other as he asked her questions about the children and her extended family and his. They talked for more than an hour without stopping. Meanwhile, Kim-Cuong broke out cooking utensils, some rice, dried meat, and tea. She prepared it for the two of them as they continued to chat and reacquaint themselves with each other. Quoc looked at this wonderful creature and said a silent prayer of thanks.

At one point, Kim-Cuong, smiling, whispered gently to Quoc, "I understand there is a stream nearby. You can take this soap and get cleaned up." Quoc grinned and rushed out of the hut. He returned quickly, and then they made love for the first time in two years.

They fell asleep in each other's arms. That night, their dreams were uninterrupted by either guards or prisoners. Their world was the only world that existed.

Quoc and Kim-Cuong remained together for three more days. Each day and night were filled with joy, conversation, and physical pleasure that kept the realities of the camps at bay.

The officer in charge of Quoc's part of Bu Gia Map was the one who had decided to allow wives to remain overnight. Other sections of the camp had not been so fortunate. In those cases, if the men were not allowed to sleep with their wives, the women would always band together during the night for security.

Each morning, a guard would come to the main barracks at the camp, waking the men for their daily exercise. He would laugh and say, "Wake up, and make love to your wives!" The men appreciated the humor. Many concluded that the government wanted the wives to get pregnant and settle in the New Economic Zone with their husbands. What the camp leadership did not appreciate, though, was that the majority of the women who visited their husbands at Bu Gia Map were city girls, who had no desire or inclination to settle on farms – husband or not, pregnant or not.

Though there were no reported rapes at the camp, there were continual cases of young guards approaching the women with lurid comments. Guards came on to the wives, saying things like, "Your husband is a criminal and a prisoner. Why do you stick with him? You're so young and beautiful, you could marry someone else."

The wives would gently deflect the comments so as not to arouse the ire of the guards. After all, the Communists still carried weapons and the husbands were still prisoners. One day, though, an especially obnoxious guard pressed his case to one of the wives, asserting, "I am a soldier of the Republic of Vietnam. I make good money. You should come with me!"

The woman icily stared him down and then replied sternly, "Look young man, I could sell just my lingerie and feed my husband for 10 years!"

The young guard gulped and skulked away.

As their time in Bu Gia Map progressed, the men realized that, in many respects, they were living a charmed existence. At least for the first three months of their stay, the camp had been devoid of senior leadership. The commandant had allegedly been on leave and junior subordinates were running the camp.

The captain, the ranking junior officer, was lenient and seemed motivated to try to bridge the gap between former enemies. His second in command – a lieutenant – was the exact opposite, exhibiting many of the same tendencies that the men had seen from the guards in Katum. This officer hated the men because he felt they were criminals. He was often heard ranting about the stupidity of allowing criminals to have conjugal visits in a military facility.

The prisoners called the captain the Good Guy, the lieutenant Bad. Good kept Bad in check for most of the time.

Except for late one night.

It was during Kim-Cuong's second visit. This time she came with their daughter, Ngan.

The men and their wives had retired for the night. Ngan was already asleep, and Quoc and Kim-Cuong were ready to retire. The prisoners had been allowed to remain with their wives in the guest quarters at the visitor center. Sometime after midnight, the Bad officer showed up. He had obviously been drinking heavily.

He fired his pistol into the air once and, with an angry and strident voice, shouted, "Everyone come out of your huts!"

"Did you hear me?" he screamed again. "I said get your asses out of the huts and into formation." He fired the pistol again.

The prisoners peered through cracks in the hut walls and saw the drunken lieutenant stagger back and forth, screaming his orders to be obeyed.

"I will shoot you right through the walls, I swear! Now get out here! And bring your whores with you!"

A standoff occurred. The men didn't know what to do. To remain in the huts was perilous. To stand before the guard carried equal risk.

Courage comes in many forms. Oftentimes, the greatest courage is choosing something other than conflict.

Quoc, his fellow prisoners, and their wives, knelt by the walls of their huts, peering through whatever cracks they could find. As they watched, one of the wives – an especially beautiful one – walked towards the lieutenant. She wore nothing but her nightgown, and then she dropped it to the ground.

Naked, she approached the drunken officer with a softness and sensuality that took a poise and control that few could have mustered. She walked towards him, gently saying, "Don't worry about those people. I am here for you. Make love to me!"

The officer staggered backwards, shocked as if he had been punched. The woman continued, "I don't care about my husband. I just want a man like you. An officer of our government and a disciple of Ho Chi Minh. Take me!"

The officer holstered his pistol. He moved towards her. He didn't notice the woman's body quiver, even though the night was warm. The young wife did not know what would happen. She only knew she had to save her husband and the others. Terrified, she could not let him see her fear.

The lieutenant grabbed her by the arm, and then pulled her body to him. She could smell his sweat and drunken breath. She mustered every bit of presence she could to appear to show interest in him. He kissed her, a sloppy, drunken kiss. She knew she would have to go through with her implied intention. The lieutenant had unwittingly called her bluff.

Quoc hugged Kim-Cuong closely. The prisoners and their wives collectively held their breath.

Then a shout rang out.

The captain came running up to the man. He tore him away from the young wife, barking, "Get back to your quarters. You are relieved."

The drunken lieutenant staggered somewhat and then moved menacingly towards his captain. The senior officer took his pistol and hit the man against the side of the head, nearly knocking him unconscious. The drunken lieutenant backed away, angrily eyeing the officer as he did. Blood ran down his face.

The young wife collapsed to the ground. Her husband came running with a blanket and gently placed it over her shoulders. He held her tightly as he helped her back to the quarters.

LATE 1977

As the year ended, the men hoped more changes would occur. However, they didn't know what was occurring outside of the Bu Gia Map province or in Southeast Asia and other parts of the world. And like most people in Vietnam, they had no sense of what was happening in the central government.

Although the men had heard about the ongoing war between Vietnam and Pol Pot's regime in Cambodia, they didn't know the enormity of the conflict and the drain of manpower and resources it took from the Communist government. The reduced number of guards and the lack of oversight by the Communist camp overseers was probably a direct function of the war. But only years later would the men make that correlation.

The Communists had likely concluded that the two-decade war had already created tremendous losses of expert manpower. The government was losing the services of hundreds of thousands of educated and capable men who were prisoners of their own country. The conflict with Cambodia was draining even more manpower from the country every day.

The prisoners were considered criminals by their government. However, the pragmatists in the Communist leadership no doubt realized that the brains, education, and experience of the prisoners could be put to valuable use for the state, providing a capable labor force for Saigon and the New Economic Zone. However, a prisoner could not, would not, embrace this view, unless he felt his family had a part in that future. The government leaders likely concluded that bringing the families into the camps would help convince the men to settle in the New Economic Zone once they were released. There, the leaders believed, they could establish new lives for themselves for their own benefit and that of the country. The prisoners eventually realized the government's intentions. Men like Quoc were key to getting the economy back on track. The New Economic Zone was the chessboard to which many would be consigned.

As this Communist strategy began to filter down to the prisoners in December of 1977, it was apparent that skilled professionals, ranging from pharmacists to doctors to engineers, would be needed to settle the Zone. Some would even be needed in Saigon.

Initially Quoc, with his maritime officer background, felt he would be released. And, he might have been, except for an unforeseen event.

Unknown to Quoc, one of his former maritime classmates, recently released to the New Economic Zone, was recruited to serve as captain of a large ship. His intention was to escape from the country. In early December 1977, using bribes to allow the escape, the captain and his crew successfully transported nearly a thousand men, women, and children to Subic Bay, Philippines.

After the government learned how the plan had come together, all former South Vietnamese mariners were ordered to remain in Reeducation Camps far away from any coast. Quoc's hopes for release, even to the New Economic Zone, were dashed.

25

WALKING THE PATH WITH LOVE AND DETERMINATION

"No one saves us but ourselves. No one can and no one may. We ourselves must walk the path."

Buddha

THE VISITS IN 1977 AND 1978

The trip from Saigon to Phuoc Long was the first leg of the tortuous two-day journey to the camp at Bu Gia Map. It was an arduous one for Kim-Cuong. She made the trip there four times, spending a number of days at the visitor center's guest quarters, or in the small huts constructed by the prisoners.

Transportation options were sparse. Neither Kim-Cuong's nor Quoc's family owned a car. Between them the families might have retained one poorly maintained motorbike, only suitable for quick jaunts around Saigon. Neither a car nor a motorbike could have taken her safely to Bu Gia Map.

Public bus was the only real option. Buses could use the un-improved roads. Buses also afforded safety in numbers for the passengers. The countryside could be dangerous, especially for women traveling alone.

Twenty years of war had seen the infrastructure of the country slowly erode. Old main supply routes like the Ho Chi Minh Trail, long used by the NVA and Viet Cong were further to the west. The U.S. had relied less on ground transport and more substantially on aircraft like the C-123 and C-130, which, throughout the war, hauled supplies, fuel, and ammunition. There had been no coordinated efforts to repair, pave, or improve the roads in the country. Highways were often no more than wide dusty trails that became large muddy impasses during the rainy season.

The buses used by the government to provide some sort of transportation network around the country were primarily underpowered diesel minivans from China. They were designed to hold eight passengers but usually carried from twelve to fifteen people, crammed double on the seats, on the floor, and in the baggage area. There were also larger buses, designed for twenty, but usually containing as many as fifty passengers.

When the bus was unable to traverse a road, the passengers dismounted and pushed the vehicle until it had cleared the mud or steep hill. Some of the buses dated back to the French occupation. They were rusty and largely unsafe for the passengers, but travelers were forced to accept the risk. There were no other options.

A few of the buses were configured with makeshift bunks for those passengers traveling during the night. Kim-Cuong was never one of them. She and her family felt it was safer to travel during daylight hours. There was limited bus service from Saigon to Phuoc Long. Passengers had to book seats, and often bribe agents, weeks in advance.

On her trips, Kim-Cuong carried as many barter items as the family could afford, given their limited funds. She crammed the items – mostly clothing, like skirts, blouses, and even lingerie – into an old military backpack. Kim-Cuong clutched the backpack throughout the journey, occasionally nodding off for a catnap. She secured it to her wrist with a piece of twine to ensure that no one could steal it while she was sleeping.

Kim-Cuong also carried at least ten pounds of dried meat and noodles or beans in order to feed herself and Quoc while she was at the camp. After the first trip, she learned that she could obtain more rice by bartering clothing for it in the countryside.

The ride from Saigon to Phuoc Long via bus was scheduled for 10 hours, but it usually took 12-14. The distance was eighty miles, but the serpentine route and impassability of the roads made it seem considerably longer. Additional minutes added up to hours each time the passengers were forced to push the bus.

Phuoc Long was the farthest Kim-Cuong could travel via regularly-scheduled public transit. Once there, she was still more than thirty miles from the Bu Gia Map camps. It was usually very nearly dark or, depending on the time of the year, past nightfall when Kim-Cuong arrived in Phuoc Long. There were no hotels or guest-houses in Phuoc Long. It was a rural area with villages scattered over several square miles. Kim-Cuong heard that in nearby villages people would take travelers into their homes.

These villagers with Buddhist backgrounds had pre-war values: Honoring a stranger with food and shelter was considered a privi-lege. Kim-Cuong respected the Buddhist traditions. She accepted gifts of hospitality with a grace and kindness that reflected the honor that had been bestowed upon her. When she entered a small village, she would choose a hut or small abode and quietly knock on a door. When the occupant cracked the door open – or for those places with-out doors – pulled a curtain aside – Kim-Cuong would bow slowly and explain that she was a traveler in need.

Without exception they would ask her to join their humble family circle. It would have been impolite to turn her down or ask her why she was on her journey, though most knew why. A small bowl of rice with some fish sauce would be placed in front of Kim-Cuong, and she was always given a sleeping mat in a dry corner of the abode.

Kim-Cuong often gave an article of clothing to the woman of the house. She would respectfully offer it, not as payment, but as a way to honor the kindness of the family. Later, if the opportunity presented itself, Kim-Cuong would gently ask if the family wanted to sell or barter any food. She was careful never to push the bounds of propriety with such a request and always assessed the family situation before even considering it. Honor meant as much to Kim-Cuong as it did to Quoc. The age-old culture and traditions of the Vietnamese people had been built on honor.

The villagers were savvy about the war and its aftermath. Unlike the former NVA and Viet Cong soldiers, most bore no anger or hostility towards men like Quoc. Indeed, they felt sorry for the treatment the men were receiving. The villagers knew that they were prisoners and how they were treated in the camps. Often they knew more than the city dwellers of Saigon. As a result, Kim-Cuong and many of the other women received special kindness and treatment during their overnight stays to and from Bu Gia Map.

The departures from Phuoc Long were always emotional for Kim-Cuong. To receive such kindnesses from strangers was always humbling and had an enormous impact on her. She always bowed respectfully and waved to her hosts as she walked away from the village. She was thankful that devout people had protected her through the night.

Phuoc Long abutted a river that needed to be crossed by a ferry, small boat, or by wading across the shallow parts. On Kim-Cuong's first trip to visit Quoc, she came to the river where two fishermen were quietly plying their trade. She asked, "Will you give me a ride to the other side of the river?"

"No, we're too busy. We can't."

"Will you help me cross so I can visit my husband? He is a political prisoner in Bu Gia Map"

With that, they acquiesced. On subsequent trips, she always obtained free travel across the river. After the ten-minute crossing, the men would wish her well and often gave her food and a drink of tea to fortify her on her continued journey.

Once Kim-Cuong crossed the river, she still had at least 30 miles to hike or to hitchhike on motorbikes through fields and forest. Sometimes this journey took two days. The path she traversed was well worn by local villagers and worn even more by the continual stream of wives visiting their husbands in Bu Gia Map. Kim-Cuong walked with confidence and purpose, determinedly carrying a pack that was far too heavy. She was powered by a single-minded love for Quoc. Her faith ensured that she never feared for her own safety. During her travels to and from the camp, Kim-Cuong never encountered anyone with ill intent.

A few times on her journey, she would link up with one or two other women, intent on visiting their husbands or family members in the camp, and passed the arduous trek in pleasant conversation. One time she joined five other women as they traveled to Bu Gia Map.

The women would trade stories about their lives since 1975: How they felt and how their families were coping. They became fast friends. They spoke of their anger about the incarceration and their frustration with the government. They related thoughts of husbands who did not fully appreciate them and what they were going through, and they spoke about the love that kept them going. They exchanged ideas about child rearing and how to stretch food for their families in such hard times. They conversed woman-to-woman in a language men never comprehend, even when they hear it.

The husbands never fully understood the privations and

challenges with which their wives lived. The prisoners seldom realized what was happening beyond the walls of their jails. Though they
tried their best to shield their wives from the realities of the camps,
Kim-Cuong and the rest of the wives always knew.

26

A SECOND CAMP IN BU GIA MAP

"Joy came back to us as we sat around the campfire and sang."

Quoc Pham

EARLY 1978

After the release of some prisoners to Saigon and the New Economic Zone, the remaining group of men was transferred to another camp. The move came as quickly as all the other moves preceding it. One day they were told to pack their belongings and were then marched further into the forest of Bu Gia Map.

Although they were still confined, there were also some positive changes for the prisoners. Life became even more relaxed. The men received real food rations from their captors. A terrible smelling dried fish was routinely given to the men. Although they hated the smell, they appreciated the nourishment. Most of the men did not gain weight – the ration was simply not sufficient to provide that benefit – but including protein in their diet helped improve their health, and was a welcome relief from consuming insects.

The fish also gave the prisoners something with which to bargain.

The villagers considered the fish a delicacy and gladly bartered portions of it for ample amounts of rice, potatoes, and other foodstuff.

Something else was markedly different at the new camp in Bu Gia Map. The camp was located in an isolated forest far away from the nearest city, but there were local people living nearby. A tribe of highland people – the Tien – had lived in the area for centuries. They showed no signs of ceding ownership of their land, or the trails they walked each day, to the Communists.

Each morning, Tien natives traveled through the camp where Quoc and the others were working. They walked with purpose on the well-worn path to begin their daily chores of farming and hunting. Their route was worn into a footpath that was now nearly three-feet wide. Every morning and early evening, the villagers guided carts pulled by donkeys or water buffalo.

The villagers were not unfriendly, but they seemed indifferent to the camp's existence. The prisoners were startled to see the young women of the village walk along the path topless, as was the Tien custom. They were not going to change just because a prison camp had been constructed on their land.

For the prisoners, the presence of women alone provided enjoyment and quasi-normalcy to their daily lives. The fact that the women were topless undoubtedly raised other interests in the prisoners as well. The women's first appearance shocked the men. On subsequent days, the men calibrated their stares to be less intrusive yet still provide some viewing pleasure.

When the villagers walked through the camp, the prisoners remained respectfully quiet and avoided direct eye contact with the men and their wives and daughters. After the villagers passed, there was always a measure of quiet sexual innuendo. None of the prisoners was ribald or graphic, but their comments expressed their renewed feelings of being alive.

Within days of their arrival, imaginary fantasy banquets ceased, replaced by real food. Pots of rice and beans or fried potatoes and vegetables were realities. And, for the first time, the guards did not steal food from the men.

Their improved lives continued. Family visits, though not officially sanctioned, were usually allowed if the guards were appropriately bribed. Because the new camp was even farther from the Communist headquarters, the guards readily accepted the bribes and allowed the visits without repercussions.

Additionally, visitors smuggled in contraband and cash to procure sufficient food, even some alcohol. One man's wife brought her husband an old guitar.

At night, men and women sat around a small fire. Sipping whatever alcohol they had procured, they listened to the guitar player and sang well into the night. They sang mostly love songs but also included pop hits and even some country tunes they had learned from American G.I.s. Anything the men heard was better than the martial music they had listened to for two and a half years. Even the guards seemed to enjoy the music. The music and alcohol no doubt contributed to more than a few romantic evenings.

After spending Vietnamese New Year with the family, Kim-Cuong made her third visit to Bu Gia Map. Quoc and Kim-Cuong spent a week together in a small hut Quoc and a friend had constructed. It was like the honeymoon the couple never had. Quoc was still a prisoner and expected to be involved in his daily work details at Bu Gia Map, but he was usually done before noon and came back to the hut for an afternoon of lovemaking, followed by dinner.

When Kim-Cuong visited, the couple often invited some of Quoc's fellow prisoners to dinner. The men laughed with each other and enjoyed the company of a beautiful woman. They sought, like all men do, to impress her with stories of the camps and their exploits as prisoners. Kim-Cuong dutifully listened and smiled because she had something, at least for an evening, that bordered on normalcy.

Occasionally, a guard who stopped by the hut would be surprised to be invited in for tea and food.

Kim-Cuong always came prepared to barter with the local highlanders. She brought a small satchel of brightly colored blouses and skirts that could be exchanged for food from the villagers. One beautiful skirt could easily be bartered for twenty pounds of rice.

Kim-Cuong was a good trader and made excellent use of the clothes as currency to barter. So much so that one of Quoc's fellow prisoners at dinner one night quipped, "If our wives keep selling clothes to the natives, they'll be wearing blouses and our wives will be topless!"

It was heartening for Quoc and Kim-Cuong to laugh once again with others. Humor had long been a distant memory at the prisoners' earlier camps. Here, how very quickly it emerged, bringing joy to men who had experienced none for so many years.

At the end of Kim-Cuong's and Quoc's first week together, one of the guards stopped by their quarters and said to Kim-Cuong, "It's time to go now, sister."

Quoc was prepared. He already had learned from his fellow prisoner, that a pound of Thuoc Lao given to a guard would buy the couple another week together. The guard walked away without a word.

After two weeks, Kim-Cuong had to leave. The parting was sorrowful, but their two weeks together reunited them as a couple once more.

Everyone is a sexual creature in his or her own right. Katum had denied that part of a prisoners' being. When a man is starving and fearful of a daily beating, sexual desire disappears, but when normalcy returns, it is reignited. In this new camp, prisoners realized that life was not ending for them.

Nearly half of the prison population – all professional men – had been released in December. Quoc hoped he would be released too. By the end of February, visits from the wives, the late-night song sessions, and the nods by the guards allowing alcohol all came to an end when a new officer took command of the camp.

Quoc would receive one more visit from Kim-Cuong in Bu Gia Map.

In mid-March of 1978, Quoc was surprised to see Kim-Cuong arrive at the camp, and he knew instantly that something was terribly wrong.

27

JOURNEY HOME

"Life is a temporary stop. Death is a journey home."

Vietnamese Proverb

APRIL 1978

It had taken just milliseconds to realize it. Perhaps it was the energy around Kim-Cuong that was different. Or the way she carried her body. Whatever it was, it emanated from her entire being.

There was worry in her eyes and dark circles beneath them. They reflected her many sleepless nights. He intuitively knew she had cried until no more tears were left and undoubtedly had cried some more.

"Who was it?"

"My mother and your father." She hesitated and then spoke again. "Both of them – they're gone."

Kim-Cuong embraced Quoc. The embrace was one that sought strength and comfort, as only Quoc could provide, but it fell on Kim-Cuong to provide for both: Quoc's legs had buckled at the news. The man he admired most in the world and the woman who had raised the wife he loved, were no longer alive. They no longer existed except in memory. The finality of it was larger than anything he had known.

At that moment, Quoc's anger overwhelmed his pain. The Communists had taken so much from him – his freedom, his health, his wife, and his children. Now they had taken away the most fundamental thing a human being can experience – the right to say goodbye to a loved one.

Husband and wife held each other for more than a minute, each providing unspoken support for the other. As the embrace ended, Quoc backed away slightly and gently asked,

"What can I do?"

"Come back to Saigon – I've gotten you a pass to come home."

The words shocked him. They carried meaning far beyond a visit back to his remaining family members. They signaled a seismic shift of sorts in the attitudes of the Vietnamese government, who were finally allowing passes – albeit due to tragic circumstances – back to the prisoners' homes.

Kim-Cuong spent that night with Quoc. They talked well into the night until both collapsed in exhaustion.

Quoc learned that his father, Xuong, had died of a stroke. He collapsed at home while reaching for the front door handle. He remained in a coma for ten days with no signs of recovery. Vo wanted Quoc to return home during that period, but the authorities refused. With no sign of brain activity or physical movement, the family made the difficult decision to authorize the removal of his respirator. Xuong died within an hour, what was left of his life slowly ebbing away.

The doctors, some of them former South Vietnamese officers, were sympathetic. They told the family there was nothing that could have been done; his death was caused by cardiovascular conditions. But Vo, to her dying day, fervently believed that Xuong died of a broken heart.

Like countless others, Xuong's life was torn apart after the fall of his country. His family had been dispersed to Reeducation Camps and bankrupted financially.

The harmony that could have assuaged his pain had been disrupted by arguments with his son Phuc, who continually spoke about the virtues of Communism and often referred to Quoc as a war criminal.

While Quoc was a prisoner in a camp, Xuong was held captive in a far more pernicious one. He spent his last days in a prison of shame, poverty, and disharmony within the family. It was no wonder, Quoc thought, that he died so suddenly.

Kim-Cuong's mother, Tot, succumbed to cancer. She experienced a long and painful death. Most of her family members believed that the stress of the war and its aftermath had taken a terrible toll on her health. Her death was emblematic of the war's ultimate consequences.

The next morning, Kim-Cuong and Quoc awoke, but were not well rested. Though their eyes had been closed, their minds were filled with the enormity of the deaths. It would take years to cope with their pain and anguish, which would be triggered by any reminder of the war and what they considered to be their parents' untimely deaths.

The guards would not allow Quoc and Kim-Cuong to travel together. Quoc could accompany Kim-Cuong the 30 miles back to the river at Phuoc Long, but he had to pledge to return. Even though Quoc had an official pass from the government, it was as if the Communists still needed to exert some control over him. It was not surprising to Kim-Cuong or Quoc that the guards' compliance was also malicious. Sadly, Quoc and Kim-Cuong had become inured to such cruelty.

Kim-Cuong promised that Quoc would not use his pass to escape. She committed her family's honor. She also believed that retribution against the family would be forthcoming if either of them violated the terms of the furlough. Based on his experiences, Quoc knew it with certainty.

Quoc ensured that Kim-Cuong received safe passage across the river and saw her successfully catch a ride on the back of a motorbike. He waved to her and turned back. He hiked about a mile towards Bu Gia Map when he flagged down and hitched a ride with a military convoy headed in the direction of the camp. From his clothing and his physical condition, the soldiers recognized that Quoc was a prisoner. As Quoc bounced along in the bed of the truck, he thought ruefully that they were happier to return him to camp. Someday he promised himself, he would be free.

After another sad, lonely and sleep-deprived night, the guards allowed Quoc to leave the next day. After verification by the camp guards and a careful scrutiny of the written pass he carried, Quoc was allowed to hitch a ride on a military truck to Phuoc Long. He spent the night there. The next day he used some of the money Kim-Cuong had smuggled in to buy a bus ticket back to Saigon.

The bus driver readily identified Quoc as a political prisoner and told him to sit in the back of the bus. About 15 miles from Saigon, the driver told Quoc to get off the bus. No reason was given. He then hitched rides, first on a horse-drawn cart, then on a small carriage pulled by a water buffalo. Quoc's last ride was on the back of a motorbike, arriving in Saigon late that night.

As the motorbike sped along the city streets, Quoc saw a noticeable difference in his native city. The traffic had diminished. The vibrancy was gone. A malaise hung over Saigon. The buildings had deteriorated and many were abandoned. There was a strong military presence, with soldiers and their equipment evident on every block, including the ever-present loudspeakers strategically mounted every few streets.

Quoc met Kim-Cuong at his in-laws' home. Hung, Ngan and

Khanh were there. He hugged his children for as long as they remained still, with tears streaming down his cheeks. Neuroscience has determined that children do not remember the way adults do. Their early childhood memories are less about their own experiences than the stories they hear from their elders. Kim-Cuong had continually told them about Quoc, and they delighted in seeing him, but he knew that any memories were limited. That didn't diminish his joy in seeing them and knowing his prayers for their safety had been answered. They were still alive and relatively healthy and for that, he gave thanks.

In the camps, Quoc's thoughts of homecoming were confined to his immediate family – Kim-Cuong and the children, as well as his parents. He had spent little time thinking about interactions with his or Kim-Cuong's extended families. He was unprepared for the level of tension among family members. A number of relatives and friends now avoided Quoc. Some did not speak to him or, if they did, gave short, perfunctory answers to his questions. Eye contact was limited. When they did look at him, some seemed fearful. They had suffered a lot in the past three years and clearly didn't want to be identified as collaborators with a known traitor or criminal.

One day, at Kim-Cuong's father's urging, Quoc stopped by to see his wife's grandmother. They had always had a good relationship, and she always welcomed him into her small home with cordiality, good food, and respect. This visit was markedly different. She refused to let him in the house and yelled to other relatives to serve him a cold lunch of some rice and fish sauce. She said, "He better eat quick and then get out of here!"

Quoc left the food untouched and quietly walked out, feeling violated and betrayed.

Kim-Cuong told him of the hateful comments she received from her family. A close relative said, "You always wanted to marry an officer. Well, this is what you got for it." Another told her, bragging,

"My husband was only an enlisted man, and you don't see him in jail do you? I'm glad he is home with me."

Quoc was appalled by their behavior, especially as he struggled with his father's death. Only years later would he appreciate the fear and concern each felt for their own family's safety at the time. A country governed by a military regime with a philosophy of retribution was one that instilled fear in all its citizens at all times. That fear created mistrust, which affected every relationship.

His children were with Kim-Cuong's family during his visit, so each night he slept there. He didn't spend much time there, though, as the reception was chilly, and the conversations were limited. He usually went to his mother's house every morning. Hung went with him, because he had spent a lot of his time there in the past three years. To him, it was home.

The reception at his mother's home could also be strained. Only his mother and younger sister talked to him at length. Phuc refused to talk, choosing not to repeat the pattern of arguments he had had with their father, but nonetheless continued to stake his claim to the superiority of Communism.

The others engaged in limited discussions. He didn't know why, though he imagined that they looked at him with sadness, seeing his physical condition and the toll the years had taken on him. Kim-Cuong's sister, Dong, looked at him and cried. Seeing his skinny frame, she couldn't help but remember the man who was strong and full of energy when he had left in 1975.

He and his mother talked at length about his father's last days and his death at the relatively young age of 65. Vo repeatedly emphasized that Xuong had died of a broken heart, and Quoc could not disagree. She related the continual arguments with Phuc, recalling how Xuong would become enraged, his face red and eyes bulging.

When their conversation waned, Quoc often saw his mother looking at his own emaciated body and sallow face, hearing a noticeable sigh escape her lips, her eyes moist with tears. Life in prison was never brought up. His mother seemed to know that he couldn't bear to speak about it. No doubt she didn't want to hear about the suffering he had endured. Better to let it remain silent than remember it out loud.

Quoc painfully listened to the account of the funeral preparations that followed his father's death. The family still retained plots in the cemetery that had been used by their relatives for several generations. The Communists hadn't confiscated them yet.

Nevertheless, their impoverished condition manifested itself in a tragic way. There was no money for a casket. The family used furniture, scrap wood, and even packing crates to build a primitive coffin for the interment. Xuong was buried as a pauper, with the simplest of ceremonies. The funeral, while brief, was emotional. Quoc listened mournfully to the description of the day.

Later that week, Quoc paid a visit to the gravesite with one of his female cousins, Khuong, and her brother whose name was just one letter, Y. Khuong and Quoc had never been close during his childhood, perhaps because she was about seven years older. During this visit, she took Quoc under her wing. They prayed together, standing before the fresh grave. Emotions swirled around Quoc as he silently contemplated what had happened to the patriarch of his family.

Khuong stood near him, quiet and respectful. As they walked away from the grave, Y expressed his condolences. The three were together for only two minutes, and yet it became an inflection point for Quoc's eventual escape.

Y said, "Quoc, you have considerable experience as a naval officer. You know that men like you are in demand."

Quoc's eyes flickered acknowledgement but didn't verbalize his thanks. The cousin added, "And you know, no one wants to stay in this country. A lamppost would leave this city if it could."

Then he added, almost as an afterthought, "Quoc, when you get out of the camp – however you get out – see me. I'll connect you with the right people."

That was the extent of the conversation, but it was nonetheless the passport to a future. As he prepared to go back to the camp, Quoc guarded Y's words in his heart like a man holds a map with directions out of a dangerous country.

28

LAI KHE - THE NEW ECONOMIC ZONE

"People say that time goes by; time says that people go by."

Vietnamese Proverb

MAY 1978

Quoc knew he would have to return to Bu Gia Map. Kim-Cuong's life depended upon it, though there were still a few snide and unkind comments from family members, such as,

"You are stupid. Why are you going back?"

"Disappear. No one will ever know."

Quoc did not bother to answer. He just carefully prepared to return. He filled a large duffel bag with nearly 60 pounds of food to share with his fellow prisoners at camp. He would do everything he could do to drag the bag back to his friends.

Parting from Kim-Cuong was always painful, but they were hopeful that several factors were coalescing that indicated a loosening of the Reeducation Camp system. The massive releases in the fall of 1977, followed by his own 10-day pass, indicated that the system was changing. Perhaps in the near future, they would be back together as a family.

Quoc took a bus back to Phuoc Long. This time he was not tossed out by the driver. Once across the river, he hitchhiked on a military convoy to Bu Gia Map.

When Quoc returned, there were just a few prisoners there. Most had been sent out on one, to two-week assignments in other camps. During the next few days, the men returned, and were appreciative of the food brought by Quoc.

In many respects, the return to the camp, as painful as it was, brought him back to a group of military men with a shared experience. They weren't afraid of talking with each other, nor did they judge one another. A mutual respect borne by common deprivation existed among the men; something they would never share with those in the civilian world, not even among close relatives.

Quoc began to hear rumors from the guards that he would soon be released to the New Economic Zone. At one point in April of 1978, he was prepared to go on a two-week work assignment, but it was cancelled, because his release was regarded as imminent. The decision was postponed for nearly eight weeks, supposedly due to an impending currency devaluation. The wait seemed to last forever.

Nearly 50 men were in the same category as Quoc, just waiting every day for their release. They weren't even given work assignments in the camp. The guards did not allow more than three men to meet together at a time, so the men often just remained on their sleep mats or in their hammocks. Even more so than usual, it was difficult for the men to maintain their sanity during this time of uncertainty.

The day finally came. Quoc was awakened at dawn. Along with a group of about 50 other men, he was ordered to report to the district headquarters, ten miles away.

After a two-hour trek, the prisoners arrived. One by one, they were presented with release papers. They were then asked to sign a book, and make comments for posterity. It was another test to elicit support from the prisoners. The guards watched as each man stood in front of the book and entered a message. Most wrote an innocent phrase like, "Long Live Ho Chi Minh!"

While some scratched out, "Thank you for your hospitality."

Quoc thought for a brief moment and then wrote the most popular propaganda slogan that he had heard almost every day for the last three years, "Nothing better than freedom." It was a final expression of resistance. No one caught the irony.

Goodbyes were exchanged with the remaining prisoners. Quoc had mixed emotions. Although his assignment was in the New Economic Zone, it was still not a release from a captivity of sorts. He knew imprisonment in the camps would be replaced with still another forced separation from his family.

Attached to the release paper for Quoc and the others was a 10-day pass back to their homes, and orders to report to a specific location in the New Economic Zone. Quoc's new assignment was Lai Khe, a village about forty miles from Saigon. There, though still under the supervision of local police and militia, Quoc was assigned a two-acre plot and told to make a new life. It was July 1978.

Over the next months, he built a small hut in Lai Khe. Loc, his brother, joined him. Vo sent some money with which they procured farm implements, some seeds, and a few chickens. The main crop was rice, but they also grew bananas and yams. They were forced to give most of their crop to the village leaders as payment for the privilege of working the land.

Loc worked side by side with Quoc, ensuring that they eked out enough for their own needs, as well as a little extra for the family back in Saigon. Kim-Cuong came several times and, when she could, brought the children. Obtaining bus tickets was difficult. The conditions were primitive in Lai Khe, and the environment was less than suitable for children. There were mosquitoes and a plethora of

other insects, along with poisonous snakes. It was so dark at night –
and combined with the sounds of the jungle – the children could
hardly sleep and would wake up terrified. For Quoc it was different.
Anything was better than life in the camps.

In Saigon, the police stopped by and asked Kim-Cuong when
she was moving her family to Lai Khe. She smiled and nodded, but
Quoc knew Kim-Cuong could never make the transition to such a
rural existence. Quoc knew he could not produce enough food to
sustain a family and that there was no real future there. He knew,
though, that it was important to convince the authorities that he
and his family were permanently relocating to the village. In the
meantime, he and Kim-Cuong began to formulate a plan of escape.
It would take both of them working together and would involve both
subterfuge and deceit.

Every evening at around midnight, the local militiamen stopped
at Quoc's hut to ensure he was still in Lai Khe. He was required to
report to the village police chief every ten days, where he was once
more harangued as a criminal and a traitor to his country. Quoc
dutifully told the police chief of his excitement about relocating to
the area and often brought Kim-Cuong with him, and she voiced her
enthusiasm as well. Quoc, through his mother Vo, was able to purchase two more acres of land, which he and Loc began to clear. Loc
also helped him erect new walls for his hut, expanding it for the supposed permanent relocation of his family. From all appearances, the
village authorities seemed convinced of Quoc's and Kim-Cuong's
commitment to the region and the Communist cause.

However, Quoc was there less than four months when the village chief called him and three others to his hut. A fifth person,
the chief's son, was there as well. Of the five, three were former
Reeducation Camp prisoners. The chief announced, "I need three
volunteers for a short assignment."

He smiled as he said it. He knew who he was going to pick. It wasn't going to be his son or the other villager. He laughed and pointed at Quoc and the two other former South Vietnamese officers, "I think it will be you three. Don't worry. It will only be about five days."

A chill went through Quoc. He remembered the last time someone had promised that he'd be away from home – at that time, just 10 days. That had been in June of 1975. He wondered, "How long will it last this time?"

29

BARBARIC WEAPONS OF WAR

"Landmines are among the most barbaric weapons of war, because they continue to kill and maim innocent people long after the war itself has ended."

Kofi Annan
1938 –
Seventh Secretary General of United Nations

LATE 1978

It was as if a railroad tie had slammed against his head. His brain did not immediately comprehend what he felt. Then Quoc processed it. An explosion had occurred.

He pieced it together. The man next to him had just stepped on a landmine. In that blinding flash, a human being had ceased to exist. There were pieces of flesh and blood and something that resembled a leg, but there was nothing else left of him.

He had stepped on the spot where Quoc just slept.

The guards began to yell, "Stay in place. Don't move!"

Quoc froze, recognizing how stupid it had been to put the prisoners in an area that was a known minefield. He felt like screaming at such idiocy, but he couldn't argue or complain. He only considered the pitiful incompetence and stupidity of the Communist leadership, who, with malicious intent, used him and his fellow prisoners as tools in a vicious game called retribution.

This time, the prisoners were used as tools to clear minefields placed by the Cambodian Army to stop an invading army from entering their country.

He woke at dawn. The activity near the Cambodian border was different from what he had experienced before. Military trucks loaded with troops travelled through the roadway area. The sounds of diesel engines roared, and in the far distance Quoc could hear the distinct sound of artillery. They were muffled by distance but sounded like 122mm Howitzers.

Vietnam was preparing to invade Cambodia, otherwise known as Kampuchea. Their leader, Pol Pot, had been victorious in the Cambodian Civil War on April 17, 1975, less than two weeks before the fall of South Vietnam.

The two countries seemed poised for a long-term détente. However, within weeks they were at war with one another. In May of 1975, Pol Pot's forces invaded the island of Phu Quoc. This was ironic. It was the very island where Quoc Pham had held his last Navy duty assignment.

Battle between Cambodia and Vietnam would be on and off for the next three years. The war reached a crescendo at the end of 1978 and the beginning of 1979, when a full-scale invasion of Cambodia by Vietnam successfully overthrew Pol Pot, and the Vietnamese occupied the country. More than 150,000 soldiers were part of the invasion, including a significant number of political prisoners. Quoc Pham was one of them.

Quoc and the two other residents of Lai Khe, who had been volunteered for the assignment, were transported for hours in a long, tortuous journey by truck, stopping the convoy along the way to pick up more volunteers to help the cause against Cambodia. The task for which they had been volunteered was unknown to them. Until they came to the land mines.

The convoy stopped late at night. The men had no idea if they were in Vietnam or Cambodia. They thought they were located well to the west of Saigon, near Loc Ninh. The scene was so similar to the other ones that Quoc had experienced in the previous three years. Hundreds of men, perhaps even a thousand, were scattered throughout a forested area that had been cleared. The men were told to bed down with their sleeping mats wherever they could find space. Quoc and the others ate a few morsels of food they had with them and then settled into a troubled sleep. Quoc wondered what his duties would be and how long he would remain in this new camp.

Southeast Asia may well be the area of the world with the most landmines buried by defenders. Most are still undetected, and children and adults are routinely killed and maimed by them every year. Today it is estimated that about 20 percent of the land in Vietnam still contains landmines. As a result, more than 100,000 people have been injured and killed over the years.

Pol Pot's generals knew that an invasion by the Vietnamese was planned. They also knew, through well-understood topographic analysis and bitter experience in warfare, the likely avenues of advance by an invading army. They had spent the three years of the conflict placing thousands of land mines throughout these areas.

Equally experienced military strategists from Vietnam knew that to successfully launch an attack of more than a hundred thousand men, the army needed to clear areas to provide wide pathways and avenues of advance for infantry, artillery, and armor units. Using prisoners to clear the mines was their solution. The prisoners, as traitors, were expendable. Why not have them die for their country in the noble cause of invading Cambodia? A more poignant restitution could not be imagined.

After the prisoner died from the mine where Quoc had slept

the previous night, the walk out to the minefield to safer ground was psychologically tortuous. They crossed a minefield with escort guards armed with and ready to use AK-47's. Once on safe ground the men considered how to organize themselves.

The men largely self-organized into units of about 50 men apiece. There was a cross-sectional representation of enlisted men, and warrant and commissioned officers. There were also a significant number of young people who claimed allegiance to the Communists. Quoc wondered if they had been volunteered or had actually offered their services to the cause. He was reluctant to speak to the other prisoners: He still feared such conversations would be relayed by spies back to the camp leaders. Quoc was locked into self-imposed silence and therefore unable to trade information with the others in his group.

There were no reeducation classes. There was just focused urgency exhibited by the guards. Quoc figured the guards were under orders to prepare for the imminent invasion of Cambodia.

The day after the death in the minefield, the guards called everyone into formation and ordered, "All former officers of South Vietnam raise your hands."

Though he momentarily considered not doing so, Quoc realized he could not trust the men around him and grudgingly raised his arm.

Quoc and the other officers were taken to a section closest to the border. There were about a hundred in his group. An officer told them to pay attention. They had been chosen, he said, for a very delicate mission that would prove their allegiance to Vietnam. They had been selected to clear a series of minefields to clear a path for the Vietnamese Army. It would be safe. They would be well trained to clear the minefields, he assured them. The training would be short, but intense and it began immediately.

Quoc had been surrounded by injuries and death during the

previous three and a half years. After the culmination of so many trials during that time, Quoc was now being forced at gunpoint into a minefield from which some men would not return. Today Quoc was facing the high probability of his own maiming or death. Primal feelings surged through him.

The training course to detect mines consisted of a briefing on how to use a bamboo stick with an aluminum tip on its end. The officer demonstrated and said, "Take your stick and push it gently into the ground ahead of you. If it goes into the ground easily, continue pushing until it goes in at least eight to 10 inches. If there is no resistance, gently pull it out, then push the stick back into the ground about six inches ahead of you. Then clear the areas to each side of your lane, some six inches apart."

The men were incredulous. Many were former Army officers who had been trained in landmines, had used them, and knew how sensitive they were. They knew the designs varied. Some mines could go off with the slightest pressure, others were magnetic and exploded if ferrous metal came near them. Quoc was not knowledgeable of mine warfare, but he intuitively realized that there would be no good outcomes to this task. He had managed to survive brutality and deprivation in the past years, but now he wondered, "Is this be how I will die? "

His thoughts ran to escape, but how would he do it without getting shot?

One former officer raised his hand and said as diplomatically as possible, "I have a little experience with mines. This is not the way you go about it."

The instructor looked at him with an icy stare, "You will do it how I tell you. You don't do the thinking around here, I do. As far as I am concerned you are all traitors, and you are all expendable. Are there any other questions?"

The men were then issued their bamboo sticks and escorted to a field by armed guards. The first part of the field had a series of green flags, lazily fluttering in the breeze. There were a few yellow flags and perhaps a dozen red ones in the field too. The men were told to avoid the yellow and the red flags. The yellow marker meant a possible mine; the red marker, the certainty of one.

Other men had obviously already been at work clearing the mines. Quoc noticed that there were a few areas that had small craters showing fresh dirt. They were like a mini-version of a crater from a bomb dropped by a B-52, only they were about three feet wide and about a foot deep.

The men were lined up, some ten feet apart, in an area more than a hundred yards wide. They began the painstaking and nerve-racking process of pushing the sticks into the ground. The sticks were no more than six feet long, and Quoc did his best to push it as far forward as he could, trying to visualize what he had never seen. He imagined the mines must be some sort of cylindrical object with a spring mechanism on top.

Quoc pushed the stick into the ground the first time at about a 45-degree angle and gently pressed it into the earth. The ground yielded; he felt no resistance or bending in the stick. He pushed some more and came into contact with nothing. He pulled the stick out and tried another area a foot to the right – no resistance again. He pushed further, nothing yet. Quoc was sweating profusely in the cool morning air, and he felt himself shaking. All he could think of was Kim-Cuong and the children. After all these years, he was likely going to be killed by a Russian – or American-made landmine in a jungle far away from home. He would be buried in a common grave along with the thousands of others who had died since April 1975.

Behind them, a dozen guards stood with their rifles at the ready. There would be no escape forward into Cambodia for the former Vietnamese officers and no escape backward through the guards. The men had no choice but to continue their dangerous task.

Quoc glanced at the other men. They moved in much the same way as he did, gently pushing the sticks forward and gently pressing them into the ground. So far, no one had placed a yellow or red flag. They had positioned only small green flags. And yet, across the line, they had advanced no more than 10 feet. The field in front of them appeared to stretch out for half a mile.

A guard blew a whistle after half an hour and yelled for the men to return for a break. It seemed to Quoc that they had been there for years. Quoc gently retraced his steps in the path he had made and willed himself to be as light as possible. Though he weighed just 80 pounds, he knew any pressure could trigger the devices. As he tiptoed back, he glanced to his right and left and saw the same movements by his compatriots. No one was running, and everyone walked with the delicacy of dancers.

Then an explosion occurred. A man two lanes to the right of Quoc had stepped onto a mine. He was thrown into the air and fell to the ground, most of his lower body torn off. Shortly thereafter, another man further away hit a mine and sustained serious injuries. Severely injured, he lay there and moaned.

The very ground the men had just walked on, and supposedly cleared, was now dealing death and dismemberment to the group.

The guards ordered other prisoners to pull the dead and injured back to the starting point. The guards themselves didn't dare to venture into the minefield. Quoc pulled one man back whose left leg had been blown off. The man was bleeding profusely and Quoc wondered if he would die. Then he was certain, as he heard guards yell, "Just leave him there!"

Quoc had never been so afraid. The only way for him to control the fear was the promise he had made to himself: No matter how and no matter what it took, Quoc Pham would escape from this country that considered him a traitor. And he would take his family to safety in the process.

The men were forced at gunpoint to continually repeat their perilous task throughout the long day. Some men continued to inadvertently explode mines. A few men were lucky enough to detect mines without detonating them. These they carefully marked with the red flags. Each time the men were pulled back to the starting point, explosions occurred, even when they followed the exact same route they had carefully marked as they walked into the field.

At the end of the day, around 5:00 p.m., as the sun began setting, the men had progressed perhaps a hundred yards towards Cambodia. Thousands of yards remained ahead of them.

The tally of dead at the end of the day was, by Quoc's reckoning, about 15 men out of the hundred who had started that morning.

Quoc remained sleepless that night. While the previous four years had been a cycle of exhaustion, deprivation, and cruelty, sleep had come as an escape. Though the dreams had been torturous, he was able to fall into a semblance of rest during those years. It allowed him to survive the pain of each day, but now his mind raced, trying to calculate the odds of survival. About 15 percent of the men had been casualties the first day. In seven days, at the current rate, his death seemed imminent. It could happen tomorrow. He was caught in a quandary new to his experience. Clearly, his life was like the minefield. There was no clear path ahead.

That night, he couldn't visualize an escape plan, but he knew he would have to develop one. He prayed that night for an answer.

The next six days were a repeat of the first. At gunpoint each dawn, about a hundred men were forced into the minefield. Each day, as few as 10 and as many as 20 men were injured or killed by the mines. Usually a severe injury to legs or outright maiming occurred. Some died immediately. Those who were injured or killed were hauled away by military truck. Their fate was never learned. Quoc's bitter experience informed him that the injured men were probably consigned to death, likely with severe infections or gangrene.

Perhaps those who died immediately were among the more fortunate, he thought.

Each night, men tried to escape. While some might have succeeded, their fate was never known. Most were shot by the heavily armed guards, suffering deaths no better than those in the minefield.

Quoc barely slept that week, terrified that his life would end in the minefields of Loc Ninh.

30

QUOC ESCAPES INTO A NEW ROLE

"I still don't know how we survived it all. It is true that the human being is a remarkable creature, capable of great adaptation and having a strong survival instinct."

Carina Hoang
Boat People

LATE 1978

At dawn on the seventh day, Quoc received an answer to his prayer. He and 10 other men were assigned to pick up material at a supply depot several miles away.

An army needs a continuous stream of supplies – tons of them – everything from rations to uniforms, to razors, even toothpaste. Most of the supplies were now coming through Chinese supply channels.

Quoc discovered that the Communist district chief – a former Viet Cong leader – served as the distributor of goods and services, even to the army. The chief's nickname was Chu Tu – Fourth Uncle – and it was said of him, "He ruled the region with an iron fist and an open palm."

Chu Tu made a fortune selling goods on the black market. He did it under the eyes of the Communist leadership. His allegiance to their cause provided him with immunity from suspicion or punishment during the war years and after. Quoc knew little of the chief, but he knew there was a hierarchy within the region and, like everywhere else in the country, an underground economy existed.

Up to that point, the vagaries of imprisonment hadn't changed Quoc's lifelong values. Quoc had always been chided for his scrupulous honesty and his adherence to rules and regulations. Two oddly disparate factors were about to change that: Quoc's desire to avoid the minefields and his knowledge of the chemistry of Chinese toothpaste. The first was very understandable; the second, a bit more mysterious.

During his years in captivity, Quoc had learned much about many things. As they had smoked Thuoc Lao tobacco at Bu Gia Map one night, he listened to a man talk incessantly about how the Chinese were unscrupulous about their quality standards for products. The man went on and on about Chinese toothpaste in particular. He said that one of the main ingredients in their toothpaste could be deadly in sufficient quantities. Even if it didn't kill you, it might cause deathly illness and virtual paralysis. The man said, "Once you get to the New Economic Zone, that could be your ticket back home. If the Communists think you aren't healthy enough to work, they might send you back."

Quoc hadn't heard the scientific evidence. What he and the other prisoners did not know was that the Chinese used diethylene glycol – also known as diglycol or diglycol stearate – in their toothpaste. It was a cheap alternative to other sweeteners.

The United States had established the Federal Drug (and Food) Administration (FDA) in the 1930s after more than a hundred Americans had died consuming an elixir that contained diethylene glycol.

Despite its known health risks, the Chinese had continued using it.

Quoc hadn't thought about the man's comments since that night in Bu Gia Map, not until he walked into a large warehouse that day. He and the other men were instructed to load various products into a waiting truck. One of the products was toothpaste, Chinese toothpaste. Intuitively, Quoc made the decision to steal some of the toothpaste containers. The guards were largely illiterate and unschooled. Quoc took several of them to the stack of toothpaste boxes. He counted out loud, "One, two, three, five, six, eight, ten, eleven, fifteen, sixteen, seventeen, eighteen, nineteen, twenty-one...twenty three...thirty-four, thirty-five, thirty-six, thirty-seven, thirty-eight, thirty-nine, and, twenty"

And then said, "Take these twenty boxes to the truck."

He then proceeded to miscount another twenty. When he finished, he signed for 100 boxes and had secured an extra twenty for himself. Quoc now had the material with which to finance an escape from minefield duty. He just needed to seal a deal.

If politics makes strange bedfellows, war makes unexpected brothers. Quoc never imagined becoming a trusted lieutenant to a former Viet Cong district chief now serving as the head of the civilian government of the Loc Ninh province.

As the supply truck bounced its way back to the village, Quoc formulated a plan. It hinged on the use of the stolen Chinese toothpaste, his knowledge of how it could be marketed, and most importantly, his ability to take on a persona that he had never before exhibited. Quoc needed to project himself as a trusted lieutenant of the most powerful man in the province. To act that role would take something from deep inside him, channeling a realization he had come to believe: He knew he might die.

The supply truck was supposed to go directly to the military camp, but first it made a stop at the village chief's headquarters, located in one of the large tents not far from the field where Quoc had first arrived. When it stopped, Quoc jumped over the rear gate and brazenly demanded, "I need to see the chief!"

The guard looked Quoc up and down dismissively and said, "He doesn't see people like you."

Quoc slowly eyed the man. He mustered every bit of courage he could. He even imagined himself in a movie role. He barked, as he would to a new recruit in the Navy, "Let him decide. Tell him I have a way for him to make some real money."

The man looked at Quoc with curiosity and then respect. He hesitated and then succumbed. Looking away, he mumbled, "Wait a minute."

A few minutes later, Quoc was escorted into the district chief's office. The setting was nothing at all like a movie, where the chief always seems to sit behind a desk. The chief, Chu Tu, was in an Asian squat, sitting in a circle with several other men his age, smoking Thuoc Lao tobacco.

Quoc never learned Chu Tu's real name; he would always refer to him as "boss." Communist leaders rarely used their real names, which was likely a carryover from the many years of guerrilla warfare in the country. It is easy to identify a person by his given name, a nickname is much more difficult to trace.

Chu Tu nodded for Quoc to join him. Quoc squatted along with the other men and waited to speak. After a few puffs of the Thuoc Lao, Quoc found himself a bit calmer. Looking sideways over towards Quoc, the chief asked and stated, all in one breath, "So you have a way for me to make me money? Tell me about it."

Quoc looked around at the other men. After a quick nod from the chief, he knew that the chief trusted the others in the circle. Quoc said, "I've been able to obtain some toothpaste for you. You might find it's useful beyond cleaning teeth."

The chief chuckled, but nodded, giving permission to Quoc to proceed.

Quoc continued, now confident and with a newfound bravado, "There are men in the camps who would gladly pay for a tube of toothpaste. With just half a tube, they will be unable to work in the field detecting mines. They will be sick enough so that they won't be able to work but healthy enough to be transported back to the New Economic Zone. There will be plenty of men left to clear the mines. But in the meantime, you get the profit. These men are desperate: They will pay you dearly to not be human mine detectors"

The chief looked straight ahead, staring at nothing in particular: He appeared unfazed and took a few more puffs of Thuoc Lao, "And what do you want for this?"

"To be your supply chief. I can make sure you get the toothpaste you need and anything else, just let me be your man."

Details followed – about the toothpaste – and how many cases Quoc had stolen from the warehouse. The chief had already heard some rumors about the detrimental effects of the toothpaste, and was not surprised by the lack of safety standards. He'd seen it in other Chinese products. He also knew that the soldiers in the supply depot were uneducated. Daily he had observed examples of their ignorance. He noted, with a look of admiration, that no one had been as adept as Quoc in using their lack of education against them.

As he was questioned, Quoc looked at Chu Tu carefully. He was heavily muscled and tanned. He was a man accustomed to using his body physically and would be capable in any situation. It didn't surprise Quoc that Chu Tu had been a chief for the Viet Cong or that he should be tapped for a leadership role under the new regime.

Quoc thought momentarily of the hundreds of other Viet Cong leaders who had smiled at American G.I.'s and South Vietnamese soldiers during the day and fought against them at night.

The chief instructed one of the men to unload the twenty stolen boxes. Inside each box were twelve individual tubes of toothpaste. They represented 240 tickets home for the men able to afford the products, and courageous enough to consume them.

The chief puffed the tobacco and pondered, pulling deep from the bamboo pipe. Quoc forced himself to sit silently without moving. Then Chu Tu broke into a smile, "I believe we have a deal, Mr. Supply Officer!"

Quoc stayed emotionless, remained silent and looked down as a sign of respect. He had successfully allied himself with one of the most powerful Communists in the region. In the next several weeks, he learned that Chu Tu commanded some 10,000 civilian laborers in a province that spanned the entire area northwest of Saigon. The laborers planted and harvested rice, provided transportation, cleared trees, hunted, and distributed goods and other services. The political prisoners like Quoc were not officially under Chu Tu's purview, but they may as well have been, given his power and authority. Clearly, his reassignment of Quoc's status was such an example. He knew he didn't need to ask for anyone's permission to do so.

It was only proper for Quoc to show silent respect at that point. Inside, Quoc didn't know whether to grimace or cheer. He had accomplished something he could have never imagined. Today, he was one step closer to freedom, and he was no longer a useless pawn. He was now someone who controlled his own destiny to a greater degree than he had since 1975.

Chu Tu instructed Quoc to return to the camp. He would be picked up each morning by guards and brought back to the chief's compound. The chief, who was not native to Loc Ninh, and his entourage, occupied large, comfortable tents. Quoc, along with countless others, slept in the open. The pressure of impending warfare precluded any organized effort to build huts or barracks. Every laborer – volunteers and political prisoners – was working for the war effort, preparing for the invasion.

The next and each succeeding day, Quoc assumed the role of chief supply officer for Chu Tu. He selected a team of five other men from Chu Tu's inner circle and routinely picked up supplies and took them back to the camp. For the first time in nearly four years, Quoc was able to eat three meals a day. Sometimes he was even invited to parties at Chu Tu's tent. There, they would eat and drink – usually cheap rice liquor – and smoke Thuoc Lao. Chu Tu always drank to excess, often falling asleep before the end of the evening.

On days when he was not busy with his supply officer duties, Quoc was allowed to roam around the area to fish or hunt. He brought any fish or game he caught to Chu Tu and he always got a portion for himself.

It was a strange juxtaposition: He moved freely around the area with two armed guards, enjoying a position of authority, yet he was still a political prisoner. The irony was difficult to process. It was the strangest of the many situations he had encountered since leaving Kim-Cuong and his family in 1975. He remembered a Shakespeare quote, "All the world's a stage." Here in Loc Ninh that could not have been truer for Quoc Pham.

Quoc's ability to cheat the supply personnel continued to be handy. He didn't always use false counting. Sometimes he just engaged the clerks in animated conversation while his men loaded extra items into the truck. At other times, he lingered long enough to bore the Communist warehousemen with tales and then just took a variety of items that he wanted. He always brought everything he stole back to Chu Tu. He knew that it would be stupid to try to cheat the man who licensed his larceny.

Chu Tu sold the extra supplies on the black market, and his profits were substantial. Not surprisingly, no commodity from the warehouses was more lucrative than the toothpaste. Careful and quiet distribution channels emerged for the men who were assigned to landmine detection duty. Unlike the camps where prisoners were often strip-searched, these men held a different status. They were considered volunteers, but many, like Quoc, had actually been volunteered. Nonetheless, this status allowed them to keep small amounts of gold, usually in rings clearly visible on their fingers. Quoc and Chu Tu had ready access to a market, where buyers paid 1/12 of an ounce of gold for one tube of toothpaste.

Quoc was never involved in distribution. That was left to Chu Tu's lieutenants who were adept in black marketeering. The exchanges always took place at night. Cutouts were employed: A third party was used to obtain the gold, a piece of jewelry or a small container of gold flakes. This person passed the toothpaste to the buyer. He knew that it was his only hope to be pulled off the deadly landmine clearing details, which continued to claim more than a dozen men each day.

Quoc knew the men who consumed the toothpaste would become deathly ill. A few would die, and some would have lingering effects from the chemical compounds that would last for years. He justified the sale of the toothpaste as something that was a lesser of two evils: Severe illness and transportation back to the New Economic Zone, versus continued work in the minefields and likely injury or death.

Chu Tu and his suppliers were adept at only selling the toothpaste sparingly, so as not to arouse suspicion from the Army guards. As a result, only eight to 10 times a week did a man become so ill that he had to be sent back. When someone was paralyzed, Chu Tu, as the civilian head of the region, quickly ordered the release of the victim back to the New Economic Zone. More volunteers and political prisoners arrived each day, so the military leaders didn't bother to conduct investigations. The illness brought on by consumption of the toothpaste was scattered and random, so there was never a pattern. Also, the men who consumed the toothpaste always buried the empty tubes so that their guards could not discover their secret.

Quoc continued as Chu Tu's supply officer for about three months. Life during this time – even for Chu Tu and his men – was not pleasant. Rampant unsanitary conditions existed due to the limited infrastructure. Frequent small skirmishes and attacks by the Khmer Rouge continued. Chu Tu drank heavily every night and cursed the Communist leadership for assigning him a role that placed him and his men in such danger. As his stash of gold grew heavier, he slept under the cover of armed guards. He pocketed a fortune during the time he and Quoc worked together. Quoc saw none of it but knew he had formed an alliance that would help his escape.

The Vietnamese invasion of Pol Pot's Cambodia began in December. The entire camp moved with the army.

In the border camps, a routine eventually evolved. The volunteers harvested rice fields and then were trucked further inside Cambodia. When minefields were located, the mine-clearing details would be assigned, with the associated casualties and deaths. There was never a time when the men felt safe: If a mine didn't kill a man, a mortar or artillery round was just as likely to land on him while we was harvesting rice.

At night, younger workers and those who had volunteered for patriotic duty naively sat around campfires, smoking and, if alcohol was available, drinking. Political prisoners like Quoc, had learned from combat veterans to spend the last daylight hours digging personal foxholes for protection in case of an attack. Pol Pot's forces occasionally attacked at night, and these foxholes saved more than one prisoner's life during mortar attacks.

In his role as the supply chief, Quoc made trips to deserted hamlets. One time he walked into a village and saw a small Buddhist temple that had been filled with manure. It was a Communist insult intended to offend the Cambodians, whose national religion was the worship of Buddha. It also offended Quoc.

One day Quoc was ordered to obtain fresh meat for Chu Tu and his men. This was problematic, as meat was reserved for soldiers, not volunteers or even civilian authorities like Chu Tu: Killing animals in a war zone was prohibited. The Communist military could court martial and sentence to death anyone for this offense. Nevertheless, Quoc left with one of the chief's bodyguards who had a rifle. They eventually found a lone lost cow more than a mile from the camp. With one shot, the bodyguard killed the cow. In minutes, he and Quoc gutted the cow for its internal organs and delivered these delicacies to Chu Tu. Quoc whispered to the chief's inner circle that there was fresh meat available and took them to the scene of the crime. Within hours, there was no evidence of the killing except for a fresh carcass and some blood on the ground.

The invasion continued, with some setbacks. In January of 1979, Pol Pot's army routed the Vietnamese forces, whose retreat took them back to Snuol, with heavy casualties inflicted by the Cambodians.

Further inside of Cambodia, the attacks increased. As the men harvested rice one day in a field at least a mile from the main camp, mortar and small arms firing increased to a crescendo. The situation seemed dire. It became obvious that the harvesters and their guards were cut off from the main body of the army. The mortar fire began to inflict casualties.

Quoc took cover behind a tree, hugging the ground next to a Communist officer. The eyes of the two men met, and they both recognized each other instantaneously. The officer had been one of the cadre at Katum and Quoc had been his prisoner. The man mouthed the words, "Why are you here?" He was interrupted by yet another volley of mortar rounds, and Quoc ran for cover elsewhere. They never saw each other again.

Soldiers ordered men to mount the trucks. Two at a time, trucks attempted to escape back to the camp, zigzagging to avoid the continuous onslaught of mortars. One truck was hit squarely by a mortar round and exploded into flames. The passengers were killed or left to die.

Quoc decided to run and eventually made it to the main road heading towards Snuol. He ran for hours and finally came upon a group of other prisoners, huddled around a small fire, with soldiers maintaining a perimeter. The men shared some rice and dried fish for dinner.

Searching for fresh water, Quoc and the others stumbled across a body of water in the pitch-black night. Pushing their mouths into the liquid, they drank for the first time in hours. At first light, the soldiers woke Quoc and the others to continue with them on their retreat. Quoc stopped at the small pond and moved to scoop up some water. It was filled with leeches, just as it had been the night before.

With no time to think, they proceeded to move again at double time, finally arriving at Snuol after some 12 hours of retreat. Hundreds of volunteers and scores of soldiers did not survive. At Snuol, the army and its prisoners were allowed to rest for three days before being trucked back to the border.

After three months, Chu Tu cursed his military superiors for putting him and his men into such unsafe conditions for such a long time. After the casualties in Snuol and Kratie, the general in charge agreed to send Chu Tu and his men, including Quoc, back to Vietnam on furlough. A truck brought them back to Lai Khe.

Quoc returned to his home in the New Economic Zone late that night. He fell asleep instantly. The subterfuge and deception demanded by his role as Chu Tu's supply chief had left him constantly on guard and emotionally drained.

Quoc knew he had to maintain his role as a trusted lieutenant of Chu Tu. If he could maintain the charade for a few more days, it could benefit his escape. However, first he had to backtrack and reinforce the storyline that he and Kim-Cuong had created before he left for the Cambodian border.

During his absence, Loc completed the construction of the enlarged hut and planted new crops in the extra acreage. He also built fences and new chicken coops. Most importantly, he also stayed in touch with the family back in Saigon. Kim-Cuong's sister, Dong, continued to assure the family that Quoc's expertise as a naval officer was in demand and that his presence in Saigon would ensure that he could play a key role in a boat escape.

Quoc was back from Cambodia for two days when Kim-Cuong arrived. Her immediate arrival substantiated their claim of wanting to permanently relocate to the New Economic Zone. Within days, the village residents and police officials welcomed the Pham family's presence.

Chu Tu had told Quoc that he wouldn't be far away and would be in touch. Quoc leveraged this: He began spreading rumors that Chu Tu was owed a significant amount of money for one of the last supply missions and that Quoc was the only one who could pick up the cash. Quoc set the date. It would coincide with his required monthly visit to the village police chief. He would explain his situation to the chief and ask for an escort to the pick-up site in Ben Cat. In the meantime, Kim-Cuong and Quoc carefully mapped out a rendezvous point and escape route.

The night before the rendezvous, Quoc and Kim-Cuong stayed up most of the night, going over details and logistics. Quoc smiled as he heard his wife go over the plan with military precision. She was bright and capable. He could not do it without her.

It was now late January of 1979. He had been captive for most of the past four years. He was weary beyond words. Going back as a lieutenant for Chu Tu was not an option. The fighting was reportedly fierce in Cambodia. Even those affiliated with high-ranking civilian officials like Chu Tu were guaranteed no safety.

Now was the time to put his and Kim-Cuong's plan into effect.

31

A WALK DOWN THE STREET

"The bird that escapes from its cage never wants to come back."

Vietnamese Proverb

EARLY 1979

Quoc walked down the street into the distance and vanished. In fewer than a thousand footsteps, he transformed from political prisoner to ghost, unknown and unseen by those in power in the country.

Quoc left Lai Khe with police escorts, headed for the pick-up point for the cash in Ben Cat. He kissed Kim-Cuong goodbye that morning and hopped on the truck.

The police escort carried rifles, and Quoc held a pass handwritten by Chu Tu. Quoc was treated with deference by the guards. His status as a political prisoner was overlooked because of the respect he received from Chu Tu.

When they arrived in Ben Cat, Quoc excused himself from the group and walked down the street, looking for the rendezvous point where he and Kim-Cuong had arranged to meet. The guards thought nothing about him walking away. He was familiar to them and a member of Chu Tu's inner circle.

And then Quoc was gone.

Quoc and Kim-Cuong met at a bus stop. She carried a change of clothes for him. He quickly changed and threw away the clothes of a prisoner. In minutes they were on the back roads. It took almost two days to reach Saigon. They used buses, walked, and hitched rides on ox carts. Whenever they saw an upcoming checkpoint or guard post, Kim-Cuong always found a route around them on back roads, avoiding any questions and the scrutiny of their papers.

They arrived in Saigon on a midday in January of 1979. Quoc had escaped. He was in limbo, but he was free.

Quoc Pham was no longer a prisoner. Now he was another kind of criminal. In addition to being a traitor, he was now an escaped prisoner. He had not been officially released from the gulag of the New Economic Zone. By escaping he compounded his crimes against the state. If and when he was caught, there would be harsh retribution.

His salvation was in not getting caught and fortunately there were several factors in his favor toward this end.

There was no central database in the country. Computerized systems for licensing and passports and other automated means of tracking were still relatively rare. Those that existed were still primarily programmed with thousands of lines of code and accessed with punch cards.

Those who were assigned to camps were barely tracked: Those who died were not recorded at all. Those who were released from camp were not necessarily given papers that identified them as having served their time. Quoc did not know for sure, but he doubted that any centralized paper repository existed. As a consequence, no police officer could check with a central registry to determine the status of an individual.

What he knew existed was an active network of police and military officials intent on identifying former South Vietnamese officers and governmental officials. Even if a professional man was released from a camp, a physician or pharmacist, for instance, he was still looked upon with suspicion. These men were routinely reported to local police or military forces. Only through acceptance into a local neighborhood, daily recognition by Communist officials, or bribes was a man able to live without fear of questioning, detention, or worse.

In a way, the system was as pernicious as a database, insofar as everyone in Vietnam who was not a former South Vietnamese officer served as someone who could identify those who were. There were many individuals who chose not to report suspicious characters like Quoc, but most realized that it was in their best interest to support the efforts of Communist authorities in order to make their own lives easier.

Disguising himself might help an escaped prisoner, but Quoc did not need a disguise. He looked nothing like he had when he left Kim-Cuong and his home four years prior. Despite regular meals while working for Chu Tu, Quoc had failed to gain weight. He weighed perhaps 80-85 pounds, down from 115 pounds when he went into the camps. He looked haggard and disheveled, wearing dark clothing that was ripped and soiled. His fingernails were long and dirty, and he seldom wore shoes. If required, he wore flip-flops.

Kim-Cuong cried as she looked at him on their way back to Saigon. He asked her why. Only after some gentle prodding, did she admit that he no longer looked like a man in his thirties: He could easily pass for someone who was sixty.

After nearly four years of captivity, Quoc had learned skills he never knew he needed or thought he would ever use. For a man who always followed rules and orders, Quoc had changed dramatically. Hardship and deprivation made this transformation possible. He now knew deceit and treachery as trusted allies, and he knew when he needed one or the other to survive. However, he never lost his caring for his fellow man.

Part of his survival had introverted Quoc in a substantial way. In his formative years and as a young officer in the Navy, he had often started conversations with strangers. He had even done this in the first camps he was in, but there had been retribution – retribution that had taught him that the best way to survive was to watch, listen, and seldom speak.

Quoc knew that there were very few people in the world on whom he could truly depend. One of those was his brother, Loc, who had remained on the farm in Lai Khe, in order to facilitate Quoc's escape. Days after Quoc had left, Loc approached the village chief with a carefully crafted story that would have convinced anyone, especially a hardcore Communist committed to retribution against a criminal who had been living in his village.

Loc pleaded, "My brother was on his way back here and was caught by the militia. They claim he was trying to escape. He wasn't, I swear. He was on his way back here!"

The chief looked harshly at him and said, "And what do you want me to do about it?"

Loc tearfully explained that Quoc was under orders to be sent North, which was widely considered by former South Vietnamese officers as a death sentence. Loc begged, "Please write a letter supporting him, and get him released into your custody!"

The chief looked at Loc for a long moment, then spit on the ground and said, "Let him rot in jail!"

Loc had thus eliminated one more way that Quoc might be tracked and found.

Another factor in Quoc's favor was the police force's own corruption and willingness to accept bribes. Over the next six months, Quoc saw more and more evidence of their corruptibility. He suspected it when he escaped, and that opinion was continually confirmed.

Kim-Cuong was Quoc's bedrock. She was his eyes and ears. She was his heart.

Kim-Cuong had provided perspective to Quoc, especially during her visits to Bu Gia Map. She told him the Communists were disorganized. More importantly, she convinced him that not everyone feared the Communists. She didn't and her courage bolstered his own.

She was determined to help Quoc escape from the country. She knew that she might not be able to leave with him, but to her, Quoc's safety was paramount. When she finally knew he was safe, she'd wait in relative safety for her own chance to leave the country and rejoin him. There were a number of countries where they might be able to settle safely, including the United States, Australia, Canada, and even France. The first step though was to get Quoc out of Saigon and out of jeopardy.

The first three nights back in Saigon, Quoc alternated between his mother's house and Kim-Cuong's family home. He always entered the homes after dark and left before dawn.

Quoc's homecoming in regard to the children was partly bittersweet. Hung remembered Quoc and readily called him Ba (Father). Kim-Cuong, with Quoc's complicity, was forced to use a level of deceit with four-year old Ngan. She had just entered a pre-school, now run by Communist functionaries. Very often – perhaps daily – the school officials would question the children about who was in their home. It was an effective means of identifying men who had escaped the camps.

When Ngan asked who Quoc was, Kim-Cuong answered, "That is Hung's father." Hopefully, the girl thought that the individual she did not know at the house was not her own father. Quoc and Kim-Cuong felt that any teacher or authority figure asking would be far less suspicious of such an answer. They hoped Hung would be able to keep the secret. Still, it was one of the most painful deceits that Quoc practiced.

He passed his days wandering the streets of Saigon, spending time in coffee houses, mingling with other nondescript men, who could well have been fugitives like Quoc. Whether they were or not did not even interest him. His job was to blend in, not to start conversation. He always suspected that every stranger was a government informant.

Dong, Kim-Cuong's sister, became Quoc's guardian angel.

Dong worked with a high-ranking administrator for the Communists. Her specialty was government acquisition of private real estate, and the legal maneuverings that effectively wrested ownership of residents' homes and businesses and gave them over to the State. Dong was good at it. Her legal training prepared her with the knowledge and gravitas to support such actions. She also knew that by working with the government, she could make things better for her own family and that would help them all survive.

Like so many others, Dong was as captive by the system as Quoc was.

As someone linked to a government official, Dong had a vehicle supplied by the state that was readily identifiable as government car. She even had a driver assigned to her.

When Quoc stayed at Kim-Cuong's family home, Dong often had her driver park the car out front; and she would be the first person to answer the door if a policeman knocked to ask about Quoc.

She would send officials off with a stern look and harsh words.

32

CAPTAIN SKILLS IN DEMAND

"Do the thing you're good at. Not many people are lucky enough to be so good at something."

John Green
The Fault in Our Stars

SPRING 1979

True to his word, Quoc's cousin Y approached him one day, less than a week after he had arrived in Saigon. Y worked for a man who was building boats specifically to transport people of Chinese descent out of the country. The government, still in the midst of trying to purge the country of Chinese nationals, sanctioned the enterprise.

Dong, too, encouraged Quoc to meet with the man. His name was La Tu. He was in the process of redesigning and rebuilding boats to sail on the ocean. He met Quoc for an informal interview about 40 miles outside of Saigon, on the Long An River. During their conversation, Quoc was persuaded that La Tu knew his business well and was quality-oriented.

La Tu knew who Quoc was and had asked his contacts about him. He knew of Quoc's maritime training and expertise. He also knew that Quoc was on the run from the Communists. La Tu, a pragmatic man with no particular love for the Communists, only cared that Quoc would be a capable captain.

Moments into the interview, La Tu also asked Quoc to supervise the reconstruction of the vessel. Quoc's pay would be an ounce of gold a month, a sum at least five times higher than he had received as a South Vietnamese naval officer. Quoc's only request, "I need to take my son with me," was met with a nod of his head and a laconic reply, "That goes without saying."

Quoc quickly agreed to the arrangement with La Tu.

Quoc's qualifications were enviable among mariners. He had received both extensive merchant marine and naval training as a ship's officer. In maritime parlance, he was a deck officer, meaning he was an expert in the many skills required to command, navigate, and operate a vessel. He was qualified to operate everything from the smallest vessels to the largest ships afloat.

He also had above average navigational skills. Fortunately, he had continued exercising his knowledge while teaching celestial navigation to his fellow prisoners in Katum. He was also one of a very few mariners skilled as a river pilot, which was required to motor the 40-mile stretch from Saigon to the open sea. He knew every twist and turn of the waterway and was completely familiar with its shallow points and areas of treacherous currents.

A maritime pilot's local knowledge can only be obtained one way: through real experience with another pilot and extensive study and memorization of every aspect of a waterway. This is coupled with the ongoing – almost fanatical – collection of new knowledge about storm damage, man-made obstacles and anything else that will impede a vessel's safe passage.

To this day, even in an age of GPS and computer navigation, every port in the world has a cadre of pilots. They are all trained as ship captains and then further trained as pilots in the particular geographical area for which they specialize. Quoc's near-unique knowledge of Saigon's waterfront and the passage to the sea was an achievement that made him a valuable commodity for those planning escape. It was the reason La Tu already knew about Quoc when Y recommended him.

La Tu was an entrepreneur who recognized that there is opportunity in crisis. Chinese business people and merchants had suffered under the Communist rule, and those with money were seeking a way to escape. The Vietnamese regime did not sanction their own people leaving their country; however, their xenophobic dislike for the Chinese provided an opening for La Tu and a few others. They asked for and received permission to build or refit boats to provide safe passage out of the country. The Chinese were allowed to leave the country if they forfeited their money, homes, and other property to the Communist government. As for La Tu, he would receive 12 ounces of gold from each passenger.

This enterprise, along with dozens of others, was sanctioned and licensed by local Vietnamese government representatives. No one doubted that local palms were being greased to expedite approval of the various schemes for escape by sea. As a result, the seaworthiness of the boats and expertise of so-called "mariners" captaining them was always in question. When a boat departed with its cargo of refugees, no one knew for sure whether the occupants made it to safety. Everyone had heard stories of tragedy and death at sea, but those reports were unsubstantiated and largely ignored by people desperate to leave the country.

La Tu told Quoc he could live on the boat that was being refitted. In one day, Quoc purchased two sets of identification cards: one identifying him as Chinese; the other, Vietnamese. The name on the cards, Trung Quoc, was nondescript. When conversing with others, he didn't use the name "Quoc," instead taking the name used in his family to describe his birth order, "Anh Ba" (Third Brother).

The ship was located on a canal outside the central part of the city. Y advised Kim-Cuong not to visit Quoc in order to ensure his anonymity.

Quoc – or Anh Ba to those around him – was the construction supervisor and chief scrounger for hard-to-find boat parts. La Tu also instructed Quoc to brush up on his Cantonese. There were distant Chinese relatives on Quoc's father's side from whom he had learned some of the language. Soon he was speaking simple Chinese.

The boat was directly behind a street filled with shops adjacent to a wide canal, traversed by a bridge 300 feet long. Coincidentally, the canal was less than a quarter mile from one of Quoc's uncles and his cousins, who lived on the street. Quoc never stayed with them overnight. His visits were limited to brief conversations on a street corner after dark, followed by his quick trip across the bridge. The family lived in fear that Quoc would be identified and taken into custody and would continually warn him, "Quoc, be careful. They are after you." The "they" was the local police chief, who recognized Quoc in the first week he began working for La Tu.

Quoc was unaware initially that La Tu bribed the chief, who remained silent and happy during the six months Quoc lived on the boat. The chief often passed by Quoc and used Quoc's former military title deferentially, smiling, "Hello Lieutenant. Good morning to you!"

Quoc was uncomfortable with the chief and always worried that he would change his mind, despite the bribes, and turn Quoc into the authorities.

Nonetheless, La Tu made sure that Quoc – the expert who would guide his modified vessel to safety – was safe and secure. Protection by armed men and bribed officials was almost always available.

The redesign and refit of the vessel was extensive. The craft was about 100 feet long and 15 feet wide. It had been built for the shallows of rivers and had no keel, which was the first modification undertaken. A keel is critical to compensate for the roll of the ocean and to prevent capsizing. In order to add a keel, the boat was placed on stays and dozens of workmen were hired to accomplish the task. Quoc also ordered a flying bridge to provide a cockpit for the vessel, which originally had none, and a steel-reinforced superstructure to be built into the vessel to withstand heavy seas.

Progress was steady. At night Quoc brushed up on his navigation skills. He also procured old navigation charts for use in navigating on the open ocean. La Tu paid him regularly, and for the first time in more than five years, Quoc was able to send money back to his family for food, clothing, medicine and other necessities.

By early July, Quoc and La Tu were just weeks from launching the vessel with its cargo of 800 people. Quoc began to actually believe he and Hung would soon be headed for safety.

Ever since Cambodia, Quoc's fate had consistently moved in a positive direction towards a successful escape from Vietnam. However, its arc was interrupted. Unknown to Quoc and La Tu, the Chinese boatlift from Vietnam had now numbered hundreds of vessels. Tragically, hundreds of Chinese had died in unsafe boats. Some of the vessels had rotten timbers or were so overcrowded that they had no hope of staying afloat. Others were sturdy and seaworthy, but the captains themselves were incompetent imposters who had falsified their training records or experience.

The United Nations stepped in and put international pressure on the Vietnamese government to put a halt to the boatlift and replace it with an orderly departure program. Despite repeated denials of the magnitude of the disaster, the Communists eventually succumbed to international pressure. When they did, they moved quickly, reversing course from quick approvals and open bribery for the boatlift enterprises to an official stance denying any government involvement in any departure. Thereafter, all departures would be carefully controlled.

In addition, entrepreneurs, whose bribes had been welcomed by the government, were now being treated as criminals. The police, under mandate from their leaders, set about arresting these business people, their captains, and laborers. Bribery thereon would be even more clandestine.

One night the police headed for Quoc's boat. La Tu was informed just ahead of their arrival. He raced to the vessel in a jeep and yelled for Quoc. "Get in, Anh Ba, they're coming for us!"

They sped off into the night. La Tu melted into another of his ventures. Quoc went back to the streets of Saigon. Most of their workers were not as fortunate. A number of them were taken into custody.

Quoc's hopes for escape from Vietnam were dashed.

33

WHAT MONEY CAN'T BUY

"What money can't buy, more money can"

Vietnamese Street Saying
Quoc Pham

MID-1979

Quoc was homeless again on the streets of Saigon. He joined an ever-growing population of those living on the fringes of the law. Doubtless, many of them were escaped prisoners like Quoc. Whatever their story, each knew that their social interactions were limited to smoking together, commiserating about the weather and cryptically discussing topics which in no way could help identify them to each other or the authorities.

It was understood that no backgrounds would be questioned or discussed. It was enormously draining to manage the paradox of appearing to be casual and carefree yet remaining close-lipped about who you were. Ever since the early days of the camps – and especially his experience with Thai – Quoc had guarded himself around everyone except Kim-Cuong. This remained his standard mode of operation throughout his time in Saigon.

Quoc always waited for nightfall and made his way to Kim-Cuong, spending the night, but leaving before dawn. Kim-Cuong's family – with the exception of her sister, Dong, and her Uncle, Ut Duc, who had warned him so many years ago that he would be a prisoner until he had grandchildren – remained guarded and distant and largely shunned him when he was near. It was like he had a disease that might infect them. Intellectually, Quoc understood their viewpoints but he couldn't contain his bitterness as he saw them rushing out the back door of the house or realized that they remained in another room while he visited. Kim-Cuong felt torn between her family and her husband. Ut Duc would sit and chat with Quoc and relate his own experience. Men like Ut Duc had been largely pushed aside when the Communist professional soldiers from the North had taken over the governmental roles.

The saying that "All politics is local," was true in the most adverse way for families throughout Vietnam during these times. It was among one of the most difficult periods a country and its citizens could endure, for local could indeed reach all the way down to individual relations between two family members. Their former and current political beliefs had to coexist with their ever-present struggle for survival.

One evening, Quoc and Kim-Cuong visited her cousin. Shortly after their arrival, the police pounded on the door to the house. Quoc climbed out a second story window and remained on the roof for hours. When the police finally left, Quoc came back in, even dirtier than normal. Another time, after leaving Kim-Cuong and the children, Quoc was picked up by the local police and subjected to hours of questioning. He used his Chinese identification card and stuck to the story that he was of partial Chinese descent and was trying to make his way out of the country. The authorities, though lacking evidence, were not convinced, but weren't able to ascertain Quoc's true identify. A quick intervention by Dong got him released, but he suspected it would get more and more difficult for him as time passed.

As he roamed the streets, Quoc developed a network in the underworld, where discreet queries for boat captains surfaced in cryptic conversations. The UN's mandate and legitimate concern for the safety of ocean-going refugees did not negate the political and economic situation in the country and the desperation of both Chinese and Vietnamese nationals. Those who desired to escape knew that the risks of remaining in the country were, in some respects worse than the prospect of an unsafe boat passage into the sea. Escape by boat was a topic that boiled beneath the surface every day in Vietnam, and it was always on the top of Quoc's mind.

Saigon was essentially a port city. The Saigon River twisted and turned its way like a serpent to the east and southeast out of the central part of the city and was eventually joined by the Nha Be River, and then widened and flowed in a meandering course towards the East Sea.

The river network from the city to the open sea was about 40 miles. Quoc knew every turn of that waterway. He would soon get a chance to apply and strengthen that knowledge as a result of a dictate made by the central government.

Under the Communist Vietnamese regime, a mandate required every young man and woman in the country to serve the country for two years. It could be in any capacity and not necessarily a military one. A centralized system would place individuals into jobs where there were specific needs. Communist countries couldn't depend on the supply and demand of free trade and needed the steady hand of centralized planning, however cumbersome or inefficient it might be.

One area of Vietnam critically in need of manpower was Vung Tau, the port city where the Nha Be River met the East Sea. Vung Tau meant anchorage. The port had been used as such by ships involved in trade and fishing for nearly a century. There were a number of new industries in Vung Tau, including the beginnings of oil exploration. A predominant industry was lumbering, where hardwood stands provided ready access to wood for construction materials, particularly for fine furniture.

Young people – primarily young men – were selected to train and work as lumberjacks. Most came from the area around Saigon. Only a few were trained to carry weapons. The easiest way to transport the work crews to the lumber operations was by boat. The government lacked a fleet of boats, so a cottage industry arose at the docks of Saigon. Riverboats and their crews ferried work crews in and out of Vung Tau, working under licenses granted by the government. Thus, Quoc officially became a riverboat captain.

Each day, dozens of boats would cast off from the port, ostensibly carrying work crews to various locations downstream, including Vung Tau. However, every day an unknown number of the vessels were filled with those who became known as Boat People, who had paid the operators to escape the country. It was commonly known by the police that the practice was taking place: It only took one thing for them to turn a blind eye to the practice, and that was the inevitable bribes, which were an integral part of the economy. A Vietnamese saying encapsulated it, "What money can't buy, more money can."

A significant number of the boats escaping to the East Sea were not successful. Each family with a loved one involved in such escapes always established a code that could be sent by telegram to those remaining in Vietnam. The telegram would be sent from whatever port of safety they took refuge, including Singapore, Malaysia, and occasionally the Philippines. After a boat departed, weeks would go by. Frantic family members visited the telegraph office each day, anxiously waiting for the message that their loved one was safely out of the country. Sadly, many families never got a telegram. Sporadic reports on the BBC, and through the network of mariners who heard of or saw the flotsam of vessels destroyed in storms, cast a pall over the escapes. So too did the continued reports of vessels being attacked by Thai pirates, with the men on the ships killed, the women brutally tortured and raped.

None of the stories dampened the desire of refugees to escape to freedom.

Officially, Quoc was a riverboat pilot, but also in demand as a captain for Boat People. Those who attempted escape knew that the knowledge and skill of the captain would be the ultimate arbiter of a successful escape. Captains who left port with an empty bag of experience and a small bag of luck seldom succeeded. Better to have a full bag of experience and a modicum of luck.

Quoc was pragmatic. He wanted to ensure that any middleman looking for his services knew ships and had a respect for the sea. He also wouldn't captain a boat he considered unseaworthy or one with an underperforming engine.

Desperate but unknowledgeable people make decisions that can place them in jeopardy at sea. Those who are knowledgeable but desperate know that one set of risks does not mitigate the other risks. Risks can actually multiply. In any means of transportation – from airplanes to buses to ships – risk analysis plays a critical part of every decision. Any knowledgeable person involved in transportation knows the importance of calculating all the risks and weighing them against the odds.

Quoc continued to look to the sea for his own escape. He knew it afforded him the most viable means of leaving the country. His expertise would serve as an insurance policy against the challenges he and any crew would face.

But on which ship would that be?

34

CAPTAINCY FOR QUOC

"The real weight we were carrying was in our heavy hearts. We knew it was for the best. There was no future for us in Vietnam."

Cao Luu
Boat People

OCTOBER 1979

Di did not immediately recognize him. Quoc's time in the camps, the sickness, and the weight loss, combined with the rags he wore and his unkempt condition, all caused Di to look warily at Quoc. That wariness slowly evolved to a look of recognition and then a look of sadness at what had become of Quoc. Quoc knew what the man saw and appreciated that he said nothing. Quoc looked like an old man. It was no longer a disguise. It was a mantle he wore each day.

After escaping the police earlier that year, Quoc had lived on the streets of Saigon for three months. Di, who was a childhood friend, sought him out. It took a few weeks to find Quoc, as invisible as he was to those around him. Di offered Quoc the opportunity to be captain of a boat, ostensibly designed for a government contract to ferry workers downriver but really meant for escape. Quoc looked at him and said, "I don't think you can afford me."

The comment was not fueled by ego. Quoc knew he was not in a position to bargain, but he knew that he needed to make enough money to feed his family after he escaped. They discussed compensation. The going rate was around twenty ounces of gold. Di, who was in the initial stages of his own enterprise, could not afford to pay Quoc that amount.

Instead, Di asked Quoc to instruct him how to pilot a seagoing vessel. Di lacked the skills and experience Quoc had, but he hoped a short course would help him launch his escape. He would hope for the best as he headed toward landfall in the Philippines, Malaysia, or Singapore. This was all Di could hope for and afford.

Quoc knew Di had limited chances of success, but he knew his expertise might give his old friend a better chance of survival. Quoc realized his friend could not pay him what La Tu provided. Quoc's pay would be just enough for meals each day, with perhaps some money left over to buy food for his family. The offer was still more than nothing and was generous for the work he would do. Although it would not move him towards his ultimate goal of escape, it still kept Quoc in the maritime game, where a small network of men continually sought out expertise and nautical knowledge. This job would help improve his chances of getting the job he really wanted.

From then on, Quoc taught navigation and seamanship to Di in coffee houses and nondescript places, often speaking in whispers. He also tutored him at the pier, where two men talking about the sea was as natural as sports fans chatting at a soccer match. Quoc didn't have textbooks with which to teach Di. He instead imparted his lifetime of knowledge, using notepads, his hands, and other physical objects.

Di was bright and eager, but Quoc wasn't sure whether Di actually understood all the material he shared. It ranged from piloting down rivers, to rudimentary seamanship, light and flag signals, radio procedures, and sea conditions. Quoc continually quizzed Di on what had been covered in previous lessons. "Now tell me how to identify Polaris," he would challenge Di. "And what do you do when it's cloudy at the time of a star sighting? Tell me about sea states. What angle is the best way to approach waves? How do you handle passengers who are panicking?"

Several weeks into the training, Di suggested that they visit his boat. He also said that the boat was nearly complete and should be inspected by someone with Quoc's experience.

They took a motorbike to the heart of Saigon's waterfront, probably a mile from where Quoc had last walked the naval yard in 1975. There, under the eyes of the Communist authorities and no doubt with their complicit approval, Di had had a 37-foot boat constructed. It was allowed to sit there on its stays, poised like a large marine mammal ready to take to sea.

It didn't matter to Quoc how Di had managed to get the boat built. Other things were going through his mind. Mariners love the lines of ships just as an equestrian loves horses or a pilot adores airplanes. Di could see it in the way his friend's eyes gleamed and noticed Quoc's wide grin when he saw the boat and smelled the newly varnished wood. Even the distinct smell of the diesel fuel seemed to excite Quoc.

Although the boat was still on its stays in dry dock, it had the beautiful lines of a vessel that could carry itself in heavy seas. She had something about her that inspired confidence.

Di looked at Quoc, "I've come to a decision in the last few months."

Quoc looked at him inquiringly.

Di went on, "I've studied hard, but I am never going to know what you know and be able to do what you do. What you've taught me has given me more respect for the ocean and an understanding of what I will never know. I can't just hope for success. I need to give all of us the best chance possible. If you're willing to captain this vessel, I can give you five seats on it. That will get you and some of your family out of the country. Would that be payment enough?"

Quoc was dumbstruck but never hesitated. Smiling and laughing, he nodded in agreement. Once again, God was smiling on him, and he had a new way out of the country by ship. At that point, those five seats were worth 15 ounces of gold for those willing and able to pay it. Quoc could never have raised that much money to pay for the space, but his skills were an even trade. Over time he knew he could leverage the extra money to leave his family in Vietnam with enough resources, but that would come later.

The vessel was not as large as the hundred-foot ship he had been preparing for La Tu, but it was well-built. By Quoc's reckoning, it had an excellent chance of making it down the river and into the East Sea. There would be challenges, but Quoc's confidence soared, as he looked at the little craft, proud that he would be her captain. Together they would provide the means of escaping from Vietnam.

Di introduced Quoc to Loi, who would serve as the onboard mechanic. Loi told Quoc that he had served as a seaman – a machinist – in the Navy. Quoc discerned that Loi lacked even the most basic knowledge of ships or their power plants. However, Loi was Di's trusted lieutenant. Without him and his contacts and connections, it wouldn't have been possible to build the boat right in the heart of Saigon. Loi had no idea how to grease the bearings on a propeller shaft, but beyond doubt, he had the skills to grease the palms of the authorities. The fact that the ship sat there on its stays was testimony to it.

Quoc later learned that the bribes to the Vietnamese authorities for allowing construction of the boat and turning a blind eye to the escape totaled nearly thirty ounces of gold. In later years, Quoc realized that Di had barely broken even in his venture. This wasn't a financial business for Di: It was a desperate act to get his family to safety.

Quoc recognized Loi's strengths and his limitations. Nonetheless, he needed someone to serve as a mechanic. He worked with his underground network of mariners, and he eventually found a man named Dung, who had served on a cargo vessel as an engineer. He also had several years of experience at sea. Dung had served a few years with Phuc, Quoc's brother, on an ocean station vessel owned by the South Vietnamese government. Quoc could tell by the way he carried himself and the manner in which he carefully examined the engine that he was an experienced mariner. He would be instrumental in the escape.

Di was clearly the front man as the boat's construction continued. Quoc became vital, but he publicly remained transparent to the effort. He looked like an older man and was regarded as just one of many workers putting the finishing touches on the boat. No one would have recognized him as a naval officer, let alone the master of any vessel, but the day came when the little craft was launched. As she slid into the water, Quoc couldn't hold back his emotions as he felt the sturdy 37-footer bob gently on the river. She seemed to tug at her lines like a puppy urging her owner to take a walk. It didn't take long before Di joined Quoc and Dung in the boat and heard the small diesel engine turn over and watched the lines cast off. The boat was now operating on her own. Di looked over at Quoc with a look of gratitude as he saw his captain man the helm with a steady hand. The impatient puppy yielded to Quoc, as he steered her out for the first time.

Within a week, Di had the boat working in the service of the government, ferrying workers downriver, primarily to Vung Tau. Any uncertainty about Quoc's skills having deteriorated over the years quickly disappeared. Quoc's knowledge and instincts converged into the professional acumen that demonstrated his great skills as a mariner. On a number of the trips, Quoc trained some of Di's passengers in the duties of helmsman, so that he would have their help when they joined him in the escape.

While one of his friends steered the boat downriver one day, Quoc simultaneously kept a steady eye on him, the boat, the current, and the traffic. A young worker, an armed militiaman, moved over to Quoc and said, "Uncle, I believe you are an expert in seamanship."

Quoc glanced towards him, then cast his eyes downward, saying, "I'm just an old man who loves the sea."

The militiaman smiled and then challenged Quoc further, "I believe you are planning to escape in this boat."

Quoc frowned and shook his head, "Definitely not."

The militiaman continued to smile and then went back to gazing at the shore.

Quoc would see him again. Indeed, his fate would hang upon that one young man, whose name he would always remember, Lam.

35

HEART-BREAKING DECISIONS

"It is vain for the coward to flee; death follows close behind; it is only by defying it that the brave escape."

Voltaire

LATE 1979

Thoughts of Kim-Cuong and his family occupied his mind as Quoc captained his tiny vessel down the river for the first time. Truthfully, they had never been far from his thoughts and they were always in his heart.

Despite his inability to live with them and to even be acknowledged as the father of his daughters, he always felt a degree of solace and joy in the thought of a future together as a family – laughing together and sharing meals and memories in their own home.

Sadly, the intervening months of Quoc's freedom from the camps and forced occupation in the New Economic Zone had been replaced with a new type of incarceration. Ironically, he had no more freedom than he had experienced in the previous four-plus years. He was still not free. Quoc was still a captive, a captive of circumstance and the political winds that were not abating.

The consolidation of power by the Communists in Vietnam had fundamentally altered the political and economic landscape of the country. While some people continued to live their lives as they always had, most of the citizens of Vietnam were experiencing a new reality that bore little resemblance to their previous lives. For Quoc it was a fundamental shift that offered no hope for change. He, along with his fellow officers of the South Vietnamese Armed Forces, was a pariah. All of them would always be considered criminals and outcasts. It was a culture that, like so many, was defined as much by those who were reviled as those who were revered.

As the warm breeze generated by the boat's forward motion struck his face, Quoc became mentally preoccupied with the many terrible and heart-breaking factors of leaving versus staying in Vietnam. It was a matter of facts and emotion, head and heart and the connection between both. Quoc might consider staying if it meant that he could live as an outcast. However, if staying meant that he would always be considered a criminal and subject to incarceration or forced to live in the New Economic Zone, then that was not a life that would sustain him. While his health was somewhat better now, he knew he wouldn't survive physically living as a criminal on the streets and hiding from the law. He looked and felt so old. What would he be like in five or ten years?

Quoc had ceased to be bitter. He did not hate the Communists. Nor did he hate the officials who represented them. He had become hardened to his reality. Quoc realized that his energy was wasted on any feelings of hatred. Hate offers little in the way of solace and less in the way of hope. Hate can become an end in itself and stand in the way of the better use of energy. Quoc's chosen path was survival and the need to concentrate on hope for the future.

The little two-cylinder diesel's rapid tuk-tuk-tuk-tuk sound spoke to him. The water parted by the bow rippled smoothly along the sides of the vessel. He saw the vegetation slowly change the further south they motored and the color of the water shifted from a brown to a dark green. While physically engaged with the boat, Quoc was engrossed with the contradictions he and Kim-Cuong were still struggling to overcome.

Kim-Cuong had helped Quoc realize there was no future for him by staying in Vietnam. In 1975 he had hoped that any take-over by the Communists would be followed by an acceptance of all former combatants and that together they would be a unified country working toward common goals. He had let those feelings overcome rational thought. Ten days of Reeducation Camp that had evolved to nearly five years of incarceration and outcast status had changed him.

Uncle Ut Duc, whose words of warning had so chilled him after the fall of the country, had become a confidante since Quoc returned to Saigon. Ut Duc often encouraged his nephew and confidentially told him, "If I could leave with you, I would." Quoc told Ut Duc he would never again let wishful thinking overcome what he knew to be reality. Now he had options. He would select the best of the difficult paths before him and then use hope to sustain him on that course.

Only Kim-Cuong had intuitively recognized how bad the situation would be for him in the Reeducation Camps and afterwards, but it might not have been just intuition. Kim-Cuong understood people far better than most, and appreciated that their family was representative of what was happening in the rest of the country, divided as they were on politics and nationalism. It was Kim-Cuong who had reluctantly, but lovingly, directed him toward escape with Hung on the South Vietnamese Navy Fleet that April night in 1975.

He still felt the pain of that night, as they had clung to each other and cried. The decision had been a joint one between husband and wife. He had changed his mind without consulting Kim-Cuong. He often mentally replayed the sight of Kim-Cuong the day after he was supposed to have escaped. She had been angry and tried to pound his chest before bursting into tears and hugging him, sobbing with fear of the future. And yet, she had never stopped loving him.

Quoc didn't fully understand Kim-Cuong's ambivalent emotions. In 1975, he had pretended to be strong and had the illusion that whatever he faced he could weather. The intervening years taught Quoc that no person could withstand every storm. The cumulative impact of the events he experienced over the years now put him on another precipice. The reality before him – to escape – was something that gave him no joy or thoughts of happiness. Joy and happiness did not come close to how he felt. The thought of escape might have been better defined in just one emotionless word: Necessary.

If escape was necessary, then it had to be carefully planned and executed. Quoc had an engineer's mind and always felt that reasonable options could be developed from calculated risks. It was logical, for instance, that so many escape attempts failed, because most were attempted by unskilled mariners who too often relied on luck to escape successfully. Quoc would bring knowledge and skill to his mission and leave luck at the bottom of his mariner's toolkit, to be relied on if nothing else was available. That had been Quoc's focus for months, but his heart struggled with the logical conclusions of his mind. Quoc's heart anguished over everything he might lose if he stayed in Vietnam – his health, his freedom, his home life, his life itself – and everything he might lose if he left – his extended family in Vietnam, incarceration or death by the militia if caught, or death at sea. Only a man who has faced such extreme choices can understand the conflicts Quoc faced.

Quoc understood that Kim-Cuong had to also agonize over and internalize her own complicated and heart-rending conclusions, which she, with Quoc's help, would determine with logic guided by her heart. Kim-Cuong had always been better at connecting her heart and mind, but what they faced was nonetheless as difficult for her as it was for Quoc. He knew she was devoted to her family in Vietnam and that they had four young children, the oldest, Hung, just nine. After his return to Saigon Kim-Cuong had delivered another child, a son, named Cuong, after his mother. Cuong was barely two months old.

Yet maternal love can become an unseen and powerful factor in decision-making and inevitably becomes the deciding factor in any decision, especially when it might mean leaving home. Kim-Cuong often thought of the mothers of previous generations who had faced such difficult junctures in their lives, and she put that into perspective: Hers was not a forced evacuation or deportation. In reality, unlike the Jews in Nazi Germany, the entire family was not at imminent risk if they stayed. Quoc was the one who was living in fear of incarceration or possible death in a camp, not the rest of the family. That seemed harsh to her, but it rang true.

Kim-Cuong knew that not all of the small boats filled with escapees actually made it to safety. The rest may have been lost in storms or captured by pirates off the coast and never heard from again. The thought of getting on a boat with such odds terrified Kim-Cuong and her family. They imagined the babies falling prey to the winds and the seas and never being able to live their lives.

Kim-Cuong also weighed the risk of other means of escape. At that point, there was no scheduled air service out of Vietnam to countries friendly to refugees. Even if possible, escape by air would be enormously expensive, and they would be even more prone to capture by authorities along the way. With a seagoing escape, only a handful of militia or police needed to be bribed.

If she stayed, life would be difficult for Kim-Cuong, the girls, and their newborn son. But Kim-Cuong's families had the advantage of having some support within the government and were not tainted in the way that Quoc and his family were. Her family had survived over the past five years and many family members had been allowed to work within the constraints of the new economy. They were eating regularly and had a roof over their heads.

Each night, Kim-Cuong cried herself to sleep thinking about the possibilities and the realities she faced. The man she loved was not able to live with her or even work in the country. He would be jailed if the authorities were even a bit more organized or if Dong was not able to intervene. If Kim-Cuong tried to escape with him, some of the family – or all of them – might not make it to safety. However, she could not have Quoc remain in Vietnam and be confident he would survive.

Quoc and Kim-Cuong wrestled with a number of scenarios and possibilities to inform their final decision-making. The top priority was always to ensure the safe transport of their children. Once, Kim-Cuong proposed using the Chinese horoscope to determine who should escape on the boat with Quoc. Quoc had reluctantly agreed. As he had been taught by a fellow prisoner in the camps, he mapped his children's birth signs to the Chinese horoscope and eventually determined the outcome upon which they had already decided: Hung was the only one who would go with him on the boat.

Although she may have been skeptical of Quoc's reading of the horoscope, Kim-Cuong accepted it, because it agreed with what they had already discussed and she knew in her heart: Quoc would not be able to take care of any additional child besides Hung. The unseen and ancient power of the horoscope conveniently coincided with the logic that had already informed their decision.

Quoc loved Kim-Cuong more than anyone. He felt he was sensitive to her feelings. He appreciated her and recognized that he would not have survived without her love. He knew her love for him was absolute. They had a strong connection, but Quoc knew their time together had often been interrupted by separations, events, or other people. It always took time for them to reconnect; seldom were they afforded that time.

The ability for Kim-Cuong to talk and reason with Quoc was sometimes a challenge for her: She suspected he could not understand her woman's heart. And, too often, Kim-Cuong tried to decipher what Quoc was thinking and feeling and projected her own emotions on him, herself and their families. Such periodical lack of clear communication on occasion undermined the connection between them and, like so many other marriages, caused them difficulty.

Nonetheless, this time, their hearts and minds connected in a powerful way. Each, from different perspectives, had reached the same final decisions and shared the same bitter paradox: They knew Quoc had to leave Vietnam, and they knew without a doubt that they wanted their family intact, no matter how long it took.

Quoc's mind focused on Kim-Cuong. He respected her as much as he loved her. That was perhaps the deciding factor for him and what ultimately cemented their mutual decision to separate, in hopes of a reunion at some undefined time in the future.

When they finally made the terrible, but necessary decision that December night in 1979, it was filled with as many tears as the April night so many years before. This time, though, the tears flowed from even deeper emotions and more scars.

After they finally made the terrible but necessary decision, other concerns arose, among them, which other family members might accompany Quoc on the escape. They depended on how Quoc would utilize the five seats that Di granted to him as payment for captaining the escape.

The arithmetic was tricky. Di was selling each of the places on the boat for three ounces of gold per passenger. Part of Quoc's allocation had to go to provide escape for family members; part to leave money behind for Kim-Cuong and Vo. One of the five seats was dedicated for Hung. Quoc had a very real need to sell at least one or two of the remaining seats to leave his family with money after his departure. Unspoken, too, was the fact that any money he left with Kim-Cuong and Vo might be needed for possible bribes to obtain Quoc's release if he were captured.

Quoc's mother, Vo, wanted her tenth child, a daughter, Muoi, to escape with Quoc, but Vo became uneasy the more she heard stories about Thai pirates and the rapes of young women. The next in line was Quoc's brother, Cuu. Cuu had determined that he had a limited future in Vietnam and wanted to make his way to the United States. He figured his youth and hard work would serve him well in making a new life. Cuu was in his early twenties and not yet married. Being a man would not necessarily make it easy if pirates captured him and the others, but in Vo's mind, it was preferable to the thoughts of what would happen to her daughter Muoi.

Kim-Cuong and Quoc both knew that a woman's influence and perspective would be needed during and after the escape, to take care of Hung until Kim-Cuong could join Quoc. However long it might be, Hung would need nurturing while away from his mother and Quoc would need to find a job and make money to send back to the family for their additional support. Both Kim-Cuong and Quoc were surprised when Kim-Cuong's sister, Dong, said she wanted to join the group that would escape. She was a smart and strong woman who had made her way into the confidences of the Communist authorities. Yet, she felt that it was worth the risk to begin a new life outside of the country. She wasn't yet married, and she was young and strong enough to make the arduous trip. The job with the Communist government helped the family's security, but they weighed that with the very real reward of having her join in the escape.

When the family presented the same arguments about Thai pirates that Vo and Muoi had heard, Dong was steadfast in her determination to leave. Her father, Hung, was decidedly not in favor of Dong joining the escape. He rebuked her for even thinking of such a "foolhardy act." As a widower with only daughters, he told her he would only have considered sending a boy on such a hazardous trip, but consider sending a young woman? He would not stand for it.

He also told Kim-Cuong and Quoc pointedly that he would stand in the way of their taking his grandson, Hung, away from the family home.

After all she had done for him, there was no hesitation on Quoc's part to give Dong one of the valuable seats to freedom, but her father remained firm in his decision to stand in their way. Quoc and Kim-Cuong ultimately conspired with Dong to stage an argument between Dong and her father. This would give her a plausible reason to leave his house. As to young Hung's departure, that would be a challenge requiring stealth and finesse.

So three seats were gone. Quoc and Kim-Cuong quietly conveyed to the other close family members the possibility of escape, without offering details. No other takers requested passage. That left two for Quoc to broker for gold to give to Kim-Cuong and his mother, as well to procure necessary supplies for the trip. At no point did Quoc consider making any profit from the sales. Selling the two seats was necessary to procure what he needed for his family and for the trip.

Then, Kim-Cuong received an inquiry from her Aunt Tuyet Hong, her mother's sister. She and her husband, My, secretly confided to her that if Quoc was captaining an escape vessel, they wanted to be included. Quoc only had two tickets, but he approached Di and convinced him that two more seats should go on sale in order to finance the purchase of a sextant and supplies. At this point, Di realized that his venture was not going to be a moneymaker. He also recognized that navigational instruments and other supplies were needed to help ensure a successful escape. Di agreed to sell four seats to Hong and her family.

Through a mutual contact, Quoc received one other request for a seat. He recalled the name immediately. It was Thai, who had escaped murder in Katum. One incredulous look from Quoc told the man that transportation for the Communist spy would not ever be considered.

Quoc ended up with six ounces of gold. He promptly gave two ounces each to Kim-Cuong and to his mother, Vo. He and Di together spent most of the remaining two ounces for necessary equipment and supplies.

After all the emotional and logical thinking, the contradictory insights, the assessment of risks and rewards, after every thought and word had been exhausted on the subject, a final irony was an unexpected confidante and co-conspirator. Quoc's brother, Phuc, who had long voiced sympathy towards the Communists, sat down with Quoc and said simply, "How can I help you in your escape, Brother?"

Quoc was surprised by the question, but knew right away how Phuc's expertise could be useful. Despite Phuc's political beliefs, Quoc trusted him. Phuc had been a radio operator, knew Morse code and understood the science of meteorology. Together, those talents would provide the final expertise necessary for a successful escape.

The splash of another boat's wake brought Quoc back to the river and the trip downstream. The strong sound of the engine somehow assured him that the terrible decisions he and his family had made were the best they could do and that providence would bring them all to a safe place in the future.

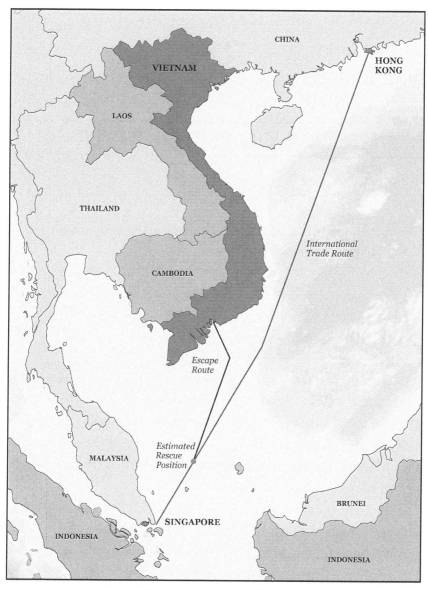

Quoc's Escape Route into the East Sea

Map created by Hung Pham

36

ESCAPE DOWN THE RIVER

"Goodbye my loved ones, I miss you already even though I haven't yet left."

Farewell
Traditional Vietnamese Song

JANUARY 1980

New Year in the West came on January 1, 1980. There were no real celebrations in Vietnam – it wasn't the New Year holiday there – and anyway, there wasn't a lot to celebrate for most people. That date's only real significance for Quoc was that it marked the beginning of the fifth calendar year the Communists had ruled Vietnam and that he had been denied his freedom.

That day, the front page of the New York Times concentrated on the Iranian Hostage Crisis. There were three articles on the Soviet war being waged in Afghanistan, and two articles about the U.S. economy. There was no mention of Vietnam. Occasional news articles about Vietnam had long since been consigned to the inside pages of newspapers and magazines throughout the world.

Sometimes, there were articles about the continued escapes to sea from Vietnam, but one would be hard-pressed to conclude from most news outlets that it was a crisis. Based on this coverage, it would be impossible to realize just how tragic and how personal the situation had become. Hundreds were dying in their attempts to leave. Each month, more people kept trying to escape from Vietnam. UN authorities at that time verified numbers that ranged from 5,000 to more than 13,000 people every month.

The United Nations High Commissioner For Refugees (UNHCR) would report in August of 1981 that, in the six years since the war ended, a total of 393,394 Vietnamese boat people had been settled in other countries. The vast majority escaped by sea. There are no accurate figures on how many failed in these escape attempts, but few now doubt that thousands perished at the hands of pirates and the vagaries of the ocean. Sadly, no one will ever really know.

Quoc had some idea of the refugee situation, but at that time, he had no perspective on the exodus. Nor could he focus on such numbers. His obligation to his family members and to the other escapees on his little boat depended upon him keeping only the tactical view in sight. To the captain of any vessel, his ship is the whole world. He can't concentrate on anything else. If he does, he will lose focus, and focus is the primary trait that a mariner learns. Quoc needed every bit of that focus for his planning and execution of the mission.

Quoc continued his purchases. Using the black marketing skills he had learned in Cambodia, Quoc approached a stevedore helping to unload a cargo vessel at the Port of Saigon. He sized up the man and then asked him if he wanted to earn some money. He would pay in gold. The man did not seem surprised. Such was the culture of the country at that point: It was not a matter of who was on the take, just how much they charged.

Quoc explained to the man that he was in the market for a sextant. The man replied, "I don't know what that is."

Quoc sketched out a diagram of the device, describing its hard angles, multiple mirrors, and lenses and then simply said, "If you happen to run across a good one, I would pay up to an ounce of gold." Quoc didn't tell him that it was a necessary instrument for sighting the sun and stars for celestial navigation at sea. The man might have guessed, but Quoc didn't want to confirm, that the instrument was a critical tool for escape.

The man silently nodded, gave a quick wink, and headed back onto the ship. At the end of his shift, after darkness had fallen, he rendezvoused with Quoc and held out a new sextant. He showed off his trophy, but didn't hand it over until the gold appeared. Quoc took out an ounce of gold leaf and handed it to the man. The stevedore then relinquished the single most valuable tool Quoc needed for navigation. Without being asked, the man simply said to Quoc as he walked away, "It's interesting what you can find on the bridge of a ship!"

Quoc spent his money carefully on a number of other necessary items. The most fundamental tool on any ship is a compass, and Quoc needed one that was mounted and visible in the cockpit. Again, through acquaintances on the dock, he was able to obtain a large compass with a brass case that he stowed away until he was ready to set sail on the ocean. The compass was too valuable to use for river cruising and could easily develop legs in that environment of equipment procurement that was all too common during that period. It was also unnecessary for river navigation.

An emergency signal mirror was procured that had a hole in the middle with a reticle that could be used to focus on another vessel, and then use the sun to flash into the eyes of an observer. Though just four by six inches, the tool was incredibly effective and had been used for decades around the world. It was especially useful in the Pacific, with its continual days of sunshine and relative calm, allowing signaling at long distances. This particular mirror was not glass but highly polished metal with chrome on it; Quoc was told that it was designed to be picked up by a ship's onboard radar. Quoc didn't know if it would work, but he figured it wouldn't hurt to have every advantage on the high seas.

To further help identification on radar, Quoc had a metal frame added above the wheelhouse of his boat, along with a ship's bell that could be rung to get the attention of mariners that they might see on the East Sea.

Other survival items Quoc obtained included a flare gun with extra cartridges and a sea anchor labeled U.S. Army that had been part of the gear left on an LST – or Landing Ship Tank, one of the thousands of pieces of military gear and transportation devices abandoned by the Americans. Quoc was also able to obtain a good set of binoculars for sighting ships. He even procured Communist uniforms for himself and the crewmembers on the boat for the initial stages of the escape.

Quoc accomplished a near-miracle as he spent the last few months of the year converting a 1971 nautical almanac so that he could use it in 1980. Most modern mariners knew celestial navigation, but the advanced mathematics required to derive the interpolation of celestial bodies and their position in the sky was not taught in many curriculums. A French instructor named Ducasse had instructed Quoc and Quoc had demonstrated that knowledge in his final exam more than a decade before, even though he never expected to use the skill. He accomplished this painstaking effort and produced a series of handwritten tables used to help determine the boat's position as they navigated the sea towards their destination.

Quoc's plan was to head southeast into the East Sea and then turn due south towards Singapore. That would put him in the heavily travelled shipping lanes between Hong Kong and Singapore. He would try to locate an American ship or some vessel flying under a flag friendly to refugees and then get safe passage to Singapore. Absent that, he planned for enough fuel for a voyage all the way to

Singapore, which was about 660 nautical miles from the mouth of the Saigon River. He calculated that it could take at least a week to make the trip.

Quoc split the remaining four ounces of gold between Kim-Cuong and Vo. In the economy of Vietnam in early 1980, two ounces of gold would likely buy food for a family for as long as six months, including badly needed milk for young children. As he gave the gold to his mother and wife, it was left unsaid that it could also be used for bribes if Quoc and Hung were captured.

Quoc and Kim-Cuong's extended families continued to work together. They were still blood relatives and committed towards a common goal, saving Quoc from his current plight.

There was military precision in the planning and, like any operation of that kind, very real compartmentalization and plausible deniability in case the plan was compromised. For instance, while Phuc knew that Quoc was planning the escape, he never knew for sure who would travel with his brother, or when the mission was planned. He just knew that Quoc needed his help with a forecast of wind, weather and sea conditions so he could decide the date of departure.

Like so many other times in the past five years, Quoc had to hide his emotions and to ask his family members to do the same. Part of this compartmentalization of information also included succinctness in relaying necessary details. Each member of the family also knew that they should never ask for any information they did not need to know, or the timing of the escape. That way, if a neighbor overheard or saw one of the families speaking, they wouldn't notice clandestine behavior, lengthy conversations or heightened emotion.

Though necessary, none of their precautionary measures served to eliminate the pain and tears of Quoc's impending escape attempt. Those emotions were exiled to the late-night hours of sleeplessness that every member of the family experienced. Regularly, tearless days became tearful nights as the fears and concerns of each person emerged.

One of those most concerned was Kim-Cuong's father, Hung, for whom Quoc's son was named. He knew – for all the reasons the others did – that Quoc had to make the escape attempt and supported that effort, but he steadfastly refused to sanction any other family member's departure.

In the meantime, Quoc, Dung, and the rest of the crew continued to motor their government-paid route, transporting workers downriver, primarily to the lumber company near Vung Tau. By day, the little boat – still unnamed by Quoc – picked up a cargo of 15 to 20 young men and a few women and took them to their worksites, where they would spend the night. During the dawn hours on the next day, the crew headed back upriver, docking their boat after sunset.

Quoc usually steered the boat away from the pier and then allowed other crewmembers to man the helm. He didn't want to be identified as the captain, though it was difficult for him to hide his practiced eye and skills. Those attributes belied his own knowledge and experience. For most observers, he might appear as just an older man, but those who carefully observed his actions realized he knew his way around a boat.

He continued to think about the militiaman, Lam, who had confronted him. The challenge still echoed in his mind. He had not seen Lam again but knew the young man had suspected an escape.

More and more boats had been heading out to escape from Saigon since December. The numbers escalated as January began. The reason for the increase no doubt centered on the weather. Its inevitable uncertainty and unpredictability in the winter was valued as a masking agent for escapes. The captains were willing to risk the dangers of heavy seas in exchange for avoiding the watchful eyes of the authorities. Bribes alone could not guarantee success.

Just to maintain their credibility, the police had to catch a few boats attempting to escape. Quoc did not intend for his boat to be one of those captured. He continued his rigorous preparations and practiced a variety of boating techniques he had not used in years. He ensured that the boat was as well equipped as possible. He and Di also decided how they would accommodate the nearly 50 occupants on a boat designed for 20.

They determined that all but critical crewmembers would be housed below deck. It would be extraordinarily cramped with no room for lying down. All the occupants would be sitting on the bottom of the vessel, pressed close together with their backs resting against the hull. The occupants would not have room to stand. The distance from the bottom of the vessel to the decking was less than four feet.

When water splashed or leaked into the vessel, the escapees sitting inside the hull would be soaked. There were two sets of bilge pumps on the vessel, but if these failed, the passengers would need to bail with buckets and small tin cans. These would be passed through a small bulkhead that entered into the wheelhouse, a small covered area on the boat that held Quoc and a few others.

There were no toilet facilities on the boat. When possible, a pail would be used by the escapees, passed through the small hatchway, and poured into the ocean. Once at sea, even that would not be feasible, because the heavy seas probably would not allow it.

Quoc and Di planned for most of the passengers to be brought aboard in small groups and then positioned below decks, through one of two main hatchways on the deck. Once all were inside, the hatches, which were designed to conform and blend in with the normal decking, would be nailed shut. If boarded, it would look as if the only occupants were a few crewmembers and a handful of passengers – the routine load for trips downriver to Vung Tau. Any indication of a large group would be effectively camouflaged. Once the vessel left the Vung Tau anchorage and headed to sea, those 10-15 people above deck would be placed below decks and the hatches re-nailed.

The passengers were required to bring their own dried food, that could be consumed without cooking. Drinking water would be carried in metal cans and shared between the passengers stuffed in the cramped quarters.

The trip would be painful, dangerous, and uncertain, but like Quoc, the Boat People of Vietnam felt they had no choice. They were choosing to gamble everything – their livelihood, their homeland, their families, and even their lives – to find safety for themselves and to establish a beachhead to bring the rest of their families out of the country.

Quoc designated certain able-bodied men to help with steering duties, and others to serve below decks to bail water as necessary. He also identified those who would serve as lookouts for ships once they entered the busy shipping lanes.

Each night in January, Quoc stopped by his mother's house before heading to Kim-Cuong's family home. Without even being asked, Quoc's brother, Phuc, would relay the weather in a few cryptic words or a sidelong glance. He would shake his head to indicate that the weather and sea conditions were considered – paradoxically – too good for an attempted escape.

At the beginning of the second week of January, Quoc walked into the house and saw Phuc motion for him to come into the corner.

"Quoc, there's a tropical depression building in the East Sea. I just heard it over the commercial ship radio frequency. By about the 17th, there should be low visibility conditions and heavy rains and seas. If that's what you need, that's what you're going to get."

Quoc said nothing except, "Thank you, Brother."

He walked out the door. As he headed towards Kim-Cuong's home, a timeline began formulating in his brain. The past four-plus years were not even a remote part of his thinking. His thoughts centered on the present. He would not allow the past to usurp or contaminate his future.

For the first time in nearly five years it was now possible for Quoc to have a new beginning, a new life for him and his family. The 17th would be the day they would escape. The time was arriving when Quoc would sail to freedom.

Quoc walked into the house and looked into Kim-Cuong's deep, black eyes. He didn't have to say anything, she just knew. She teared up and hugged him. He quietly murmured, "It'll be alright. We have less than a week."

He hugged her again. Kim-Cuong's father, Hung, glanced up from where he squatted on the low chair and looked at them both inquiringly, but he did not stir. Perhaps he knew what they were talking about – or maybe didn't want to know.

Quoc met with Di early the next morning. The boat was ready, with the exception of diesel fuel. Watchful eyes were always attentive to extra fuel purchases as evidence of a plan for escape. Over the next five days, with help from some additional bribes, they filled 20 steel containers with 20 gallons of diesel fuel each – some 400 gallons in all. It was enough for a run to Singapore. The two-cylinder diesel only had a 10-gallon internal tank, so the fuel would have to be siphoned and poured into the tank periodically by Dung.

Quoc also instructed Dung to change the oil in the engine and have it running in top condition for the escape. The engineer knew what that meant, but like so many others complicit in an open secret, said nothing.

Di knew the passenger list. Quoc did not. He only knew for sure that Cuu, Dong, Hung, and Kim-Cuong's relatives would accompany him. Di quietly put into place a communication plan that involved multiple cut outs for those involved. This involved one person talking to another and then another, each armed only with limited knowledge in the event of compromise. Rendezvous points had been established weeks before, and Di set into motion the detailed plan. Individuals would be picked up beginning the night of the 14th, and the loading would continue at points all along the river adjacent to the city through January 16. The escapees would immediately board and go below decks with their food and a few possessions. They would remain there as long as the escape took.

Quoc's job was to have Di join him, unobtrusively cruise the river near Saigon, and pick up the passengers during periods of darkness. Most were shuttled by smaller boats and taken to rendezvous points. Cuu picked some up on his motorbike. Passengers were picked up for the better part of two nights; usually between 8:00 p.m. and 2:00 a.m. Before dawn on January 16, there were some 35 men, women, and children below decks. They did their best to keep quiet; some families even resorted to dispensing cough medicine to the children to keep them sleepy.

With the boat tied to the dock that night, the escapees did their best to get some sleep in their cramped quarters, which in a few days would be even more packed. The small hatch in the wheelhouse remained available for passing the bucket used to relieve themselves. Dung or one of the other crewmen dutifully emptied it, leaving the hatch open for only brief periods.

The passenger list included 26 members of Di's family, all of whom had contributed towards the escape. Quoc knew Di and realized it had never been about money for this boat owner. It was merely a method to gain freedom for as many of his family members as possible.

There were a number of men and a few women on board who had served in the South Vietnamese military. As a result, security had been excellent. Quoc was sure that discipline, despite the privations ahead, would be maintained. He knew how to command a ship and would not be shy to issue orders to anyone, no matter what their previous rank or background had been.

Quoc made sure his position as captain would not be questioned. Those who had met Quoc already felt his confidence as a mariner on the high seas. They passed on to the others that they were being led by an experienced man, a man with a personal reason to get himself and his family members to safety.

Quoc's knowledge and obvious skill would help ensure obedience and respect, but like any group of individuals, there were always those who would inevitably question authority.

Having Cuu aboard the boat gave Quoc a measure of comfort, because Cuu had demonstrated unique survival abilities during the past five years and was quick to learn. Having a male family member there to back up Dong when Quoc was otherwise occupied, also gave Quoc some level of assurance for Hung's safety.

Duties on the boat were shared by all those above decks with passengers serving as relief crewmen where needed. Also, everyone aboard was fully prepared for any bribes that might be necessary: They carried extra gold and some Vietnamese *dong* just in case it was needed.

Late on the night of the 16th, Quoc began to feel the change in the weather. The forecast had been correct. He headed first to his mother's home. He walked in and hugged his mother, and she silently sobbed, knowing that this was the long-anticipated night. Quoc didn't say a word and silently walked out the door.

It was only after he left that Vo began a nearly inaudible wail, as she struggled to remain standing. Vo had lost so much in the war, a daughter to a tragic death and a husband as much to a broken heart as a stroke. Tonight, she would be losing two sons and her young grandson, not knowing if or when she would ever see them again. Another mother's heart was broken in a nation that was already overflowing with the sorrow of war.

Quoc headed to Kim-Cuong's home. He spotted the doorway and immediately ran into his father-in-law lying in a hammock that stretched across the opening. Clearly the elder Hung knew of the plan – Kim-Cuong must have somehow let it slip out. Hung's intent was to act as a physical barrier, keeping his grandson safe from escape. Hung did not know it yet, but he had already lost his daughter, Dong, as well. After the contrived argument the previous night, she had stayed at a neighbor's house and then made her way to the boat. Even then, Dong was already aboard and below deck awaiting the hour of departure.

Quoc did not argue with his father-in-law. He just sat there with Kim-Cuong, as they silently held each other and young Hung, hoping for a chance to get him out of the house. They sat there hour after hour, never sleeping, listening to the seconds tick by on a small clock on the wall.

Hung remained in the hammock, staring at them defiantly. Respect for the elderly is strong in the Vietnamese culture. Quoc would never consider attempting to overpower his father-in-law, but he would take any chance he could to get his son to safety. That chance came around 4:00 a.m. when Hung finally fell asleep. When they heard his determined breathing shift to quiet snoring, Quoc quickly picked up young Hung, grabbed the bag of food, silently kissed Kim-Cuong goodbye and then slipped under the hammock. He pushed through the opening and broke into a run.

Quoc never knew what Kim-Cuong went through with her father until nearly 10 years later. Hung had been angrier than he had ever been before. At first, he threatened to tell the authorities to rescue his grandson. Only after hours of argument did he finally stop his tirade and ultimately sink into a silent despair. He barely talked to Kim-Cuong and the rest of the family for weeks.

Quoc could not think about what was happening between Kim-Cuong and her father. He alternated between a run and a walk. The young boy, ever stoic, silently held onto his father. Hung was nine years old, but weighed less than normal youngsters his age. He had lived through war and the challenges of an impoverished family for too long. He trusted his father, and any sadness he might have felt for leaving was overshadowed by a sense of adventure. Riding on a boat for the first time, sailing the high seas, going to America. His excitement had built in the previous weeks; so much so that the week before, he had inadvertently told a schoolmate that he was going to America. Overheard by a sympathetic teacher who was a friend of the family, it caused Kim-Cuong to pull him out of school in the days before the escape.

As they made their way to the pier, Quoc whispered, "Son, what an adventure we're on! It will be all right. Your father is with you, and we'll get through this. You'll see your mother again, I promise." Hung did not cry. He said nothing. Like young children the world over, he just thought of how exciting the trip would be, never understanding the dangers they might face.

Quoc used multiple means of transportation to get to the pier. He jumped on a cyclo taxi and rode for half a mile, then paid the driver, walked three blocks, and flagged down another cab. He did this two more times, taking more than 45 minutes to get to a place that normally took 20.

When Quoc and Hung finally arrived at the boat, the setting was placid. It was just after dawn, and the water lapped quietly against the boat's hull. The official mission was for the boat to carry workers for an important Tet celebration at the lumber company's headquarters near Vung Tau.

Ships and boats are constructed from wood and steel. It is difficult to imagine ships being excited about a pending voyage, but mariners see their vessels – not as inanimate objects – but living entities. They almost universally give them female names and ascribe feminine attributes to them. As Quoc held Hung's hand, he eyed his little vessel and knew she was ready. She was provisioned and the occupants were, for the most part, already aboard. Looking at the boat, one could not imagine that there were already more than 35 individuals below deck, silently enduring cramped quarters and deprivation. The plan was for a four to six day journey. It would be painful for everyone aboard.

The scene on the dock was surreal. A dozen men, including a number of policemen, were eating breakfast with Di. They invited Quoc and Hung to join them. They sat there chatting for the better part of an hour, Quoc wondering, but not ever sure, if the police knew the escape was imminent. Were they all pretending to not know the plan while actually having full knowledge of it? Quoc wrestled with the idea, but played along with the casual conversation.

Phuc's forecast for bad weather on the 17th had fortuitously coincided with the Tet celebration. The workers would still be allowed to enjoy a picnic under cover at the company's headquarters in Can Gio, near Vung Tau.

Quoc and Di boarded the boat with Hung. He appeared to those on the dock as just another child attending a celebration with his father. From the black market, Di had procured Vietnamese military uniforms for the crew and for the passengers on deck. From all appearances, they appeared to be officials on the way to the party.

There was a further twist: Quoc's boat had always motored down the waterway alone, but today two other boats would travel the route with him. They would ride side by side. Quoc knew it would change his timing for the trip down the river.

Dung cast off the lines and Quoc swung the boat out to the middle of the channel, falling in line behind the other two boats. Quoc noticed the other captains motored downriver faster than normal, no doubt in anticipation of the festivities at the lumber company. Given the current on the river, Quoc's calculations of speed at his initial checkpoints along the river indicated to him that he would arrive at the mouth of the river before nightfall.

He had planned for the cover of weather and darkness to escape to the sea. Now that was in jeopardy. It was up to Quoc to figure out how to compensate.

37

BOARDED BY MILITIA

"In any game, you should play up to the last hand. There is no point of return."

Popular slogan for the Boat People
during the 1980's

The three-boat flotilla made its way downriver at a heady pace. Quoc and Di could hear singing on the other two boats as they sped along with the tide. While it provided good cover to be traveling with the other boats, they seemed to be motoring along with abandon; no doubt trying to maximize the time they would have at the Tet celebration.

Festivities in the new Vietnam were far less common than during previous times in the country's history. Doubtless the captains of the other boats wanted to get their passengers there as soon as possible, so they too, could join in the fun.

Quoc had carefully calculated a speed of four nautical miles per hour (knots) in order to arrive at the open sea at nightfall and in the forecast deteriorating weather conditions. The other two boats had a timetable that essentially was: "Get to Can Gio as soon as possible." The other captains used higher power settings and the tide to their advantage. Quoc calculated their speed at about eight knots. Using his watch and counting minutes and seconds between known checkpoints, he could calculate his speed with great precision. He used the simple equation long known to mariners: Rate (or Speed) = Distance/Time. Quoc had no choice but to maintain the same speed as the other boats.

In order to slow their progress, Quoc stopped the boat at a community gathering several miles downriver. It turned out to be a wedding party. The other two boats stopped briefly with him, but after 30 minutes, the other captains insisted they leave to get to their own party. Quoc reluctantly set out again.

The Communist uniforms gave them authenticity as they sped by a number of Communist checkpoints. Quoc, Di, and the others would smile and wave to the Communist guards, who would provide a cursory salute, showing no apparent interest in the boats or their passengers.

Quoc stood at the helm. The people on the foredeck – about 15 men and a couple of women – were passengers, but also escapees, who needed to appear on deck as enthusiastic attendees bound for the festivities.

The remaining escapees sat silently below deck, the hatches nailed shut above them. They were jammed into the bilge. The boat was designed so that the engine was in a separate compartment in the rear, but the rapid "tuk-tuk-tuk-tuk," of the straining little two-cylinder engine reverberated through the wooden hull. Quoc knew there would be water splashing into the bilge and suspected from the smells emanating through the small hatch in the wheelhouse that at least one person may have already vomited. It was not surprising, locked as they were in a dark and smelly space that rocked in a disorienting manner from the waves and wind off the river.

Quoc's boat sat heavier in the water than the other two boats. With the throttle of his engine set at its highest setting for most of the trip downriver, it was more difficult for him to maintain their pace. Dung checked below decks on the little diesel and would come up with a reassuring nod to Quoc. The two had developed a strong bond. They respected each other's unique abilities: Quoc as the experienced navigator and captain; Dung, as his chief engineer. Dung had a unique ability to perform magic with anything mechanical and especially with their little engine, so vital to them.

As they neared the final few miles, Di whispered to Quoc, "What are you going to do? We're ahead of schedule."

Quoc had thought over his options in the previous three hours downriver, "We fake an engine problem and tell them we will catch up."

There was a risk that another captain might tow Quoc's boat to the dock, but Quoc gambled that the other crew's enthusiasm for the festivities – along with Quoc's supposedly-disabled boat's relatively close proximity to shore – would dissuade the other two boats from assisting him.

At noon, some two miles from the mouth of the river, Quoc began pulsating the throttle of the two-cylinder diesel. His speed diminished rapidly then sped up and then slowed down. The wake behind the boat echoed the changing speed, with a wave nearly hitting the stern as each slowdown moved in rhythm with the throttle movement.

One boat came alongside Quoc's boat seconds before he shut down the engine entirely. The captain waited patiently as Quoc yelled mock orders to Dung, indicating his displeasure. Quoc did not readily acknowledge the other boat, instead focusing wrath upon Dung, who willingly went along with the play-acting, yelling from below decks, "The engine ran out of fuel. I just have to fill the tank. I'll have it going in five minutes. Be patient!"

Quoc barked, "You fool! What are we paying you for except to keep that engine running? Now get it going right away!"

The other captain nodded to Quoc, "You okay? You need a tow?"

Quoc just pointed below deck and frowned, "No, the idiot just forgot to keep the tank full. He'll have to siphon some diesel from our extra tank, but we should be underway in a few minutes. Go enjoy yourself: We'll join you shortly."

The other captain gave a knowing look, a short salute, and then accelerated away from Quoc. The passengers waved merrily.

Quoc kept up the appearance of anger as long as the other two boats were within sight. As soon as they rounded a bend, he began the process of transferring the rest of the escapees below deck.

First, Di used a small crowbar to pry up the nails on one of the main deck hatches. He and Dung spent a couple of minutes emptying buckets filled with human waste and vomit, quickly rinsing them in the water and handing them back below decks. Then the remaining escapees jumped below decks, grimacing or frowning from the stench and the crowded conditions in the hold. They did not know how long they would be in that hellhole, but it was their only means of getting out of the country.

The weather had grown increasingly windy in the past few hours, true to Phuc's forecast. The waves no longer rhythmically rocked the boat; now they were erratically pitching the boat in various directions, and no doubt adversely adding to the discomfort of those below.

Quoc was amazed that no sounds came from the escapees. He admired their stoicism and their ability to endure such privations. As a prisoner, he had endured similar conditions on the truck rides between camps. During every convoy at least one person vomited, which triggered the same reaction in others. The smell of vomit elicited a visceral response from another person, then another, until a chain reaction took on a life of its own as the smell, taste, and gagging became a common experience throughout the confined space. The only antidote – on the convoys and now below deck – was fresh air - and that was denied.

As captain, Quoc hated to put his passengers through such a painful and uncomfortable journey. Necessity impelled him. Ironically, Quoc's passengers were willing prisoners on his boat – they had volunteered and paid for the journey – but they were still prisoners.

Quoc's plan was to stay in a sheltered place along the river until nightfall and then make for the sea in the darkness and the lowered visibility brought on by the impending storm system. It was not a particularly advantageous plan, because the river lacked estuaries where even a small boat could hide. Nevertheless, if he stayed by the shore, he would be less likely to be spotted. Quoc had a real fear of being boarded by police, who might detect the passengers below deck. If that happened, he figured that by wearing a uniform, he would be the first to be executed on the spot.

Quoc restarted the engine and began motoring to a place they could hide until nightfall. Within minutes, though, two boats appeared out of nowhere and approached at high speed. A quick look through his binoculars confirmed Quoc's worst fear: The men appeared to be militia. He and Di could tell they were armed.

Quoc felt a wave of panic. He looked over at Di, who held his head down in abject despair. Quoc's heart was breaking. He was about to fail in his attempt to save the 50 souls on board his vessel before he had even gotten them to the sea. After nearly five years of his small steps forward and huge ones backwards, freedom was again in jeopardy: now, not just for himself but for the others as well.

He said a silent prayer. If a man can actually scream a silent prayer, he did that too. The prayer was as much informed by hope as it was fear, searching for some sort of divine sign that they would survive this boarding. "This is it. Please save my soul," Quoc prayed to God, to Buddha, to whoever might hear him. He repeated the words to himself again and again as the boat approached.

Quoc looked at Cuu. Cuu could see the concern etched on Quoc's face. Quoc said, "Pray for us, Brother. If something happens, use your best judgment to protect Hung, whatever happens to me." Cuu gave a curt nod. Di wrapped himself in a poncho and then calmly told Quoc in a soft voice, "Show them where my neck is so they can end my life quickly."

The words of prayer echoed in Quoc's heart as he redirected his attention to the militiamen who came alongside in two boats. Then suddenly Quoc heard an answer to his prayer. It was not God's voice. Instead, someone spoke for God in a familiar voice with a grin and conversational tone, and asked, "Uncle, is this the day?" Shocked, Quoc immediately recognized Lam, who had confronted Quoc weeks before and had rightly identified him as the captain of a vessel destined for escape.

As the two men instantaneously recognized each other, an odd exchange occurred between them – respect, followed by understanding. It transcended that of soldier and boat captain. The only time Quoc had experienced that from someone in authority over the past few years had been in Bu Gia Map, when the good captain had befriended the prisoners.

Another man standing next to Lam appeared to be his confederate. He said, "Uncle, we're going to take you to our dock where you'll be away from the eyes of the police." He produced a large straw hat and instructed, "Have your people fill this up with Vietnamese currency and valuable jewelry. You won't be needing them once you leave."

Lam clearly was not the only one who knew Quoc's real plan.

Quoc quizzically took the hat and passed it to Di, who had also heard the order. Di passed the hat below deck through the hatch in the wheelhouse and told everyone to comply with the instructions from the militia. Quoc himself had no idea if it was a legitimate order by an organized militia or a blatant act of robbery – either way he could see no options. They were armed while he was not and he had the slower boat.

Quoc was relieved that the militiamen showed no concern that there were an unknown number of people below decks. They must have known.

Quoc glanced over at Di who looked back with a sigh of relief – they hadn't been summarily executed or taken away in shackles – and they were still free. Clearly Lam and the other men had a plan, and it did not appear to hold the dire military consequences Di, Quoc, and the other men in the wheelhouse feared.

Lam grinned again and then loudly ordered, "Follow our boat!"

Then Lam gunned his engine and motioned for Quoc to follow in trail. They motored along for 25-30 minutes with Di and Quoc speculating quietly about what could still happen and how they would protect the escapees. Di spread word that gold had not been demanded and that none of them should even hint if they had it or any other valuables aboard.

The local militia base was located at a small dock on the west side of the river. It was a little over a mile from the mouth of the Saigon River to where it met the East Sea.

At the base, they were met by the militia leader and other armed men. The leader was a handsome man of about 30. He smiled broadly and said, "Please follow me to the hall, we have an important meeting with the whole group."

Armed militiamen secured the boat to the pier and motioned for Quoc to accompany the leader to a hut near the shore. Quoc motioned that Di would accompany him. With no argument, the militiamen nodded their assent.

The two men followed the young leader into a big hall. As the leader entered, a large group of people – perhaps a hundred – rose. They looked younger and less military than the men who had first intercepted their boat.

The leader sat down easily. Quoc had observed many men in powerful positions during his time as a prisoner. This man appeared to be nonchalant and relaxed, almost as if he was not in a military chain of command. In some respects, he seemed to display the independence and confidence of Chu Tu, the district chief who Quoc had served. He almost carelessly balanced a rifle, first on one knee and then the table. Quoc recognized now that this man and his cadre of militia were in business for themselves.

Quoc realized that his optimism was growing. He knew enough to dampen that feeling with brutal pragmatism. A man with a rifle whose actions lack threats and contain implicit kindness is still a man with a rifle. And a rifle spells mortal danger. Still, something told Quoc that the danger was passing. He firmly held that thought. It gave him strength.

The leader chatted for a few moments with some of his lieutenants. He stood up and walked to a makeshift podium, where all eyes followed him. He had everyone's full attention. Then he announced, "I've collected a large sum of money from people who won't be needing it." He paused and said, with a quick wink towards Quoc, "For where they will be headed."

He surprised Quoc with his next announcement. "There will be a lottery to draw out three names from this hat. Whoever is lucky enough, they will be chosen to make a little trip with this gentleman." Then he smiled again and whispered to Quoc, "Right, Uncle?"

Quoc could only smile weakly and nod agreement. The leader's final words, "Whoever is not lucky enough to win the lottery will share the proceeds of the donations from the boat." This time he pointed to the hat that held the money confiscated from the hidden escapees.

The names of every person in the room had been written on small slips of paper and put into a bucket. Every eye in the room stared at the bucket in anticipation. At that moment, no lottery in the world could have been more popular.

As Quoc watched the drama play out, he realized the enormity of concern and unrest that had settled over his country. Here were young people; most had come of age after the Communist victory in 1975. They all seemed desperate to leave. Nevertheless, they still obviously respected that Quoc already had a full load of passengers aboard and, as a result, they had limited the drawing to only three names.

"How easy it would be to pull the escapees off the boat and take their places," Quoc thought.

Even in the midst of such obvious desperation, a kindness blossomed in the hearts of these men and women. It was a grace that Quoc often feared was no longer part of this world. He was heartened it still thrived. He casually brushed aside a tear from his eye so as not to raise attention.

The drawing didn't take long. As each name was called, a quiet but pronounced gasp emerged from the winner. Within minutes there were three smiling faces, all men. The rest of the young militiamen and women sat there with their heads in their hands or stared ahead with dispirited looks. There was little joy when the Vietnamese *dong* was distributed.

The three lottery winners, in full military garb, walked to the dock with Quoc and Di. They carried side arms, rifles, and even hand grenades. Though disquieting to Quoc, the men assured him they would use the weapons only if needed to defend the boat from pirates or if it became necessary against boarding by authorities.

They also pledged to discard the weapons when they had reached safety.

The men hopped onto the boat and two took up positions on the foredeck just ahead of the wheelhouse. Their rifles at the ready, they effectively transformed what had appeared as a party boat a few hours earlier into an armed vessel. One of them used wires to attach a large steel cooking pot over the end of the diesel's exhaust. Quoc had seen the technique before but had not thought about it in his planning. It would mute and echo the exhaust. That would make it difficult to pinpoint the boat's position in the coming dreary weather and darkness ahead.

Quoc heard the footsteps of someone running very fast behind him. He saw a man dart onto the boat and disappear below deck.

Quoc recognized the man. It was Lam.

None of the militiamen on the dock or those already aboard the boat reacted. They went about their business, readying the boat for departure. The next day at sea, Lam would tell Quoc that he had wanted to leave from the minute he met Quoc. Quoc's courage and confidence had inspired him. Quoc couldn't help but like Lam and felt reassured by Lam's vote of confidence in his seamanship.

A final surprise came as darkness fell at the dock. A small boat appeared and tied up to the transom of Quoc's boat. Out jumped a young man who announced, "Captain, do you need an experienced hand?"

Quoc's crew of knowledgeable seamen was slim. Only two men – he and Dung – had experience in the open ocean. Quoc had seconds to size up the man. Relying on intuition alone, Quoc decided that this man had the skills and the confidence they would need. Quoc knew he alone wouldn't be able to expertly man the helm for days on end. He looked at him sternly and said, "You know we're headed out to sea to escape, don't you?"

The man nodded. He assured Quoc that he had two years of

experience as a mariner but cautioned Quoc that his night vision was poor. Quoc reasoned that one more body would not sink the already heavily laden boat and that the man probably had some skills that could be pressed into service.

They took the man, Thong, aboard. Counting himself, Quoc now had 55 souls on board a vessel designed for 20.

A little after 7:00 p.m., with full darkness covering their departure and the predicted storm developing, Quoc pulled away from the dock and headed towards the East Sea. Di, Quoc, Cuu, and Dung were in the wheelhouse. The rest of the escapees were secured below decks, the hatches nailed shut. The three winners of the lottery stood guard on deck, rifles at the ready. They took the time to provide Quoc with a valuable piece of information; the location of huge fishing posts mounted near the mouth of the river, each with hundred-foot wide nets strung between them. Without that piece of information, Quoc knew he could well have been sunk or capsized when he ran into them.

The local militiamen stood there at the dock in silent witness to the courage of the 55 passengers. They were risking everything to gain what they valued most. Freedom.

38

THE OPEN OCEAN

"The ocean was waiting with grand and bitter provocations, as if it invited you to think how deep it was, how much colder than your blood or saltier, or to outguess it, to tell which were its feints or passes and which its real intentions, meaning business."

Saul Bellow
The Adventures of Augie March

Rivers flow. They don't usually churn or roll or create waves that can engulf a boat or ship. True, rivers each have personalities and bring challenges to the mariners who navigate them, requiring a vast knowledge of each of the two shores, the shallow spots, the bridge abutments, the quirky currents, and challenging winds along the winding path of the waterway. Yet rivers eventually give up their secrets to their friends. Those friends are the mariners, the pilots, who come to know and respect them.

Quoc was a friend to the Saigon River. He had carefully memorized the many facets of the route from Saigon to Vung Tau. He respected the waterway and loved its personality. The river, in return, had repaid him with safe passage during his many journeys downstream.

However, there is a boundary between where a river ends and the sea begins. The boundary, called by mariners, "the bar," moves with the tides, with the seasons, with morning and evening fog banks, storms, and tropical depressions. The bar can extend for relatively short distances or fan out for miles. A trained mariner respects it with a practiced eye and a knowledge borne by days and days of entering the sea. The bar is not known to extend the hand of friendship to anyone. A mariner must pay homage to it, knowing that his own knowledge and skills and the strength of his vessel must carry him through that boundary of currents, weather, and tides to the open ocean beyond.

As Quoc entered the bar that evening, the sky was only partly clear, with clouds rapidly forming. The wind was blowing better than 20 knots. Quoc characterized it in his mind as a "6" on the Beaufort scale, with a "strong breeze" and "long waves" beginning to form. The forecast had been correct.

British Royal Navy Officer Francis Beaufort originally devised the Beaufort scale. It is used by mariners to describe both the wind conditions and the relative sea state. Today, 12 levels are typically used on the scale, ranging from "0", with the wind being described as "calm" and the sea state "like a mirror." Conversely, level "12" describes hurricane force winds, with the seas having "huge waves."

Quoc knew that the conditions could rapidly climb through the levels of the Beaufort scale, but he did not know just how high. Though he had heard the weather forecast, he knew from long years of experience that meteorology was an inexact science. He would have to rely on his maritime skills and his little boat to get his precious cargo to safety.

Quoc's destination was the international shipping lanes between Hong Kong and Singapore. If not rescued by a ship in the lanes, he had enough fuel to make it as far as Singapore, about six to seven days away. That country afforded the best laws and protection for the Vietnamese refugees.

In 1978, the Singapore Government and the United Nations High Commissioner for Refugees had entered into an agreement "to provide refugees with international protection." At that time, the country had agreed to set up a transit camp at a place called Hawkins Road, allowing "a maximum of 1,000 refugees to stay for a period not exceeding 90 days at any given time." UNHCR representatives were required to facilitate a permanent resettlement solution to a third country during that period.

Indonesia was another destination for many refugees and served as Quoc's second choice if he could not make it to Singapore. On Quoc's boat, the countries were within a day's journey of each other.

Other places, like Thailand and Malaysia, were not known to be sympathetic to the massive boat exodus from Vietnam. Thus, Quoc had no plans to venture to these places. Quoc's navigation skills and ability to take sightings with his sextant and use his personally modified almanac afforded him an advantage most Boat People did not have. For the majority of the refugees, obtaining a boat and heading out to sea were the highest and often only priorities. Most were not trained in the ways of the sea, and many would lose their lives as a result. Estimates ranged from 25 to 50 percent of the boats not making it to safety, with many succumbing to pirates or foundering in the sea.

For Quoc, a skilled mariner, having the tools and navigational abilities were critical to arrive at a pre-planned destination like Singapore. Along the way, he would ensure that he traversed the heavily travelled sea-lanes in hopes of being rescued by a larger vessel.

Quoc's plan was to establish an initial course line of 135-degrees for about twelve hours and then swing almost due south. The initial course was indirect but would guarantee two things. He would steer well clear of the Communist-controlled Con Son Island due south of Vung Tau, and it would ensure that his boat entered the shipping lanes before taking up a course towards Singapore.

If divine providence smiled upon Quoc, he would encounter an American vessel and request assistance on the high seas. If that did not occur, he would try to escape detection and continue on a course towards Singapore.

Escaping detection for his boat would be partly luck, but it also helped that a small boat is more difficult to spot in heavy seas. Quoc knew that and took some comfort in it. Vietnamese allies like Russia, China, North Korea, and a number of Eastern European nations required their flag vessels to immediately return the refugees to Vietnam for punishment if they were intercepted at sea. He could only hope – and pray to God – that he could elude them.

Many others had tried the same gambit. Quoc had no illusions. It would be perilous, but he had no other choice.

As they traversed the bar, the boat began to encounter three to four-foot waves. The militiamen quickly went below decks where they would stay for the next four days. They, along with the other escapees, were soon overcome with seasickness. The odor of vomit permeated the little vessel, and the smells wafting up through the small hatch in the wheelhouse soon had the men on deck gagging and vomiting periodically. Quoc was able to avoid seasickness for the most part. But he succumbed at times, too, heaving over the side of the boat into the ocean.

Quoc and the others threw their Vietnamese uniforms overboard and donned coveralls.

Looking at the little boat from a distance, an observer would wonder how it could make headway in the high seas. But it chugged along confidently, its two-cylinder diesel – nicknamed by the Vietnamese as two silver heads – driving the boat to a speed of about five knots. Its bow, with painted eyes, seemed to convey confidence as it proceeded into the open ocean.

As they moved away from the mouth of the river, Quoc and Di caught sight of a Vietnamese patrol boat. Quoc shifted his course and prayed that the boat hadn't spotted him. With the roll of the ocean, the wave tops often obscured Quoc's craft, as it pitched into one valley and then the next. Quoc used the waves to his advantage, aiming for the troughs of the waves as much as possible. It covered the boat with salt spray and water, but hid it from the eyes of those who would intercept them.

The patrol boat shadowed them for more than an hour. Then it appeared to change course, heading away from Quoc, towards Can Gio. Quoc attributed their move to the inability of their crew to pinpoint the exhaust sound from his boat. He acknowledged the good fortune of having been intercepted by the militia and joined by the lottery winners. Their new muffler on the exhaust was a significant contribution to the mission.

Quoc turned the boat back to the original 135-degree magnetic course line and set the throttle to a steady speed of five nautical miles an hour. He thanked God for sparing them from interception and thought back to other divine gifts they had been given prior to the departure that morning. A few weeks before, the propeller shaft had broken. Dung had installed a replacement. As a precaution, Dung affixed a spare shaft to the hull of the boat and dragged it along with them. It provided an insurance policy in case another shaft failed. Dung tried to never leave anything to chance.

The seas continued to intensify, with the waves now exceeding six feet – now likely approaching "7" on the Beaufort scale. It would stay that way for most of the next three days. Now the sea was fetching up and transformed into wind-driven white-crested waves shipping the sea over the gunnels on the starboard – right side – of the boat. The onboard mechanical pump seemed to be keeping up with clearing the bilge of the water, vomit, and human waste.

Quoc intuitively knew, by looking at the sea and the sky, that the weather would continue deteriorating further. This increased his anxiety for the escapees locked below deck. Most had never been on the open sea. Di and Quoc had not been able to procure enough life jackets for everyone on board. Besides, Quoc had reasoned, if they became necessary, who would be there to pick up survivors floating in the open ocean?

The ocean is ever changing and an experienced captain can usually read it. Oftentimes in darkness, the sky can give some indication of what the sea might be churning up, but by watching the water's surface, a knowledgeable mariner can also see what the wind is doing. For instance, the wind drives wave actions that may be completely opposite of the long swell action of the ocean.

There are times when a mariner can't discern the wind and the waves accurately due to a fast-moving squall from a cold front or the gradual development of clouds associated with a warm front. Everything a captain does must focus upon the boat and its cargo of human beings.

Quoc held the fate of the passengers in his hands. The most precious passenger for him was Hung. Dong sheltered him in her arms below deck. Quoc knew he could not afford to worry about Hung, Dong, and Cuu, but he did allow moments of reflection about the enormity of the decision they had all made. Adults who decide to move towards peril is one thing, Quoc thought, but taking a child on an unknown and incredibly dangerous path almost seemed unconscionable.

That night, as the sea state continued to worsen, Quoc was pleased to see his little boat weather the conditions better than one would have imagined. However, the noise made by the waves crashing against the hull of the boat was terrifying for nearly all of the occupants. Quoc was unable to provide words of comfort to his passengers: The sounds of the seas crashing on the boat were simply too loud.

Above deck, the sky was completely dark, with low menacing clouds. Sheets of rain periodically soaked everyone and reduced visibility to mere feet. Quoc stayed at the helm the whole time. Earlier he had allowed Cuu and two others to take turns, vainly attempting to teach them techniques to follow the compass to maintain a 135-degree heading. However, he was never sure they were able to stay on course.

The boat was at times thrown about like a leaf; other times it stalled between two large waves. The waves alternated between peaks, at the crest of the wave, to troughs, at the lowest point. Sometimes it seemed the vessel gasped like a swimmer struggling against the waves. Traveling with them, the boat would bog down, as the waves moved faster than the boat. And when Quoc headed into the waves from the peaks, the boat experienced vertical drops that felt like a slap of a hand on a table. Alternatively, when he hit a wave in a trough, the effects were teeth jarring. The ocean didn't try to engulf the vessel so much as it worked to bury it, but each time the little craft emerged from the depths, demonstrating a determination to continue into the storm.

Quoc's mind focused on the course line and the proper handling of the boat. He refused to contemplate the very real possibility of the boat foundering and sinking in the East Sea. Mariners are trained to compartmentalize their thoughts and fears. Only after the storm – hours, days, or even years later – does a professional contemplate just what the outcome could have been. Even years later a professional mariner's night could be disrupted by the possibilities of what could have happened on such a stormy night.

Quoc reasoned that the sea state was such that his initial estimate of twelve hours on the 135-degree heading should be extended.

At dawn on the second day, Quoc's boat surprisingly passed almost directly between two fishing boats flying the Vietnamese flag. The boats did not initially appear to spot him. Quoc reasoned that they must have heard his diesel chugging along, because both vessels began to give chase. Quoc turned 90-degrees to port, driving directly into the six-foot waves. The boat shook violently, then staggered as the bow acted as a battering ram against each trough. Every wave engulfed the ship as it plowed forward. It soaked Quoc and his crew and sent the ocean water below deck.

The passengers had no protection from the water and dampness. Many, like Hung, were developing fevers from the filth below, seasickness, and the continued drenching from the Pacific water. Although the temperature of the water was in the low 70's, the continued drenching and inability to get dry made the escapees continually shiver.

The fishing boats were slightly larger than Quoc's. They too must have suffered as they strained their engines to intercept Quoc. As his little craft struggled and plowed ahead, he would look back and see the two vessels disappear for long seconds, then rise from the waves like a submarine as it surfaces. Although he could hear their engines over the waves, they had little success in closing the gap between their vessels and Quoc's.

After an hour, the two boats broke off the chase. Quoc continued on the same northeasterly heading for nearly an hour, occasionally slowing or stopping his engine to listen for the engine noises of the other boats.

As he brought the engine to idle at one point, he noted a sound missing on his own boat. The mechanical bilge pump attached to the boat shaft was no longer working. It had been designed by Loi and never appeared adequate to Quoc. A forward bilge pump had already clogged due to debris from the passengers below decks. The boat was quickly filling with water.

Quoc yelled for the able-bodied men to begin using a hand pump to clear the bilges. The militiamen and other male passengers sprang into action and bailed in shifts throughout the days ahead.

By dawn, Quoc had been manning the helm for twelve hours and was too exhausted to continue. At that point Thong volunteered to take the wheel. Thong's abilities, it turned out, equaled or exceeded Quoc's, and his stamina was phenomenal.

In Vietnamese, Thong means Clear or Knowledge. When Quoc saw him steer the boat, he recognized that Thong had been appropriately named. Quoc came to view Thong, who was just 20 years old, as his guardian angel. Thong steered the boat with an effortlessness borne by experience. He never said a word as he carried out his task. The steering by now was completely by reference to the boat's compass, as the winds, waves, and rain reduced forward visibility to zero.

In time, Quoc became so confident of Thong that he could nap for more than minutes at a time. Thong continued at the helm for 12 hours that day and each day thereafter. He seemed to relax as he sat at the wheel, braving the heavy seas that continued to pound the little vessel.

Near-disaster struck late that afternoon. The boat's diesel engine coughed once, and the engine appeared to overheat. Immediately, Quoc shut the engine down to prevent damage. Acrid smells arose from the engine compartment.

The sudden silence alarmed the passengers below decks. The terror in their voices was apparent, as they demanded to be released. Quoc knew that if he let them all on deck the boat would become top heavy and potentially capsize. This was a time where a captain needed to stay cool in the face of panic.

He leaned down through the small hatch in the wheelhouse and stared at the terrified passengers. Some screamed at him, threatening harm if they were not released.

"Look, we're going to fix the engine. Remain calm while Dung works on it. These things happen, people. Dung knows what he is doing – we'll get this thing started right away."

"You're holding us prisoner. Let us out. We'll swim for it."

"You'll do nothing of the kind, now just stay down there and shut up."

Dung jumped down into the engine compartment. He quickly determined that the abrupt and repeated movements during the last day had dislodged the oil dipstick. With the heavy roll and pounding of the waves, along with the normal oil pressure essentially pumping the oil out of the hole, the oil had slowly been depleted from the engine. As a result, the engine had nearly seized. In layman's terms, the pistons had almost frozen in place inside the cylinders, lacking the microscopic layer of oil to cool and lubricate their movements that keep any engine running.

Quoc looked down to Dung. They wordlessly and mournfully communicated. Absent oil, the engine would not run. Dung shook his head to the left and right, dropping his gaze in a sign that he had no idea how to get the engine fixed. Even with all of the planning, extra oil had not been stowed aboard. As if in answer to a prayer, though, Dung's lowered gaze fixed on a five-gallon container of old motor oil sitting in the corner of the compartment. He had changed the oil in the engine just prior to departure and, in the rush to board passengers, had inadvertently failed to dump the oil. The drained oil would now be their salvation.

He carefully poured the dirty but still useable dark viscous fluid back into the diesel and carefully replaced the dipstick. In minutes, the engine coughed to life. They were underway again, this time at a slightly reduced power setting, as Dung cautioned Quoc that the engine had likely sustained some damage. Nevertheless the engine began its determined tuk-tuk-tuk-ing. To Quoc, it sounded as if it turned the propeller with renewed enthusiasm. He guessed that the boat was now traveling at about four knots.

The passengers calmed down, though they were shaken by the experience. They still harbored anger towards Quoc. They remained painfully uncomfortable. The water clung to their skin and clothes. The stench of vomit and human waste permeated the compartment in which they were virtual prisoners. Quoc knew that no person could survive such conditions for long. The terrible weather and sea conditions were protecting Quoc and his passengers from capture, but it also threatened to destroy the boat and eventually kill them all.

The boat continued on the 135-degree heading, plowing through the heavy seas all night. Quoc, Cuu and the two others took one to two hour turns at the helm, straining to see the compass in order to hold the heading. Thong went below to sleep and was fully prepared the next day to handle a solo 12-hour shift as the heavy sea state continued.

At one point that day, they spotted a large ocean-going vessel, far off to their right. With no sun to use for the signal mirror, Quoc attempted to set a controlled fire in a steel drum on top of the wheelhouse. He successfully lit some diesel-soaked rags, which billowed black smoke. The effort failed, and the boat disappeared over the horizon. The heavy seas toppled the drum, nearly catching the boat on fire. Only the spray from the ocean saved them.

By the morning of the third day, Quoc estimated that they had progressed far enough to the southeast to avoid Con Son Island. They were now probably close to the shipping-lanes. He wasn't able to take a sextant sighting of the sun, stars, or planets because the cloud cover remained thick and impenetrable. He could only use basic calculations and dead reckoning to determine how far they had come and where they might be in the East Sea. Quoc turned the boat to due south. Thong took over and steered for another 12 hours.

By this time, Hung and several other children had developed high fevers. Early in the day, Dong came to the small hatch opening and handed Hung over to Quoc, pleading, "Quoc, he's not going to make it down here. You'll have to take him."

Quoc gently lifted Hung. He held him throughout the day, as the young boy cried softly in his arms. He pleaded for his mother and asked to get off the boat. Quoc tried to warm the boy, who shook violently from a high fever. Hung and Quoc sat perched on the wooden sextant case, clinging to each other: The father comforting his child with strong arms and gentle whispers. That afternoon he was able to get Hung to take a few sips of juice, but he knew the boy needed medical attention.

That same day the sea became a bit calmer and the winds abated slightly. Late in the afternoon, slight patches of blue began to appear above them. The boat now strained less and seldom buried itself into the waves. The crew and passengers had not eaten for three days. The drenching seas and seasickness had greatly reduced the desire or ability to eat. With the calmer seas, Quoc encouraged the passengers to share their food. He was rewarded with several rice cakes and water that he devoured as he sat and held Hung. He tried repeatedly to get Hung to eat but only succeeded in getting him to sip the juice.

During the day, they were also able to bring other children up to the deck for short periods of time for fresh air. After what they had all been through, even an hour of the fresh air was a tonic for them. Their moldy and ragged clothes were falling off their bodies. Some of the children lay on deck virtually comatose. They only opened their eyes and began to cry when a wave crashed over the boat and completely drenched them. Their pitiful cries and torment pained Quoc. He had no ability to improve their situation and no other way to move them to safety other than to continue on, through winds and sea and deprivation. He wondered just how long they could survive the ordeal below deck.

39

IMPRISONED BELOW DECKS

"Time is like the ocean; you can only hold a little in your hands."

The Summer
Josh Pyke

She drew fresh air deep into her lungs for the first time in more than four days. The short respite revitalized Hong Ngoc. At least for a while it relieved the disorienting motion sickness that had continuously nauseated her while crowded into the dark, smelly, claustrophobic hold.

As she stood there with the other children, the small 13-year old girl gaped open-mouthed at the enormity of the ocean and the fragility of their own tiny vessel. Their boat was just a small brown dot on an expanse of ocean – the color an uninviting dark green – with a sky that was still gray and threatening. She looked out at the waves that had calmed considerably. They were still more than three feet high. She couldn't comprehend how they all survived the punishing three-day storm, with its six-foot seas, torrential rain and hurricane-force winds.

Hong Ngoc was ordered below decks again. She slipped through the hatch, observing momentarily the holes on the forward hatch where it had been nailed shut those four long days. She settled into one of the two hammocks in the hold and immediately fell asleep.

It was a dream-filled sleep, but it seemed real and it evoked emotion in her. She felt the excitement in the dream before she even saw the vessel. It was a huge gray ship that at first sailed by their boat and then miraculously turned around. The ship came alongside their small craft, and she was hoisted aboard. She felt the strong arms of sailors lift her safely to the deck. Then she was helped to a shower of clear, fresh water and seemingly unlimited soap. She felt the water splashing onto her head and down her back; she giggled from the soap bubbles tickling her. A large, dry towel was wrapped around her, and she felt a fresh clean cotton T-shirt against her skin. It seemed so real, as did the doctor examining her, gently asking her to open her mouth, and letting him look into her ears. She tasted fresh fruit and juice and saw the other escapees smiling and holding each other, taking joy in their salvation. She laughed and smiled with them and felt like dancing on the deck.

Then Hong Ngoc woke up.

She smelled the dank hold with its sickening motion. She realized they were still in the dark confines of their own small vessel with no apparent hope of rescue. The pungent aroma of mold, human odor, and filth still filled her nostrils, her mouth, and even her skin. The dark, claustrophobic conditions held her like a shroud; she shivered, drenched from the water that always seemed to be in the hold. She noticed several of the passengers who lapsed into hallucinatory states. They chatted with long-dead relatives and some apparently even imagined family gatherings, with meals and celebration. There was the incessant sound of the boat hitting the water, and the loud, rapid, and erratic machine-gun sound – tuk-tuk-tuk-tuk-tuk of the engine filled her senses.

Despite it all, exhausted from the long journey and the storm, Hong fell asleep again.

Hong Ngoc, just 13, was a slightly built young woman with raven-colored hair and large bright eyes: All the world was new to her. She had known nothing but war during her first eight years. Since the fall of South Vietnam, she had lived every day with the feeling that escape by boat was inevitable. Two older brothers had made their way to the United States in 1975. Ngoc's father had arranged the escape. The rest of the family had long planned to join them.

A common conversation in Hong-Ngoc's home was, "Oh, the neighbors escaped last week. It looks like those people are next. I'm not surprised. It won't be long for us either now, will it?"

Her parents never mentioned the failed attempts at escape by the Vietnamese Boat People, or the continuing stories of death and rape at the hands of pirates.

It came as no surprise that January night when they heard a soft but incessant tapping on the door of their home in District 6 of Saigon. It was about 8:00 p.m. They were told simply, "It's time." Her parents whispered quietly but authoritatively to Hong Ngoc and her brother Hoang, "Get ready. It's time to see your brothers in America."

Each member of the family had prepared one small bag with basic necessities and some foodstuff. There would be no room for anything else. Neither of the children had sufficient life experience to complicate uncertainty with fear. The escape was just an unknown for each of them. Unknowns were adventures for children.

In 20 minutes, the family left their home for good. Cuu met them. It was so dark that they could only identify him by his voice. Cuu directed them, speaking softly yet firmly. He motioned them towards what smelled like a waterway. They heard the sounds of a small boat slightly bobbing against its mooring lines. They could not see the boat as much as they could sense it. It was a leap of faith as they walked up a small gangway, really just a small wooden plank, onto the deck. As they boarded, they were immediately directed towards an opening that seemed small even to a child. Paradoxically, it was a place filled all at once with sensory deprivation and sensory overload.

The sound their feet made when they hit the flooring of the hull was akin to the sound of a rubber mallet gently striking a wooden keg filled with liquid. The sound was overshadowed by other sensations and an enormity of strange newness. In some respects it was like being locked into a dark closet. The hold was absolutely dark. Other senses compensated. Initially, a slight fishy and salty smell filled their nostrils. It was as much a taste as it was a smell.

The family found places to sit on the floor of the hull. They allowed the silence to cover them like a blanket. Each wondered who else was below deck with them. It was so dark that they could not make out faces.

There was no conversation. They had been ordered not to make any sound so as not to arouse attention of anyone – authorities or otherwise – who might be near the boat. The only sounds were the quiet breathing of other passengers. The smells of human perspiration and respiration were mixed with something foreign to Hong Ngoc – a sense of uncertainty and discomfort.

Fear occupied the hold equally with uncertainty.

Hong Ngoc and her family slowly realized that one person recognized their presence. It was Dong. She had arrived on the boat some hours before. Knowing there was another family member aboard gave Hong Ngoc comfort and a sliver of confidence that she held like a good luck talisman.

None of the family members aboard had spoken openly to their children of the risks inherent in an escape by sea. They dared not voice their fears of the possibility of pirates, rape, murder or drowning in the ocean. They tried to convince themselves that by not naming fears, they were less likely to happen. The same was true of the ever-present possibility of being caught and jailed by the police.

Instead, their focus was on the prize: The safe passage to Singapore or to a rescue ship in the East Sea.

As Hong Ngoc and her family sat there quietly, the dark did not lessen. It became blacker. There were no flashlights or candles below decks. Occasionally, the sound of one of the small hatches being slid aside was followed by an almost imperceptible glow like a waning moon in its last days. That slight illumination was accompanied by more footsteps moving across the deck above and then the sound of people stepping through a hatch to join them below deck. Over the next several hours, between short catnaps, Hong Ngoc heard as many as thirty more people enter their tight, smelly compartment. Each time, the new passengers would jostle and move into position, shifting everyone else into tighter confines. Hong Ngoc didn't know any of them, but she sensed that they might know each other, as imperceptible whispers and occasional hugs could be discerned. She would later learn that more than 20 of them were part of Di's family.

Hong Ngoc realized that some of the escapees were relieving themselves on the floor of the deck. They had no choice. There were no bathroom facilities or buckets that could be used. The small vertical hatch that remained open into the wheelhouse did not allow easy access to the deck and the captain could not readily allow transit through his command position. The urine smell was relatively slight at that point, but the sound of the urine stream hitting the deck was yet another new experience for her.

They waited. It seemed like days. Perhaps it was only four or five hours. Hong Ngoc heard a strange sound as the engine turned over for the first time. The engine wasn't in the compartment where the escapees were imprisoned. A bulkhead separated them from the smell of diesel fuel or the exhaust. The bulkhead only slightly muffled the initial groan of the engine, then the overpowering initial tuk.....tuk....tuk...tuk, which bravely turned into a rapid-fire tuk-tuk-tuk-tuk. The little engine would dare to try to propel them to safety.

As the sun rose, a slight glow came from the small vertical hatch in the covered wheelhouse, located just aft of amidships. Occasionally, Quoc allowed the passengers to crawl to the opening and get a whiff of fresh air. Only one or two could stand there at a time. But the air couldn't find its way into the compartment and the light was so dim that the passengers felt only a sensation of the sun, without its brightness or warmth.

Hong Ngoc heard a slight splash against the hull and a few footsteps above her. The sounds of water gently lapping against the wooden hull soon built in volume. It sounded like a gurgling brook. They knew the journey had begun.

It was then that quiet conversations began to fill the darkness and calm the fear. A large part of the group appeared to know each other. Hong Ngoc's family, along with Dong and Hung, talked with the other passengers, beginning the process of building friendships.

With the movement came a gentle rocking, and the rocking in the darkness brought on the beginnings of disorientation, vertigo, and motion sickness. The technical description, mal-de-mer, the French term for motion sickness at sea, is both physiological and psychological. Seafarers are fully aware that a ship in motion can create an imbalance within the inner ear, which can manifest itself as severe dizziness that induces vomiting. The condition will not go away until the seas calm and the ship ceases to roll violently. In the words of an experienced mariner, "First you think you're going to die. Then you pray you won't. I have seen grown men beg to be thrown from a ship when they are suffering from seasickness, while others have said, 'Give me a gun and I'll shoot myself.'"

Hong Ngoc was one of the first to succumb. Within an hour of departure, she felt her head spinning and a sick feeling in her stomach. She begged her mother for help. Tuyet opened a small plastic bag and held it for her daughter as Hong Ngoc emptied the contents of her stomach. Hong Ngoc gagged from the taste in her throat and on her tongue. She continued to dry heave. Hong Ngoc was perplexed that the feeling of nausea did not immediately go away once her stomach was empty. Instead, repeated heaving and nausea overcame her in waves. However, she was fortunate, because her seasickness eventually subsided and did not recur.

Others did not have bags readily available. The smell of the vomit and the rocking motion in the dark cabin quickly triggered others to become ill, who gagged and puked just like Hong Ngoc. The hold took on a stench that would stay there for the duration of their voyage. They grew used to it.

Hong Ngoc and her fellow passengers had no knowledge of what was happening above deck. They didn't know the route the boat would follow or who might be following them. They didn't even hear what was said between crewmembers. They only knew the continual splashing sound against the outside of the hull, the rapid 'tuk-tuk-tuk-tuk" of the engine, and the overwhelming and bleak disorientation within the rocking hull.

As they proceeded along a route unknown to them, they occasionally heard the engine stop and the boat come into contact with a dock. The silence was terrifying. They would all collectively hold their breath, wondering whether the boat would be boarded and they would be taken into custody by the authorities. They intuitively realized by the tone of Quoc's words that their first stop was not a place to fear. The steps on the deck were light, and the tone of the words they heard through the wheelhouse hatch were friendly. Still, they sat there in total silence, knowing they couldn't disclose their presence, lest they be discovered and turned over to the police.

Then they were underway again.

After almost a day of travel – at least it seemed like a day – the engine stopped again. They could hear a distant muffled voice with a tone of inquiry, followed by Quoc's voice, muffled but discernible, "He forgot to put fuel in the tank. We'll get it going and meet you in a few minutes!"

This was followed by the sounds of at least two other boats with engines similar to theirs fading into the distance.

Then they were alone.

In minutes they heard their engine start again, now solo in its loud staccato song. The splashing began again. This time the motion of the boat was noticeably different. They fetched and rolled in a way that was even more nauseating than before.

At least another hour went by. They heard another boat engine's sounds – bigger and more powerful – and muffled voices. Once again they immediately understood the intent, if not the words. The voices were not questioning: They were commanding. And Quoc's voice was noticeably quieter and sounded to Hong Ngoc as if he were acquiescing to orders, not giving them.

Sounds of heavy shoes – perhaps military boots – hit the deck, with repeated movements on and off the boat. Words were exchanged and commands given. They sat there fearful, silently wondering what fate awaited them. Then Di's head leaned into the hold through the wheelhouse hatch, "These men want all of your Vietnamese currency. Fill this hat, please. Don't ask any questions. Remain here."

The passengers had no choice but to comply. They filled the hat with currency.

More than an hour went by. Again, they heard the sound of heavy boots hitting the deck and another exchange of words. The engine started, and there was one final sound – it seemed like a person jumping onto the deck. Muffled voices spoke, and they were underway.

Over the next night and day, the rocking of the boat became more violent and erratic. At one point, the engine's volume grew in sound and intensity, and the boat moved faster, then careened from side to side. More passengers became ill, as they were tossed about in the cramped space, trying to hold onto each other but with little success.

Frightened people can easily be moved to panic. When the patrol boats were chasing Quoc's boat, the escapees below screamed in anger and demanded an explanation or appeasement. They were quieted, but not wholly calmed with a shouted command from above, "Be quiet, we are trying to outrun the police. Calm down. We'll make it."

Shortly, the boat seemed to settle down, the engine slowed, and the careening stopped. The sea still rolled the boat. Occasionally, Cuu or Quoc would lean in and tell them what was happening, "We're past Vung Tau, headed out to sea. It's going to get very rough. There's a storm coming."

As the sea became higher, they felt the boat pitch, then roll unexpectedly. Their soaked clothes began to disintegrate in the dank space. Their clothing afforded little in the way of protection from the abrasions on their skin caused by the inside of the oak hull. Open sores were evident. Tuyet had brought some herbal balm and helped her family and others by rubbing it into their wounds. It calmed the burning, but didn't eliminate it. The family sat next to an open barrel that held fresh water. Hong Ngoc's father, My, poured some fresh water over his children to help ease the sting of the salt.

The intensity of the storm increased. The water no longer splashed against the hull. Instead, the sea hammered the timbers of the boat like a sledge. The random poundings sounded as if the hull would be crushed. The ocean mercilessly flexed its might against the small craft and its passengers. Seawater flowed freely through the hatch with each rise and fall of the boat. The main hatches had to be closed. Once again, they sat in the dark, in fear and in peril.

Water still found its way into the hull and the main bilge pump failed. The small hatch below the wheelhouse was blocked by shifts of passengers who bailed continuously in three-man shifts for the next several days. Every man took turns keeping the sea from winning its battle with the boat. None complained.

During the storm, the boat would pitch up high as its engine worked to climb a mountainous wave, and then it would pitch precipitously down, sliding on another wave, the shaft spinning easily. The little boat and its sturdy engine would struggle against yet another wave then ride another and another. Valiantly, Quoc forced the boat deep into the East Sea, intent on beating the effects of the storm as he guided them towards freedom.

The boat rolled as much as 60 degrees. The passengers felt as if the boat would turn over. Some of the fresh water containers became contaminated with the contents of the hull, mixing brine, urine, and vomit into the drinking supply. It did not matter too much during the storm, because they were all so sick they could not hold anything down, even water. However Quoc had ensured that there were enough containers of water on board. He knew that a body could survive for weeks without food, but only days without water.

Hong Ngoc heard her young cousin, Hung, cry incessantly. He screamed and later moaned from a fever that overcame him two days into the trip.

As they were tossed about by the sea, the loud, steady and comforting sound of the engine suddenly stopped. Other than the storm's might, it had been their only source of constancy. They had begun to feel as if the two-cylinder cared about them and intended to propel them to safety. Without the engine, the ship just spun and

DAVE BUSHY

swirled into the uneven swells, bouncing up and down and side to side.

Sickness and misery were overcome by panic, as the occupants sensed that something catastrophic had occurred to their only means of propulsion. It was their only ticket to safety. Those who could began to yell and pound the deck above, pleading and demanding to be released from the confines of their voluntary prison. Shouting could also be heard above decks with Quoc demanding that the engine be fixed.

Around her, Hong Ngoc heard the escapees screaming like terrified animals. They wanted to climb through the wheelhouse onto the deck, to know fresh air once again, and to be given the opportunity to swim for their lives. Hong Ngoc intuitively knew it was irrational, but she joined in the shouting chaos as well, demanding release.

Quoc leaned into the hold. He was angry. "You will stay below, and do what I tell you! This boat will capsize if you all come up here. Now let us do our jobs and get this engine started. Shut up and calm yourselves!"

The screams diminished; the anger did not. Quiet grumbling about the capriciousness of the captain soon replaced open rebellion. They all remained still in that sordid place. They didn't dare move.

Miraculously, the engine started. It seemed not as loud or as strong, but it was running and that was all that mattered. They were underway again.

Another day and night of storm followed. The seas subsided a bit. Quoc invited the children to take turns coming on deck. It was at that point that Hung joined his father, not returning below. Edible foodstuff – mostly dried fruit and meat – was distributed. A few containers of water and juice were shared between the passengers. As they sat there in the now-relative calm of two to three-foot seas that had replaced the six-foot ones, they all began to share stories of their survival and of their own fears during the storm. A camara-derie of shared experience and understanding began to occupy the boat, replacing the anger and fear that had taken hold during the three long days.

They continued to move into the East Sea, the loud tuk-tuk-tuk-tuk of the little engine taking them to a destination and a destiny that was still not known.

40

THE EYES OF THE WORLD

"For though the story of how you suffered, how you lost your home, your loved ones, and how you triumphed is not new, it must always be told. And it must, by all means, be heard. It is the only light we ever have against the overwhelming darkness."

Andrew Lam
Perfume Dreams

By the fourth day the sea became even calmer. The clouds fully parted. Spirits rose as the wave heights lowered and allowed the escapees more comfort. They began relating stories of the challenges they had faced in the previous three days. They no longer had to hold onto each other for stability and safety. More food was exchanged and the outlook of those aboard became positive.

Quoc believed they still had several days ahead of them. He was convinced they were in international waters and not under imminent threat of interception by Vietnamese government patrol boats.

Around noon, Quoc climbed to the top of the wheelhouse, holding the sextant. He was able to see the horizon and the sun. He took several sightings; carefully noting the readings, then came down to check his almanac. After a few minutes of calculations, he felt reasonably sure of his position within 50 miles. That was as accurate as he could be on a deck that stood just a few feet above the ocean's surface, still bobbing like a float on a fishing line.

They appeared to be near the international shipping lanes. Quoc didn't know for sure and asked Di's advice. After what they had been through, Di's faith in Quoc was unwavering – he trusted him to make the decision to remain on the heading or adjust course. Di simply said, "It's up to you, captain."

Quoc pondered for a few minutes and then elected to change his course to 205 degrees, banking on the fact that they would then surely intercept the shipping lanes. Quoc's navigational skills and intuition paid off. A few hours later they spotted some floating debris and garbage, indicative of a large vessel dumping at sea. They were in the commercial shipping lane linking Hong Kong to Singapore.

At around 4:00 p.m., they spotted a large vessel some ten miles off their starboard side. Quoc used his binoculars and stared intently at the vessel. As he did, he noticed that the ship was diverging away from them. The distance was increasing. Cuu, Dung, Di, and the others on the bridge began to jump up and down, waving their hands and screaming at the top of their lungs.

The vessel continued its course, becoming smaller as they continued their yelling.

Quoc grabbed the signal mirror and jumped to the top of the wheelhouse, repeatedly signaling the international distress signal, SOS, in Morse code to the other ship. He hoped, too, that the radar-reflecting properties of the metal superstructure above the wheelhouse might help.

For long minutes he signaled. Would this be the vessel that would save them?

Would it be a friendly nation's flag?

Still the ship grew smaller.

He couldn't give up. He had been through too much. He repeatedly signaled dot dot dot, dash dash dash, dot dot dot – SOS - and hoped that the ship would see him on radar. Di looked at him with a mixture of hope and resignation.

And then it happened. It took long minutes, but the ship began a long, slow turn back towards their position. Ever so slowly it became larger on the horizon, converging now towards them instead of moving away.

Quoc put the signal mirror down and grabbed the binoculars. He was breathing rapidly and soaked with perspiration. His heart raced. None of the other men around him could contain their excitement either.

Quoc blinked and looked again and then again through the salty binoculars. He wasn't sure but thought he spotted telltale white numbers on the bow, a sure fire way to identify an American naval vessel.

And then Quoc saw it. It was a large white Arabic numeral. The number was 7. The ship was indeed American: It was a U.S. Navy vessel.

———————

It was late in the day on January 20. Captain Jerome "Jerry" Johnson sat in his elevated chair on the bridge of the U.S.S. San Jose – U.S. Navy designation AFS-7 – monitoring the many activities of the ship and feeling the gentle hum of the ship through his feet and chair.

Something more powerful than men would direct Johnson and his crew that day. Two sets of lives would intersect. And two captains would forever firmly believe that divine intervention had affected the outcome.

Johnson had taken command of the San Jose in September of

1979 in Subic Bay, Philippines. It was his first command of a seagoing vessel. He was a naval aviator who had flown A-7 Corsair combat missions in Vietnam and had since held a number of command
positions in aviation squadrons and at postings on land. He had also
gained two valuable years of shipboard experience as the navigator for the aircraft carriers U.S.S. Nimitz and U.S.S. Independence.
Johnson, a full captain – Oh-6 in military parlance – was in his 24th
year as a U.S. Navy officer.

The San Jose had been part of the fleet at Subic Bay, Philippines,
but world events had dictated a full-scale deployment west. It had
been precipitated by what came to be called the Iran Hostage Crisis.
Islamic students had captured the American Embassy in Tehran on
November 4, 1979 and 52 occupants were being held hostage in the
embassy. The crisis would linger through a failed rescue attempt
and until just after the inauguration of Ronald Reagan in January
of 1981.

The American military had developed the rescue plan. Two
carrier battle groups led by the U.S.S. Nimitz and the U.S.S. Coral
Sea were placed on station in the Indian Ocean to be pivotal to the
mission. Johnson's orders for the San Jose were part of that plan.
The holds of his ship were filled with food supplies at Subic Bay to
support the fleet and they had already made one resupply run. After
two weeks of refitting and reloading in Subic Bay, the San Jose set
out again with another hold full of food and supplies.

As they crossed the shipping lanes in the South China Sea, the
ship was proceeding at normal cruising speed towards a planned
stop in Singapore for refueling and shore leave for the men. From
there, they would proceed through the Straits of Malacca to the fleet,
not far from Diego Garcia, the U.S. naval base in the middle of the
Indian Ocean, hundreds of miles south of the Maldives. The San
Jose carried enough food to feed 20,000 people, along with a mod-
est supply of spare parts. They were superbly equipped and able to

resupply food by nets, pallets, and cable from ship to ship, as well as with two CH-46 Sea Knight helicopters that enabled them to speed up the process through what was termed vertical replenishment. Speed was always of the essence during resupply or refueling at sea, because both ships were in greater jeopardy as they held parallel courses and could not readily maneuver away from obstacles or any perceived threat.

After four months in command, Johnson had developed an intuitive feel for how well the ship was operating and was more than pleased with his crew, made up of about 600 U.S. Navy officers and enlisted men specializing in logistics. The ship was known in the Navy as a combat stores ship. That Sunday, the 581-foot, 9,800-ton vessel had just entered the shipping lanes in the South China Sea north of Singapore.

Johnson was a tall handsome Texan with dark hair, brown eyes, and a ready smile. He was a born leader. Although he had not personally witnessed the fall of South Vietnam in April of 1975, he had heard the stories of what had been happening since, informed by his fellow Navy officers and through confidential U.S. Navy briefings. Unlike most of the rest of the world, he knew of the thousands of escape attempts and tragedies that had occurred in the South China Sea as the ill-equipped and often unknowledgeable crews had tried – many tragically and unsuccessfully – to escape the country in their small wooden boats.

To varying degrees, U.S. naval vessels had been instrumental in assisting the Vietnamese Boat People. Johnson and his crew had joined that fraternity by rescuing a number of Vietnamese in December of 1979, just after leaving Subic Bay.

Commanders throughout all the U.S. Armed Forces have always been afforded a wide degree of latitude and decision-making during times of peace and war. There were no standing orders from the Department of Navy regarding the Vietnamese Boat People.

Instead, there was a longstanding maritime tradition adhered to by any ship to render assistance to vessels in distress. It was core to the culture held by the men who served at sea. And it was part of who Johnson was as a man and as a U.S. Navy captain.

The mission to join up with the Nimitz and Coral Sea was of utmost importance to Johnson and his commanders back in Washington. But the need to assist human beings in distress took precedence.

Humanitarian assistance could be rendered two ways. If there was imminent danger to the occupants or the ship was not operational, commanders were always authorized to take refugees aboard, provide food and medical assistance, and divert from their course to take them to the nearest friendly country. If there were no injuries or illness and the vessel was still operable and not in danger of sinking, then food, water, and medical supplies would be provided.

The bridge of any vessel at sea is a study in understatement and low-key communications. Navy officers, chief petty officers, and enlisted men are trained to keep their emotions in check. The key is to communicate everything calmly and not allow emotions to influence decision-making. Thus, anything from reporting an incident below decks to spotting a low-flying aircraft is passed on from the observers to the decision-makers in near-flat tones with an air – to the untrained ear – of almost understated nonchalance.

As he sat in his command chair, Johnson heard a report from the signal bridge one level above the command bridge. The local time was 4:25 p.m. (1625 hours). The even, almost conversational tone said, "Captain, we've sighted a ship in distress at bearing one-two-zero degrees relative (120 degrees to the right). She looks like a Vietnamese vessel. She's signaling SOS with lights or a signal mirror. We see people waving."

The radar room in the ship's Combat Information Center (CIC) below decks almost immediately confirmed the sighting. They characterized it as a small radar target. The duty officer repeated the reports for Johnson, who had lifted his binoculars before the man even stopped talking. In the distance, he saw what appeared to be a tiny Vietnamese vessel with fish eyes painted on the bow and the nondescript color of treated wood on the hull. There was no sail. The ship appeared to be making headway by engine, as he observed smoke coming from its stack. Johnson almost casually commanded the duty officer, who in turn relayed to the helmsman, "Come about. Set intercept course. Slow to maneuvering speed."

"Aye, aye, captain," came the replies, as the watch officer and helmsman responded in turn.

Johnson spoke into the microphone on his hand held radio and said, "Lt Derrick, send a motor whaleboat to intercept the boat and advise us of their status."

A quick "Aye, aye, Captain," was the lieutenant's response, who then proceeded to dispatch and join Chief Warrant Officer 2 (CWO2) Daniel Gavin and Seaman Mac Brown on the small motor whaleboat. The San Jose was about three miles from the Vietnamese vessel. They continued to close the distance as the whaleboat was lowered. Gavin had served in Vietnam and spoke the language.

Captain Johnson knew what he was looking at, but he wanted to use the whaleboat crew to verify and determine how he could help. The San Jose was moving now at 20 knots, slowing incrementally to 10 knots, then five, then three. It would take about 40 minutes for the intercept, allowing sufficient time to slow his ship to a standstill when the tiny Vietnamese vessel would come alongside, to the left – or port side of the San Jose. Johnson noted that the seas were about three to four feet. He could not feel the waves as he sat on the bridge 50 feet above the Pacific, but he had no doubt that the occupants of the tiny craft were even now being tossed about by the swells. Johnson thought about how much trouble they must have encountered with the tropical depression that had just passed the day before.

Several of the officers, including Johnson, left the air-conditioned bridge for the port bridge wing, where they could get a better look at the Vietnamese boat. As they closed the distance with the vessel, Johnson estimated that the boat was about 40 feet long. It carried no flag, likely indicating that it was not a Vietnamese government patrol boat. There were only a handful of individuals on deck, though Johnson knew that refugees were normally hidden – and protected – below deck.

One of the men next to Johnson, himself named Johnny Johnson, said, more to himself than to anyone nearby, "What are we going to do?"

Captain Johnson didn't put down the binoculars. He merely continued his gaze and said evenly, "What do you think we're going to do? The whole world is watching!"

The personnel standing next to the captain widened their gazes and noted at least three other ships from various nations that had slowed to watch how the drama would unfold between the refugees and the American vessel.

During the next 40 minutes, the San Jose noted a number of flares fired from the small boat and continued to receive the SOS in Morse code from a signal mirror. Johnson watched his ship's whaleboat make its way in the heavy seas towards the Vietnamese vessel. The motor whaleboat, which served a number of purposes in the Navy, from rescues to shuttling shore leave parties, was an open-cockpit, diesel-powered vessel. It was just 26 feet long, but built sturdily and ready for any challenge the sea could throw its way.

Johnson needed to evaluate if the Vietnamese boat was really in distress. At this point he wasn't sure they were. His initial observation corroborated his earlier evaluation: The boat was making headway, and there was no obvious damage or reported injuries, unlike the boat they had saved the previous month, which had been nearly foundering.

The intercept of a small vessel by a seagoing ship nearly 600-feet long is as much art as it is science. The sheer mass of the San Jose meant that it could destroy the 40-foot vessel like a matchstick if it moved against it with any force. Part of the job of safely rendezvousing would rest with the captain of the small boat, who would need to come alongside carefully once the San Jose was slowed to almost a stop. If he tried to rendezvous while the boat was moving at more than a walk, the ship's movement could effectively suck the other boat towards the larger vessel's hull, crushing timbers and sinking the smaller boat.

Right now, they were not immediately coming alongside the Vietnamese vessel. That was the job of the whaleboat, which radioed to Johnson, "The power plant appears operational, skipper. She's making headway."

"How are the people"?

"From the looks of it, they look like they need some food and water. But our guess is that there are a lot of people below decks that we can't see.

Johnson issued the order to the watch officer, who in turn contacted the ship's stores personnel: "OK, prepare a pallet of supplies for them and be ready to lower it when they come alongside."

Quoc was not privy to Johnson's thinking or the orders being issued to Navy personnel. On his own small boat, he recognized that the massive U.S. Navy ship was closing the distance and slowing. He also noticed a small boat begin to make its way towards his own. It soon came alongside, keeping station a number of yards away. It was smaller than his own boat and manned by three men.

A U.S. Navy boatswain's mate yelled over a few words in Vietnamese, "You okay?"

He then yelled in English, "What assistance can we provide you?"

Quoc was in the wheelhouse, and one of his passengers who had claimed excellent knowledge of English was standing on its roof, "We need help, we need help, please. We need help!"

The man spoke a language that was barely broken English. He kept repeating the same phrase. The answer came from the whaleboat, "OK, we'll get you some help."

The Navy personnel kept station some fifteen yards away from Quoc's boat.

Clearly, Quoc realized, the whaleboat crew did not want to tie up with his vessel, probably cautious that the occupants of the Vietnamese vessel would quickly jump onto their own, putting the whaleboat in jeopardy. They doubtless also were not yet committed to carrying out a rescue mission. It almost seemed as if they were planning to just provision him and be on their way. Maybe they didn't know just how dire the straits were for his passengers.

Quoc thought quickly. How could he convince the Americans that he was in desperate need of assistance? How could he get it across that the 55 women, children, and men aboard were in imminent danger? And then Hung, still weak with a fever whispered, "Father, you know English the best. You talk with them."

This spurred Quoc to action. He handed Hung over to Cuu. Climbing to the roof of the wheelhouse, Quoc thought quickly and yelled in English, "We have pregnant women and young children aboard in desperate need of medical attention!"

The reply was instantaneous. "Show them to us."

Quoc abruptly told Cuu to shut down the engine. It became quiet on the open sea. Quoc looked down at his engineer and nodded an unspoken order. Dung knew what it meant. He grabbed a crowbar and pried up the decking, allowing the sick and debilitated passengers to slowly emerge from below decks. Quoc told one of the pregnant women – who was very close to full term – to come above deck, along with as many of the children as possible.

In short order, a small group of women and children appeared, their clothes soaked and in rags. One woman did not have a shirt, and the skin on her back had been flayed to a bloody pulp from the immersion in the water and the repeated abrasion on the inside of the oak hull. The pregnant woman alone had six children ranging from one to ten years old.

Cuu held Hung above his head as they stood near the stern of the boat, holding him up plaintively. Hung could barely open his eyes.

Minutes before there had only been a few men and one child requesting assistance. Now, Derrick and Gavin could only see a mass of humanity, whose appearance shocked them. Many passengers appeared near death. They clung to each other and pleaded with their eyes and with gestures towards the San Jose crewmen. The Americans stood for a second, barely comprehending what they were seeing. They looked at each other with the knowledge that something had to happen.

Derrick radioed back to Johnson on the San Jose, "Captain, there are a mess of very sick people here, including some pregnant women."

Once he heard that, Johnson's next decision was easy. He ordered, "All stop" to the watch officer and then instructed them to have the Vietnamese vessel pull alongside the port side of the ship. In Vietnamese, Gavin shouted, "Follow us."

Quoc quickly restarted the engine and instructed his passengers, "Hold on, we're heading to the American ship."

They fell to the deck, holding onto each other on the overcrowded boat, struggling against the motion of the three-foot seas. There were no signs of joy or laughter, only silent hugs indicating that salvation for each of them might have finally arrived. The whaleboat sped away towards the San Jose, now a quarter mile away and closing.

Quoc recognized that the massive U.S. Navy ship was slowing and coming to a stop. He stayed on a parallel course some 100 yards from the large ship until he knew it was no longer moving. Then he came along the left side, running the engine at just above idle. He stopped making headway and the boat bobbed in the three-foot swells as what appeared to be a hundred crewmen peered over the side of the San Jose. At 5:33 p.m. – 1733 hours – a line was thrown over the side. Cuu secured it to the boat.

The ship seemed the size of an island to Quoc and his fellow refugees. They looked up with an awe that bordered on reverence.

Everything on ships moves at a slower pace than one would think. Long minutes went by as Quoc bobbed in the waves, wondering what would happen next. The whaleboat pulled up behind his boat, still not close enough for boarding. It rested below the davits that had lowered it, and then it was slowly pulled up with the occupants onboard. The three crewmen aboard disappeared onto the San Jose's deck, and still, Quoc bobbed in the waves.

A pallet of supplies that Quoc recognized as canned food, fresh vegetables, and water began to be lowered from a small crane above them.

Di asked Quoc what was happening. "What do you think?"

"I dunno. Maybe they're just going to give us some supplies and send us on our way."

"What if we just rammed the American ship? It won't hurt them, but it would disable or sink us. They wouldn't have any choice then, would they?"

Quoc cautioned, "No, they wouldn't, but it seems to me those guys on the whaleboat understood our situation. Let's wait a few minutes."

Quoc waved the supplies away, yelling in English that there was no room on his deck to accommodate the pallet without injuring his passengers. The Americans complied, pulling the net and pallet back up.

Captain Johnson then ordered that the accommodation ladder – called the brow – be lowered. The brow was the boarding ramp that is carried on every ship, slung sideways onto the deck and used in ports where such ramps are not available. It is about three-feet wide and weighs hundreds of pounds. It is raised on a pulley electrically and dropped into position using the force of gravity.

The crewmen complied with Johnson's order, dropping the ramp. It moved precipitously, falling directly towards Cuu and Hung. Quoc looked in panic as Cuu grabbed Hung tightly into his arms and rolled to the side. The brow barely missed them and struck the stern of the small wooden boat, breaking some decking as it bounced. The full force was just inches from Cuu and Hung.

The brow swung out and away from the boat, once again dizzily rotating back towards them. Dung attempted to grab it, and in the process, it struck his arm, making a sound like breaking bone. Dung fell to the deck in pain, groaning. Quoc's passengers screamed and shielded each other.

Seeing the futility of using the normal brow ramp, the San Jose crewmen raised it and then lowered a rope ladder, a Jacob's Ladder in Maritime parlance. It is much lighter, about a foot wide, and routinely used by harbor pilots boarding and leaving a ship.

Three crewmen slowly climbed down the ladder. The thump onto the wooden deck identified themselves as people far heavier and healthier than any of the occupants of Quoc's vessel. It was a distinctly American footfall.

Quoc looked at Cuu, then Di. He realized now that rescue was imminent. He could tell from the expression of the three Americans. Their eyes were misting over as they looked at Quoc's passengers. He heard one of the crewmen speak into a radio, "Chief, these people don't look good."

And then one of the Americans looked at Quoc, "Are you the captain?"

Quoc replied silently with a nod. The next words from the Americans, "Our captain wants to see you. Please climb aboard."

"I will, but please see to the safety of my passengers. Look at them, please!"

"Don't worry, Captain. We will. You have my word."

The passengers lay on the deck. They looked soaked, sick, and emaciated. Some barely had their eyes open; others lay there in obvious pain. Quoc knew that Derrick and the others had already relayed that sight to the San Jose above, but he had not heard a reply.

Quoc looked at the men and women huddled before him. He prayed they would get the help they needed and that they would all survive.

Their ordeal had been extraordinary. They dared to escape from the only country they'd ever known. They left family and friends and boarded a small, overloaded boat. They had voluntarily been held as virtual prisoners through nearly five days of travel on the open ocean. They survived, soaked in darkness, filth, and human waste, continually drenched by the turbulent seas. They were captured by militia, chased by a patrol boat, and tracked in heavy seas. They weathered a storm for two full days that could easily have sunk them. Their engine had failed, and for a few minutes they were so terrified that they threatened to break out from the hold and jump into the sea. It had been Quoc's mission to save them even when they questioned his decisions.

Nonetheless, fortune smiled on them. They had not encountered dangerous Thai pirates or a vessel from a country friendly to Vietnam. A Chinese or Russian vessel could well have intercepted them, but here they were, on the verge of rescue by this American ship.

Through it all, Quoc thought, God has been with them.

Quoc's journey had been infinitely longer than that of his passengers. It had begun at Phu Quoc nearly five years before. Really, it had been a lifetime. His journey had been much like that of South Vietnam. Struggling to win a war. Losing and suffering the consequences. Attempting to rise from despair towards a new future.

Quoc thought about his family. He choked up as he looked at his passengers. He remembered his other children and how the world had changed for all of them and for him. He had suffered from camp to camp and been told that everyone had given up on him. He had hidden as a homeless person on the streets of the city he called home. He had seen men starve and be brutally killed by representatives of a victor that was unprepared to embrace its defeated foe, a victor that had no concept of how to use the talents and goodness of men like Quoc.

The cruelty and brutality would always be a part of Quoc's memories, but something else would be a part of it too: Forgiveness and, most of all, gratitude. Gratitude for the many kindnesses that had been extended to him and the providence that had brought him to this point.

He looked at this looming piece of steel above him. He thought of this huge American ship whose sailors were there for him, for his passengers and for their future. They had concern and compassion on their faces.

Of course, Quoc thought of one more person. The woman he loved – Kim-Cuong. At that instant, her courageous and beautiful face appeared in his mind. He sobbed. He cried for Kim-Cuong; he cried for himself; and he cried for a land from which the world had looked away.

Quoc was not the same man as he had been in Phu Quoc. He never would be. He stood there at the bottom of the Jacob's ladder for what seemed to be minutes. Likely, it was only seconds.

He made himself a promise. He told himself that he would make a new life for himself and create a place for his family that they could call home. He did not know where or how, but he would get Kim-Cuong and the rest of their children out. They would be a family once again.

Then Quoc grabbed the ladder with his right hand. He turned and took one last look. He fixed his gaze upward and began climbing the ladder. One hand, then one foot, then the next hand, then the next foot. He struggled to climb the twenty-plus feet to the deck above, as the rope ladder twisted in the wind.

Quoc was weak and debilitated. He carried not just his small frame, but also the weight of his experiences over the past five years. He carried the burdens of a lifetime of war. Each step was a battle, as the accumulation of the years weighed him down and the memories pulled against him.

As his strength began to ebb, he found himself being lifted up by the strong arms of the American sailors. He stepped foot on deck. He heard the ship's executive officer give the order,

"Use the mail net, Chief, and let's get these people aboard."

Quoc knew he had finally escaped from Vietnam. He took his first firm step onto the San Jose. It was a step to freedom, and it felt like home.

EPILOGUE

That afternoon, Hong Ngoc awoke from her sleep to see the vessel. This time it was real. To this day she recalls with awe the very real dream of their rescue that later so closely matched actual events.

Within minutes of their arrival on the deck of the San Jose, the 55 refugees were provided immediate medical assistance. They were each afforded the opportunity to use showers, and everyone was given clean clothes. In the next two days, the mess deck personnel lavished a continuous supply of fresh food and drinks upon them.

Some of the children required intravenous saline solution and antibiotics; Hung among them. For the most part, resting comfortably in clean clothes and taking in fluids and sustenance revived the men, women, and children who had accompanied Quoc on the perilous journey.

Quoc himself could not contain his joy. The photos of him and the others taken by Navy personnel that day show smiling faces that reflect just how relieved each was to be on the San Jose.

The sailors also sat and shared cigarettes, coffee, and tea with them. They listened to those who spoke English tell of their harrowing escape by sea, as well as of those they left behind in Vietnam.

Others, like Gavin, spent time chatting with the refugees in Vietnamese, recalling times when the two allies worked together during the war.

So as not to present a hazard to navigation, Quoc's little vessel was sunk by machine gun fire from the San Jose. The location – 06 degrees, 12 minutes North and 107 degrees, 25 minutes East - was just miles from where Quoc had calculated their last position.

Each escapee in his or her own way gave thanks for their rescue by the Navy ship. The American sailors, from their perspective, looked on the unexpected humanitarian mission as one of the most important undertakings they could imagine. Original photos of the rescue are to this day posted on a number of websites, with the smiling faces of Americans and Vietnamese shining from the pages of history. They mark a moment when the sadness of war and its aftermath was briefly overwritten by human kindness that transcended the horrors they had all experienced.

Di, Dung, Quoc, and the onboard mechanic, Loi, formed a tight circle on the deck. The other passengers surrounded them. Di gave a short, heartfelt prayer to thank Buddha for His blessings on the journey.

"Thank you, Buddha. Your providence guided us and sustained us through days of peril. We have so much to be thankful for. You kept us safe."

Tears flowed freely, as everyone in turn said their own silent prayer. And then Loi added with a smile, "And please, Buddha, punish anyone who tries to put us back on that boat."

Everyone, including nearby Americans, broke into grins and laughter.

Captain Johnson passed through the hangar deck repeatedly while Quoc and the others were aboard, but he did not linger. He had a large ship to run and was pressing the crew to offload the escapees in Singapore in a timely manner so that they could continue on with their mission and link up with the fleet in the Indian Ocean.

To this day, Jerome Johnson, who retired in 1992 as a four-star admiral and Vice Chief of Naval Operations, calls the Vietnamese boat rescues "highlights to my career." He notes that many of his sailors and those they saved have remained in touch through the years, recalling the enormity of the day and how their lives were shaped by it.

Quoc's story did not end on the San Jose. His journey to establish a new home for his family continued for months and years afterwards.

Within minutes of landing in Singapore, Quoc sent a telegram to Kim-Cuong and the rest of the family with the pre-arranged code, "Package safe in Singapore."

The 55 escapees had survived. Thousands of others did not, perishing to pirate attacks, intercepts by Vietnamese vessels, or the vagaries of the East Sea. The UN estimates that some 250,000 Boat People died on the high seas. An estimated 900,000 successfully reached asylum in about 40 countries around the world.

More than a million Vietnamese immigrants came to the United States via boat and air, as part of the UN Program, and in a series of Orderly Departure Programs (ODP) and Humanitarian Resettlement Programs. By 2012, there were some 1.7 million Vietnamese Americans.

The San Jose's deck log noted a mystery that is still unexplained, "Refugees from U.S.S. San Jose to Singapore. Total count 54 person (sic) debarked." The number was one less than that counted by the Quoc and verified by the crew when they were saved. No one alive today recalls the reason for the disparity.

As Kim-Cuong read the telegram, tears flowed down her cheeks. They were tears of gratitude, yes, but they were interspersed with tears of sadness. She had lost her son, her husband, and her sister to a distant land.

Quoc and the rest of his crew and passengers were processed in Singapore by government and UN officials. There, they spent time at Hawkins Road, the refugee camp established by the UN High Commission on Refugees.

Quoc was pressed to enter the maritime service in Singapore. His training and skills were needed in that economy, and he could have made an enviable wage. There was one catch: He would need to separate from Hung. Quoc never hesitated with his decision. He chose to seek relocation. They would remain as a family unit, just as Kim-Cuong and he had planned.

Quoc, Hung, Dong, and Cuu were sponsored by a Vietnamese family in Massachusetts and settled in Lawrence. Quoc attended Northern Essex Community College in Haverhill, studying electronic technology. He received his associate's degree and worked as an electronic technician for a number of computer start-ups for the next 20 years. He also worked as a part-time accountant during each tax season to earn extra money. After September 11, 2001, Quoc lost his job but ended up working for the Internal Revenue Service. His career had begun and ended with work at an American government agency. Today, Quoc still works part-time as a tax accountant.

Dong, as she had promised her sister, took care of Hung. She did it while attending community college and working full-time as an electronics assembler. Cuu also received his associate's degree and today still works in electronics.

Life was not easy. Quoc and the others lived in poverty in the United States in order to send money back to Vietnam to feed both extended families. For years there was no direct link for money order transfers or even phone calls between the United States and Vietnam. Throughout most of the 1980s, Quoc sent fifty-pound packages of supplies and clothing to Vietnam, asking that it be divided between the families. He learned later that less than half of the contents of each package made it through Vietnamese customs.

Quoc and Cuu would regularly drive nearly six hours to Montreal to arrange for the money transfers and to spend what little extra they had for phone calls to family. Canada was connected by phone to Vietnam, the U.S. was not. The calls cost $5.00 a minute.

Quoc and Kim-Cuong always talked about Ngan, Khanh, and Cuong and how they were faring. Kim-Cuong and every family member always pressed Quoc for details about Hung:

"How does he look?"

"Is he growing?"

"Is he healthy?"

"Is he learning English?"

"Does he play sports?"

"What are his favorite things?"

"Does he like school?"

"Do the girls like him?"

Quoc did his best to paint a mental picture for Kim-Cuong about their life in America. Sometimes they talked for nearly an hour. It was worth it to them: For nearly nine years it was their only means to stay connected.

Each call ended with, "Anh yeu em" I love you.

"Nhieu lam" I love you so much.

In the late 1980s, tension between the two countries began to lessen. Phone lines were opened. Mail service began. Money orders could be transferred.

In 1985, Cuu and Dong received their citizenship. Quoc delayed until 1987, hoping that maintaining his Vietnamese citizenship would help get his family out of the country. His status as an ex-internee in the Reeducation Camps and an escapee from Vietnam no doubt negatively influenced the Vietnamese officials granting emigration status to Kim-Cuong and the three children.

Quoc tried every official U.S. Government channel he could. His family pressed the Vietnamese from within the country, but while he saw other families joining their loved ones in the United States, Kim-Cuong was not permitted to leave.

Eventually the American people and politics stepped into the picture. Hung told his Methuen, Massachusetts high school principal, Arthur Nicholson, about the family's dilemma. Nicholson and another faculty member began a community letter writing campaign to Congressmen Chet Atkins, other Massachusetts congressional delegation members, and eventually to the news media. Quiet pressure was applied to the Vietnamese Ambassador to the United Nations by high-ranking members of the U.S. Senate, including Senator John McCain. Members of the Reagan Administration also worked behind the scenes and the story was chronicled on local and national TV stations.

It was American politics in action. It took time, but it worked.

In 1989, after two years of lobbying, Kim-Cuong and the three children were allowed to emigrate. Quoc's employer, Encore Computers, paid for the air tickets, arranged for a limousine on their arrival in Boston and held a large party in their honor.

It was the antithesis of Quoc's departure from Vietnam.

When his family arrived by plane on March 15, 1989, after more than 24 hours enroute, the entire family was exhausted. A large array of dignitaries, TV stations, and other press jammed the terminal at the Boston airport. Kim-Cuong and the girls at first tried to duck away from the crowd, not imagining that their arrival would be the cause of such a celebration.

Then Kim-Cuong saw Quoc. And Quoc saw Kim-Cuong. For moments, as they embraced, there were only two people in the crowd.

It had been nine years since the escape. The girls were almost grown; Cuong was nearly ten years old. Quoc could barely recognize them. They looked at him with expressions of both love and uncertainty, but within minutes, they were all hugging. It was the family that Quoc had promised himself that January day in 1980: A mother holding all of her children for the first time in a decade and a wife and husband embracing with a love that had not diminished over time.

They settled in Massachusetts and lived together as a family for 20 years.

Cuu married and still lives with his family in Haverhill, Massachusetts. Dong is still in Massachusetts, married and working as a test engineer.

Sinh, the other brother in the camps, remained in captivity in the northern part of Vietnam for 13 years and was finally able to immigrate to the United States as part of the Humanitarian Resettlement Program. He lived in Massachusetts until his death in May of 2017.

Of the five men on Quoc's original team from the Tay Ninh and Long Khanh Reeducation Camps, one never returned. Minh, who had taught them all so many survival skills, was sent to the North. He had been a professional Marine Corps officer and was regarded by the Communists as a hard-nosed lifer. They targeted him early for more retribution due to his long combat record. He died in confinement. No details are known.

Toan, whose wisdom and leadership helped sustain the team, migrated to the United States and is retired and living in Florida.

Quoc has not had contact with Son and Vong.

Dung, Quoc's chief engineer, migrated to the United States, worked as a mechanic and is now retired and living in Minnesota.

Di settled with his extended family in California. In 2004, he decided to become a Buddhist monk.

Tragically, Quoc's brother Loc was killed in a motorbike accident in Vietnam in the 1997. Quoc has attempted to help support Loc's children, ever mindful of the brother who was always there for him.

Phuc is still in Saigon. They remain loving brothers but have never reconciled their political differences.

Thai, the Communist snitch who sold out his fellow prisoners in Katum, was never able to find a boat on which to escape. Quoc heard that Thai died a violent death on the streets of Saigon about two years after Quoc escaped. The murderers were never found.

Lieutenant Duc and his family escaped South Vietnam prior to its fall. Quoc only occasionally hears of his whereabouts.

Uncle Ut Duc, who warned Quoc in 1975, fell out of favor with the Communists, as former NLF members lost their jobs to NVA soldiers and officials from the North. Ut Duc still lives in Saigon. Quoc visits him when he is in Vietnam, fondly recalling his uncle's support for his escape.

And Hung, the young nine-year old who nearly died on the escape boat? He thrived in the United States, did well in high school, and prepared for higher education. One night, over a bowl of *Pho*, he surprised his father by announcing that he had successfully applied to the Massachusetts Maritime Academy (MMA). He would follow in his grandfather's and father's footsteps and become a Merchant Marine officer. His captain, Thomas L. Bushy, would encourage Hung to tell his story and that of his father, Quoc.

Hung graduated from the academy in 1994. Today he is one of the officers for the MMA Training Ship Kennedy at Buzzard's Bay, Massachusetts.

Sadly, Kim-Cuong became ill and, in 2009, died at the age of 62. She and Quoc were married 39 years. They spent barely half of that time together. They had survived a war and its aftermath. They had raised a family. Her love had sustained Quoc in the camps. Kim-Cuong – the Diamond – had always shone for Quoc and her family. She will remain forever in their hearts.

Quoc eventually remarried to Duong Nguyen, a beautiful Vietnamese-American woman. A number of her relatives had been consigned to Reeducation Camps. She was able to escape to America. Today, Duong and Quoc live in Orange County, California. He is active in his church and continues to provide financial support through them to Vietnamese people in places close to his heart, like Bu Gia Map. For many years, he has travelled to Bu Gia Map, bringing food and supplies to the Tien people, as a way of thanking the kindness of strangers to prisoners in a convoy so many years ago. Quoc also volunteers weekly at a soup kitchen in Santa Ana. His health is better than many escapees, though his ability to walk distances is limited due to his camp experiences. Dreams and nightmares from those days often occur.

Quoc meets regularly with Vietnamese-Americans who take pride in their Vietnamese heritage and their U.S. citizenship. He attends reunions of Vietnamese whom he knew growing up and he learns more with each visit about what they went through during their times in the Reeducation Camps. Quoc and his Navy counterparts also proudly participate, in uniform, in community events around California.

Quoc's own words best tell his thoughts:

> "Now that I have lived in the United States more years than in Vietnam, it would take another book to tell the world how difficult it was to start life again in a foreign country. Even when you already speak English well, the challenges are enormous. Living in poverty in the United States has been a learning experience for each of us who emigrated from Vietnam. We ended up putting in double the effort to just be equal to the rest of the country. Because I was working full time, it took me almost four years to get my associate's degree. I was caught in the dilemma of needing to send almost my entire paycheck

home while getting a degree. It was even harder for Dong and Cuu, who worked full time and had to take English as a second language courses while pursuing their degrees. It took them each six years to do that. Now I consider the United States my home country. Vietnam is just a distant – and, at times – horrible memory. Without the generosity of the U.S. government and its people, we wouldn't be at this point at all. We all thank America for extending their arms to welcome us as refugees. There is a generosity of spirit in the American people that only those who come from elsewhere can fully comprehend and appreciate."

Quoc always adds,

"And please, remember this: If you stop hoping, you lose. Never give up."

When Quoc and the other Vietnamese-Americans speak of their experiences in the Reeducation Camps, people shake their heads in disbelief. A look of incredulity crosses faces. Few can comprehend just how "Reeducation Camp" can equate to imprisonment, deprivation, and death. After hearing questions from so many, Quoc made a decision. He would tell the story of what he had been through, to relate what had really happened to his country. To his family. To his fellow prisoners. To him.

Few people know what happened while the world looked away. Now they will.

AUTHOR'S NOTE

It was a phone call in early 2014 that triggered this book. My twin brother, Tom Bushy, then the captain of the Massachusetts Maritime Academy Training Ship Kennedy said, "You need to read a story. It's about a man who escaped by sea from Vietnam, along with his nine-year old son. They evaded the authorities and survived a violent storm at sea. I asked him to write it down for me. His son works with me at the academy."

Busy on other projects, I hurriedly replied, "Sure, sounds interesting, Tom. Send it over."

I then asked about his family, but discerned from the earnestness in his voice that the story of Quoc Pham was vitally important to my brother. The tale had touched his heart, he said, and it had opened up a perspective on the Vietnam War that neither of us had.

Both of us had graduated from high school in 1970. Tom headed to the Maritime Academy, where he obtained a Naval Reserve commission. I graduated from Army ROTC at Bowdoin College and became a second lieutenant. That was 1974. Both of us were willing to serve in the war, but we were among the fortunate: American forces pulled out in 1973. For Americans, the war was over in early 1973.

When I entered active duty as an Army officer, I served with dozens of Vietnam War veterans. Few spoke about the war. Because I did not fight in Vietnam, I was reluctant to ask questions about it, only doing so when the veterans raised the subject. Late at night on the gunnery ranges, or in reflective moments over drinks at the club, I heard their stories, felt their pain and saw in their eyes the enormity of their experience. They pondered the deaths of comrades and their own scars, emotional and otherwise.

Due to the time difference, the fall of South Vietnam on April 30, 1975, was occurring real-time as a couple of other lieutenants and I watched a small TV screen in an officer's club in Fort Huachuca, Arizona late on the 29th. I saw a small group of officers in civilian clothes – I think they were captains and majors – across the bar, watching the same screen. They sat there in silence, exchanging looks I had never seen in my life. There was pain, and sadness and regret. Their eyes were tortured, their expressions grim. They were watching defeat through the eyes of veterans. They ordered more drinks and sat in silence.

The next day, and in the days after, we all went about our Army work. Within months, initiatives were started that would transform our troops into an army of the future, an army that would be regarded as modern and capable. It was our mission to learn from the war and then erase the memories of the Army's Vietnam experience and create a new way of fighting: A new Army different from that which had existed in the jungles of Southeast Asia. In so many ways in the next decade, we succeeded.

Few spoke of the Vietnam War. Still fewer spoke of what was happening in South Vietnam after its fall. Our lives were busy and the less we heard, the less we asked, until eventually I, along with most of the rest of the country, looked away.

I received a pdf document from my brother hours after we spoke on the phone. Although not written by a native English speaker, it still detailed a story that was compelling. It spoke of Quoc's effort to evade authorities while living on the streets of Saigon, his attempts to refurbish a vessel, and his success at gaining a captaincy on a boat in which he ultimately succeeded in escaping, along with 54 other people. A storm wreaked havoc on him and his passengers; only his skill as a naval officer enabled him to captain his boat to the shipping lanes, where he was fortunate to be rescued by a US Navy ship.

My mind wrestled with Quoc's story, trying to understand its historical context. I knew about boat escapes from Vietnam, but I had no sense of the enormity of the effort or why so many had made the attempt. As I re-read Quoc's narrative, I also realized that I had even less knowledge of what had occurred within the country after 1975.

Tom convinced me to have lunch with Quoc later that month. We met at a sandwich shop in Barnstable, Massachusetts. Quoc came with his wife, Duong, the son who had escaped with him, Hung, and Hung's wife Kimmy. Language proved to be less of a barrier than my own lack of knowledge about the era. I listened raptly to Quoc's story about his life in South Vietnam, the invasion by the North, and his forced captivity in Reeducation Camps. I was shocked. After more than an hour, Quoc looked at me, smiled, and said, "Will you write my story? It has to be told."

My first thought was that I had to be able to understand it first – there was so much I didn't know about that period in history. Then I answered, "I agree that it needs to be told. But let's try a few chapters and see how it works out."

I agreed to the project, not because of what Quoc said, but because I saw in his face and in his eyes the same look I had seen nearly 40 years before in that Army officer's club. No one can describe the pain I saw, masked by Quoc's gentle smile and kind demeanor.

We arranged the first of a series of bi-weekly meetings via Face Time that extended three years, during which Quoc told me his experiences, his challenges, and his pain. We got to know each other so well that he opened up in ways that he had not previously done, even with his family. There were tears, there was laughter, and there was my persistent, "Tell me more, Quoc," followed by "I'm honored that you would share this experience."

As I wrote, Quoc would carefully review the drafts, deftly noting inconsistencies or inaccuracies. As I learned more, I recognized that research was required to verify claims made by the survivors of the camps and the Vietnamese Boat People. I wanted to substantiate these claims and understand the facts related to that era. I even researched things like toothpaste and Quoc's type of paralysis. Quoc came to realize that his own attention to detail in his escape needed to be replicated in the same way as I wrote his story. Quoc's other family members, and even the captain of the U.S.S. San Jose, Admiral Jerome Johnson, were extremely generous with their time in providing details about the period covered in the book.

In 2016, my wife Lisa, Quoc, Duong and Dick and Sylvia Pazolt, visited Vietnam. We traveled to most of the sites where there had been camps, though they no longer existed even in the memories of the local inhabitants. We retraced Quoc's escape route down the Saigon River, this time not in a small two-cylinder propelled boat like Quoc used, but in a new high-speed hydrofoil. We experienced a country where more than half of the people alive today have been born since the war ended and where the Vietnamese conflict is seldom mentioned. We also met those who still feel the effects of being on the losing side of a war, even extending to third-generation Vietnamese who are denied jobs and positions simply because a relative fought for South Vietnam or worked for the Americans.

As we had finished lunch that day in 2014, I agreed to "try a few chapters."

Quoc looked me in the eye and gently asked, "How much will it cost?"

My answer was, "Nothing." Quoc murmured thanks to a stranger. Only three years later did I realize that I have been graced with the intimate knowledge of a man's courage, the appreciation of the love of the woman who sustained him, and the meaning of family that shaped his destiny. Quoc has paid me handsomely with his story – not with money, but the riches of friendship that I will always cherish.

ACKNOWLEDGEMENTS

I owe a debt of thanks to so many women and men who encouraged and supported me on this project:

My wife, Lisa, who served as a willing editor and a source of unending loving support throughout the three-year effort. It was she who always carefully listened and encouraged me as I shared my interviews and research; and who was my willing partner on the trip to Vietnam. It was Lisa who also helped me as I made meaning of the depth of pain that Quoc and his family had experienced, and it was Lisa who assisted my initial feeble attempts to understand the heart of a woman. As we both came to know Kim-Cuong, a person we have never met, she became someone we came to love. Lisa and Kim-Cuong would have been friends. Of that I am certain.

As we have both relived his story over the years, Quoc Pham has taught me so much. He patiently related the details of his memories, as I asked question after question in my search to know every part of what he had been through. As we worked through the innumerable drafts, we came to know each other better and developed a trust and understanding that was based upon our similar ages, and something much more: A bond of common experience as military officers and a compassion for each other's perspective and our abiding love of family.

Other members of Quoc's family were always there for us, as we worked to provide the perspectives needed about their family and those who struggled to survive in the post-war economy: Duong (Quoc's second wife), Cuu, Dong, Hong Ngoc, and of course, Hung Pham, the boy who escaped with his father, who is now the man who contributes so much to his college and his profession.

No project like this can thrive without inspiration and encouragement. Those who provided a kind word, continual cheerleading or both were many: Tracy Ferguson, whose own recent book inspired my efforts; Dick and Sylvia Pazolt, who reviewed the book and accompanied us to Vietnam; Reverend Thomas Leinbach, whose spirituality and perspective helped expand my understanding of Quoc's own feelings about divine providence; Henry Moore, a retired professional photographer who works at the local copy center; and Mark Bushy, my son, who listened to the many turns and twists I experienced during the three years and always had a word of humor and caring to add at just the right moment.

My reviewers gave so freely of their time and care, I cannot thank them enough for their efforts, which never failed to make a more readable book. These included: Charlie Tutt, Mac Armstrong, Gene Conner, Jerome Johnson, Patrick Walsh, Brian Tuohy, Tim Brady, Krista Walsh, Bill Pattee, Ly Minh Vo, Bang Kim Ngo, Robin Wakeham, Admiral W. J. "Bud" Flanagan USN (Ret), John Flanagan, Dave Sexton, Jessica Flanagan Bushy and Mark Bushy. I should note that many reviewers who also consented to interviews about their Vietnam or maritime experience are former senior military officers. Their full names and ranks are listed in the bibliography. Dave Fuller acted as a reviewer and lent his technical expertise and perspective to the various iterations of the word-processing effort, often correcting author-induced issues. Appreciation also goes to my local Writer's Group, organized by Kathy Cockraft, director of our wonderful Brewster, Massachusetts Library, where the gifts of learning and joy of reading are cultivated daily; as well as Sharon Leder and the other authors, who willingly gave of their love and creativity to support the project. Special thanks to Tom Steiner, who came on my wing in the final stages and gave me the guidance I needed for the final push towards publication. I am also indebted to Gina McNeely of Gina McNeely Picture Research, who ably researched and scanned high resolution Navy photos of Quoc's rescue. Also, I owe a debt to the coaches and colleagues at the Gestalt International Study Center in Cape Cod, who have helped guide me in my life's journey and opened me up to so many possibilities, including writing. And my brother, Tom Bushy, with whom I entered the world, and share many wonderful parallels in our journeys through life, who first saw the book in his mind's eye and helped me in innumerable reviews and proof-readings.

And my sincere thanks go to my dear friend Bill Wakeham, who never failed to encourage me on my project and introduced me to Kendra Burgess, my editor. Kendra, when I approached her, intuitively understood the gift we had been given to tell the story of Quoc Pham, Kim-Cuong, their family, and the people they represent in the post-war period. Kendra Burgess's wisdom, discerning eye, and understanding were invaluable to me. I never failed to learn from Kendra and always appreciated the insights, edits, and care with which she approached the project.

And, to the many authors about the Reeducation Camps, the post-war period, and the struggles of the Boat People: I have attributed you as sources and quoted you in many places, and I hope to some-time thank you personally for your gifts to those who struggled, those who escaped, and the memories of those who died.

Everyone has given so much to me in this endeavor. You have all made it a better book through your gifts of insight and understand-ing. Any errors in this book are mine alone.

Dave Bushy
Eastham, Massachusetts
August 2017

END NOTES

AUTHOR'S NOTE CONCERNING CITATIONS:

As this historical work is a memoir, the basis of the information and facts primarily come from Quoc Pham and his personal recollections. The preponderance of the information and facts in this book are based on a series of some 65 personal interviews with Quoc Pham by the author. Where he is the sole source, I have chosen not to repeatedly cite Quoc as the source of historical facts, context and even some technical issues. However, I have included citations for historical facts and figures that might be in question, or where I need to provide context for the book. This also applies to technical and scientific facts that Quoc provided to me, yet begged further research.

The facts related to the Reeducation Camp system, including numbers of individuals incarcerated and estimates of those who died, required extensive research. A number of sources are cited, and background provided in those cases. Specific historical details, like announcements from the South Vietnamese government in Saigon, and the many epigraphs are also cited.

In some cases, the author needed to attempt a re-creation of events, such as the details of parts of the U.S.S. San Jose rescue (not known by Admiral Johnson), based on Quoc's recollection.

Finally, we could not find official Vietnamese Government accounts of the camp system, internees and that period in history. Consequently, Quoc's viewpoint and that of others needed to inform the narrative.

PROLOGUE

Page xiii – THEN IN LATE 1959 THE CONFLICT BEGAN ANEW - Interview with Quoc Pham – personal recollection.

Page xiv - NO ACCURATE ACCOUNTING EXISTS - See:

- Le Thi Anh. "Second Anniversary – The New Vietnam," undated. https://www.jim.com/ChomskyLiesCites/When we new what happened in Vietnam.htm
- Nancy Bui. "50th Anniversary of the Vietnam War from a Vietnamese American Perspective." Undated blog.
- Anh Do. "Camp Z30-D: The Survivors." *Dart Center for Journalism and Trauma,* March 1, 2002.
- Carl Gershman. "After the Dominoes Fell." *Commentary Magazine,* May 1, 1978.
- S. Grant,"9 Obscure Concentration Camps." *Listverse,* August 27, 2013.
- Murray Hiebert. "Vietnamese Reeducation Camp Victims Embark for U.S." *The Washington Post,* January 6, 1990.
- Interview with Quoc Pham – personal recollection.
- Theodore Jacqueney. "They Are Us, Were We Vietnamese." *WorldView – Carnegie Council for Ethics in International Affairs,* Volume 20, Number 4, April 1, 1977.
- "Remember: an economist co-authored with Chomsky to write these." *Economics Job Market Rumors,* undated blog.
- "Republic of Vietnam Armed Forces." GlobalSecurity.org.
- Dennis Rockstroh. "Hidden Horrors of Vietnam's Re-Education Camps." *New SaiGon,* April 2, 2005.
- "Vietnam War Info." http://vietnam-war.info/summary

CONCERNING THE ESTIMATES OF INTERNEES IN THE CAMPS:

Determining the exact number of internees in the Reeducation Camps will never be possible, unless it is determined that the current Vietnamese Government has access to and releases the figures: Most former internees believe some sort of government list of camps and internees exists, with an official count of camps and the actual number of prisoners known. Absent such information, however, many sources still cite exact numbers of internees and deaths, though none provide specific source material or analysis related to those figures.

The exact numbers will likely never be known. However, working in conjunction with Quoc Pham, we both concluded the best approach is a range of prisoners and deaths based upon facts that are largely verifiable. For instance, the number of individuals on active duty in the South Vietnamese Armed Forces in the years 1971-72 was approximately 1,048,000. (GlobalSecurity.org)

http://www.globalsecurity.org/military/world/vietnam/rvn-af.htm). This included all branches of the military, as well as the South Vietnamese militia forces. Also considered are the unknown number of former armed force members who may have been medically disqualified or beyond the normal age of retirement. One can assume that all these military members received some sort of reeducation internment. Sources indicate that internees also included government officials. See Minh Fullerton. *Thank You America! Memoir of an 18-year Journey to Freedom.* Others include religious leaders and even some Communist leaders who fell out of favor with the post-1975 regime. No verifiable numbers are available for this group, but one can easily assume, given the size of the country (17.4 million in 1975), that hundreds of thousands of individuals were considered by the Communists to have been complicit with the South Vietnamese Government or the United States, with a specific emphasis on those who worked in the South Vietnamese government offices or as employees of the U.S. Government. It is likely that a range of 500,000 to one million South Vietnamese civil servants or former employees of Americans, as well as religious leaders, were in this group.

The total potential population of Reeducation Camp internees was thus likely in the 1.5 to 2 million range. This is consistent with some sources reviewed by the author, which claim some 2.5 million internees (Vietnamwar.info), but only if one looks at the varying levels of camps that likely existed.

A number of sources indicate that there were three levels of camps, based on the former rank or role of those interned. Quoc Pham, for instance, noted that the vast majority of former enlisted men and women spent a relatively short amount of time in reeducation (three to seven days). This would have been the lowest possible level of internment and likely included a majority of the total number of internees. A middle level of Reeducation Camp internment would have been in the two to four year range and usually involved incarceration in the southern part of the combined Vietnam. The most brutal and highest level of internment was that of high-ranking officers (as described by Quoc and a number of other sources, including Minh Fullerton), who spent a decade or longer in the camps usually located in the northern part of the combined country. Some were imprisoned until the late 1980's – a few until the early 1990's. Individuals in the mid to high level (time incarcerated, and brutality of conditions) would have been officers, specialists or elite cadre, senior governmental workers and religious leaders and other high ranking civilians.

If one in five military members were either an officer or a member of an intelligence or elite unit (Rangers, Paratroopers, or Marines), then slightly more than 200,000 individuals with military backgrounds would have been subject to the longer confinement periods like Quoc's. If one in four of the civilian government workers were considered to be of high rank, then that number would range from 125,000 to 250,000. The total of internees in these two levels of camp can thus be estimated at 325,000 to 450,000 individuals, all subject to the longer and more brutal incarcerations, ranging from two to as many as 17 years.

The range of estimated internees: 325,000-450,000 - is consistent with most of the sources as an estimate of those who were interned for protracted periods of time, as follows:

- Anh: "300,000 people are being detained."
- Gershman: "In 1976, one Vietnamese official said there were more than 200,000" in the camps..."
- Gershman: "Lacouture thinks the figure may exceed 300,000, while Father Gelinas estimates there may be as many as 500,000 in the camps."
- Jaqueney: "Jean Lacouture and Tiziano Terzani, friendly toward the National Liberation Front during the war but troubled now by Hanoi's human rights policies, have estimated that the figure may exceed 300,000, a judgment shared by U.S. Analysts."
- Rockstroh: "...consigned as many as 500,000 people to extended stays in the camps."
- Seidman: "The million or so South Vietnamese who were members of Thieu's army have not been mistreated. The PRG (Provisional Revolutionary Government) merely explained its policies to low-ranking soldiers and sent them home, while higher-level officials are going through somewhat longer reeducation in centers one Vietnamese scholar described as 'more like universities than prison camps'"
- Theinfolist.com: "Up to 300,000 people, especially those associated with the former government of South Vietnam were sent to re-education camps."
- "Vietnam's Political Hostages," The Economist, 1989. "When the Vietnam War ended in 1975, about 1M Vietnamese who had worked for the Americans and the government of South Vietnam were rounded up by the victorious North and sent to "re-education" camps. Some were

kept inside for only a short time; they did their penance and made their peace with the communists. Some were freed after a year or two. But 95,000 former opponents of the regime are thought to remain political prisoners in Vietnam."

Bear in mind, too, that some 140,000 individuals and family members escaped Vietnam in April of 1975. A significant number of these could have been high-ranking individuals. Bui, Ibid. Also see, "State of the World's Refugees 2000." Chapter 4 – Flight from Indochina." *United Nations High Commission for Refugees,* p 81.

Likely, no one will ever know with certainty the numbers of those sent to the Reeducation Camps. Research and careful analysis would point towards a total of 325,000 to 450,000 or more who were subjected to incarcerations of two or more years. It is also reasonable to assume that a total population of some 1.5 to 2 million or more was sent to all types of Reeducation Camps, ranging from internments that lasted just a week to nearly two decades in duration.

Deaths:

The number of deaths in the Reeducation Camp system is even more difficult to assess, considering the unknown numbers of those who escaped or died escaping, and the deaths of those who were buried hurriedly in unmarked graves, especially during the 1978-79 fighting in Cambodia. As difficult as it is to calculate total internees, it is considerably more challenging to gauge the total number of deaths in the camps. Some sources indicate a number of "165,000" deaths. See Do, Anh. "Camp Z30-D: The Survivors." Other authors do not attempt to cite numbers.

As witnessed by Quoc and others, death in the camps was not the primary aim of the Communist leadership, though it was often an outcome for prisoners. His belief is that the overarching goal of the Communists was retribution and forced removal of educated men and women from society, to allow the government the opportunity to cement their gains in the South and prevent any opposition from arising. This in no way mitigates the fact that the inhumane treatment resulted in deaths from disease, malnutrition, punishment, poor medical treatment, minefield-clearing duty and even suicide. Quoc estimated that 30% of his camp (300 out of 1000) at Long Khanh died the night of the explosions, as a result of a fire of unknown origin and resultant explosions. In Katum, the most brutal camp for Quoc and his fellow prisoners, some five to six percent of prisoners are estimated to have died. There is also evidence from the community of survivors (reported by Quoc and other immigrants) that the death rate was significantly higher in the Reeducation Camps located in the North, due to both the treatment and also the longer-duration internments. The

Vietnamese-American community also reports that many of those released were in poor health and died after they returned to their families, which would possibly increase the death rates to more than 10 percent. The author cannot accurately hazard an approximation, but there appears to be strong evidence that tens of thousands of men died from all causes in the camps.

It is not unreasonable to conclude that 100,000 or more men died during the years the camps operated. Many more died after leaving the country, when they ventured into the unforgiving East Sea to escape the country.

Finally, there are some sources that indicate summary executions by the Vietnamese government of those who opposed the regime (see Carl Gershman, "After the Dominoes Fell." *Commentary Magazine*. The above estimates above do not include these numbers.

Page xiv - THOUSANDS OF BOAT PEOPLE – See:

- John Bowman, General editor. *The Vietnam War – An Almanac.*
- Jeff Gammage, "Smithsonian's Vietnamese Exhibit Recalls Plight of Boat People," *Philadelphia Inquirer,* May 14, 2012.
- Pam Proctor, "Boat People and Compassion Fatigue."
- Connie Tran, "Vietnamese Boat People: The Stories of Vietnamese Refugees and their Journey in Seeking Asylum in Canada during the Late 1970s to the 1980s" pp. 65-77.
- "Vietnamese Boat People," Revolvy
- Zack Paul, "Flood of Indochinese Refugees Ebbing," *The Washington Post,* March 11, 1980
- State of the World's Refugees 2000." Chapter 4 – Flight from Indochina." *United Nations High Commission for Refugees.*

Page xiv - SURREAL QUALITY TO THE REPORTING - Gay Seidman, "Reconstruction & Revolution in Vietnam – The East is Red." Also, see Le Thi Anh, "Second Anniversary – The New Vietnam."

Page xv - THOUSANDS OF BOAT PEOPLE, WHO WOULD PERISH - Barbara Crossette, "Thai Pirates Continuing Brutal Attacks on Vietnamese Boat People." Special to *The New York Times,* January 11, 1982. Also, see Jeff Gammage, "A Forgotten Past – Vietnamese Boat People in Singapore."

Page xv - APPROXIMATELY 1.1 MILLION SOLDIERS WERE LOST – For the statistics cited in this paragraph, see, Nancy Bui, "50th Anniversary of the Vietnam War from a Vietnamese American Perspective."

Page xv - THE UNITED STATES SENT – Ibid.

Page xv - SOUTH VIETNAMESE MILITARY PERSONNEL DIED - Ibid.

Page xv - RICHARD M. NIXON WAS ELECTED - "The Christmas Bombing." (President Richard M. Nixon ordered bombing of North Vietnam in 1972). *Newsweek*, March 1, 1999.

Page xvi - IN JANUARY OF 1975 – Bowman, "The Vietnam War – An Almanac," p. 343.

Page xvi - THIEU ORDERED A WITHDRAWAL – Interview with Quoc Pham – personal recollection.

Page xvi - CAM RANH BAY FELL - Ibid.

Page xvi - PRESIDENT FORD REQUESTED FUNDS – Jeff Jacoby, "What Happened When U.S. Troops Left Too Soon." *The Boston Globe*, May 10, 2015.

Page xvii - SOUTH VIETNAM OFFICIALLY SURRENDERED – George Esper, "Fall of Saigon was Death Knell for South Vietnam." *The Columbian* (Vancouver, WA), April 9, 1995.

CHAPTER 1

WILL SOUTH VIETNAM FALL?

Page 1 - THE CAMP ON THE ISLAND OF PHU QUOC – Interview with Quoc Pham – personal recollection.

Page 3 - A MAKESHIFT REFUGEE CAMP – Ibid.

Page 3 - POW INTERNMENT CENTERS – Ibid.

Page 4 - AMERICAN GMC 2 ½ TON – Ibid.

Page 5 - STATELY, CANOPIED *DAU* TREES - "Saigon needs plan to preserve again street trees: expert" *Thanh Nien News*. August 10, 2014.

Page 9 - LST (LANDING SHIP TANK) – Kit Bonner. "LST – Otherwise Known as 'Large Slow Target.'" *Sea Classics*.

CHAPTER 2

THE MOIST EARTH OF THE COUNTRYSIDE

Page 10 - DON'T LISTEN TO WHAT THE COMMUNISTS SAY - Brainy Quote.

Page 15 - VIET CONG – A number of reporters routinely mention Viet Cong without context. Known as the National Liberation Front (NLF), the Viet Cong constituted the Communist militia force in the South, founded in 1960, after hostilities began between the North and South. It was separate and distinct from the Viet Minh or Vietnam Fatherland Front (VFF), which was first organized to fight the Japanese and then the French. The Viet Minh were considered to be key to the victory against the French in Dien Bien Phu. After the 1954 Geneva Accords, the Viet Minh are not generally cited. The Viet Cong became active in the 1960s and 1970s and fought guerilla actions in the South, while the North Vietnamese Army (NVA) constituted the regular, organized fighting force. See, "Get Together Marks VFF's 70th Founding Anniversary." *Vietnamese News Agency*, May 19, 2011. https://www.highbeam.com/doc/1G1-256816950.html. Also, see "Thi Dinh Nguyen," Vietnam War Reference Library, January 1, 2001. https://www.highbeam.com/doc/1P2-18806624.html. See also: "What's the Difference Between Viet Minh and Viet Cong?" *eNotes* https://www.enotes.com/homework-help/what-differenc e-between-viet-minh-viet-cong-359807

CHAPTER 3

FATEFUL DECISION

Page 17 - YOUR FAMILY IS THE ONLY THING – Henry Ku, *Boat People – Personal Stories From the Vietnamese Exodus 1975-1996*, Carina Hoang, Editor, p. 204

Page 21 -THE VIET MINH – See references to "COMMUNIST MILITIAS – THE VIET CONG, above.

Page 21 - THE VICHY FRENCH – Ted Morgan, *Valley of Death – The Tragedy at Dien Bien Phu That Led America into the Vietnam War*. New York: Random House, 2010. P. 8.

Page 21 - AFTER THE WAR, DEGAULLE'S GOVERNMENT - Ibid, pp. 39, 51, 59.

Page 22 - THE GENEVA ACCORDS – Robert Templer, *Shadows and Wind – A View of Modern Vietnam*. New York: Penguin Books, 1998. Also, see John S. Bowman, General Editor. *The Vietnam War – An Almanac*, p. 38.

CHAPTER 4

THE LAST DAYS OF VIETNAM

Page 27 - I HESITATE TO RECALL – Tran Van Phuc, *Reeducation in Postwar Vietnam – Personal Postscripts to Peace*. College Station: Texas A&M University Press, 2001, p. 5.

Page 30 - ON APRIL 21 - "Thieu Resigns, Calling U.S. Untrustworthy." *The New York Times*, April 22, 1975.

Page 30 - TRAN VAN HUONG – Ibid.

Page 30 - HUONG WAS KNOWN FOR - Ibid.

Page 30 - THIEU HAD BEEN A FORMER GENERAL – Ibid.

Page 30 - THIEU'S REPLACEMENT, HUONG, WOULD LAST - "Gen. Duong Van Minh, 86; Briefly Led South Vietnam (Obituary)," *The Washington Post*, August 8, 2016.

Page 32 - ALTERNATE HISTORIES WOULD BE DEBATED - Interview with Quoc Pham – personal recollection.

CHAPTER 5

THE FALL OF A COUNTRY

Page 36 - DURING THE DAY ON MONDAY - AZ Quotes.

Page 37 - HIGH OF SOME 540,000 MILITARY – "The Vietnam War – Allied Troop Levels."

Page 37 - BING CROSBY'S SONG WHITE CHRISTMAS – Interview with Quoc Pham – personal recollection.

Page 37 - TRAN VAN HOUNG - "Gen. Duong Van Minh, 86; Briefly Led South Vietnam (Obituary)," *The Washington Post*, August 8, 2016

Page 37 - SOME SORT OF SETTLEMENT – Interview with Quoc Pham – personal recollection.

Page 38 - "LET US SIT TOGETHER" - "President Minh's Inaugural Address in Saigon Palace." *The New York Times*, April 29, 1975

Page 40 - LOW HOVER TO TRANSLATIONAL LIFT - Tarrance Kramer. "Rotary Revelations: Managing Helicopter Operations around Fixed-Wing Aircraft Demands a Little Finesse and a Lot of Clarity on the Part of Pilots and Controllers." *IFR Magazine*, January 1, 2017.

Page 41 - GENERAL MINH'S VOICE WAS SAYING - Interview with Quoc Pham – personal recollection. Also, "Saigon liberation: Witness recalls historic event," *Vietnamese News Agency*, April 22, 2010. https://www.highbeam.com/doc/1G1-224574732.html

CHAPTER 6

WHY DIDN'T YOU ESCAPE?

Page 43 - LIFE WAS NOT THE SAME – Tran Dinh Thuc, *Boat People – Personal Stories From the Vietnamese Exodus 1975-1996*, Carina Hoang, Editor, P. 122.

Page 44 - ALEXANDER THE GREAT - "Alexander the Great." *Encyclopedia Judaica*, January 1, 2007.

Page 45 - AT THE END OF WORLD WAR I - Donna Tillotson, "Treaty of Versailles: not exactly as planned: how the treaty 'to end all wars' led instead to numerous new conflicts". THE GREAT WAR, *Esprits De Corps*, July 1, 2009.

Page 45 - MARSHALL PLAN ULTIMATELY SUCCEEDED – George Will, "Marshall is Still Not Getting His Due." *The Buffalo News* (Buffalo, N.Y.), June 3, 1997.

Page 45 - QUIXOTIC ATTEMPTS BY THE FRENCH – Morgan, *Valley of Death – The Tragedy at Dien Bien Phu That Led America into the Vietnam War*, p. 8.

Page 45 - FALL OF DIEN BIEN PHU IN 1954 – Morgan, *Valley of Death – The Tragedy at Dien Bien Phu That Led America into the Vietnam War*, pp. 552-556.

Page 46 - POL POT IN CAMBODIA – Keith B. Richburg, "Pol Pot Admits 'Mistakes' by his Regime; But Cambodian Insists, 'My Conscience is Clear'," *The Washington Post*, October 23, 1997.

CHAPTER 7

ORDERS TO REPORT TO REEDUCATION

Page 49 - THE RECONCILIATION CLOCK STOPPED – Thomas Maresca, "40 Years Later, Vietnam still deeply divided over war," April 28, 2015, updated April 30, 2015. *USA Today.*

Page 50 - ARMED PROPAGANDA TEAMS – Herbert A. Friedman, (SGM, ret.), "The Armed Propaganda Teams of Vietnam." http://www.psywarrior.com/VNArmedPropTeams.html

Page 51 - FOOD SUPPLIES AND TECHNOLOGY- The technological advances of the South had been fostered with strong support from the United States. An example was a power station that supplied electricity to the grid around Saigon. Once the Communists took over, they decided to dismantle and relocate the plant to the North, which was starved for electric power after years of war. The dismantling process took weeks and severely reduced electricity on the South's power grid. Components were trucked north to Hanoi and the plant reassembled. Ironically, the very engineers who had designed and helped build the generation plant were no longer available. They were under house arrest or being prepared to move to remote camps for reeducation. The plant lay useless for decades – all due to the arrogance of a regime that shunned educated people in favor of those whose only intellectual talent was unswerving loyalty to the Communist regime. Interview with Quoc Pham – personal recollection.

CHAPTER 8

THE REPORTING CENTER

Page 54 - THE NOTICE TO REPORT – Minh Fullerton. *Thank You America! Memoir of an 18-year Journey to Freedom.* Lee M. Vo, 1985. 8-9.

CHAPTER 9

BEYOND 10 DAYS

Page 65 - A DAY IN PRISON IS LONGER – Proverbatim.com.

Page 66 - WESTERNERS CALL THE ASIAN SQUAT – Cate Leona. "Asian Squats to Improve Health, Flexibility and Balance," *Udemyblog.* https://blog.udemy.com/asian-squats.

Page 68 - THE STOMACH, USED TO NORMAL AMMOUNTS – Joshua Krause, "Brace yourself for the frightening symptoms of starvation." *Ready Nutrition,* October 4, 2015. Also, Interview with Quoc Pham – personal recollection.

Page 70 - FORAGING IN THE FOREST – See "Forest vs. Jungle." *Diffen.* http://www.diffen.com/difference/Forest_vs_Jungle. The selective use of forest and jungle is an intentional word choice made by the author, based on research and personal observation. The word forest is primarily used where the men are assigned logging operations, while the term jungle is more generic. Both words have very similar meanings. As described in "Forest vs. Jungle," jungle is generally considered impenetrable, but forests, while heavily wooded, are considered accessible. Both contain deciduous trees. Observing the wooded region of Vietnam, the term forest seems to more appropriately apply to cases where the prisoners were involved in logging. The fact that Quoc and the other prisoners were able to navigate the wooded areas without generally using machetes or other implements seems to point to use the term forest as more appropriate. Interestingly, according to Diffen, "The word jungle originates from a Sanskrit word jangala, meaning 'forest'." The author does use the term jungle in a generic context when describing areas to which the prisoners were sent, and some selected locations, like the New Economic Zone. Used by Quoc, these references typically connote impenetrability.

Page 71 - THE REGIME OF POL POT – Richburg, "Pol Pot Admits 'Mistakes' by his Regime; But Cambodian Insists, 'My Conscience is Clear.'"

CHAPTER 10

SAIGON

Page 73 - LIVING UNDER THE NEW REGIME – Tran Tri Vu, *Lost Years – My 1,632 Days in Reeducation Camps.* Berkeley: Institute of East Asian Studies, University of California, 1988. P.75

Page 78 - TAKE THESE LESSONS HOME – Interview with Cuu Pham - personal recollection.

Page 80 - IN 1976, THE GOVERNMENT ABRUPTLY – "Vietnam and Vietnamese Americans after 1975." Vietnamese Americans – lessons in American History. *Teaching Tolerance.* Undated. www.teachingtolerance/vietnamese. Also, Interview with Quoc Pham – personal recollection.

Page 80 - LARGEST PRODUCERS OF RICE - "Rice in Vietnam." *Vietnamese Culture Values,* Undated.

CHAPTER 11

DIAMOND

PAGE 87 - PEOPLE OFTEN THOUGHT SHE LOOKED LIKE PHUONG HOAI TAM - Interview with Quoc Pham – personal recollection.

CHAPTER 12

ALL THAT WE ARE

Page 95 - ALL THAT WE ARE - Goodreads. http://www.goodreads.com/quotes/1296640-all-that-we-are-is-the-result-of-what-we

Page 98 - HYPOKALEMIC PERIODIC PARALYSIS - "Hypokalemic Periodic Paralysis FAQ." *Periodic Paralysis International*, June 21, 2011.

Page 98 - GENETIC MUTATIONS, WHICH AFFECT – Ibid.

Page 103 - SMALL STEEL CONEX CONTAINER - "History and Development of the Container – The 'Transporter' – Predecessor to the CONEX." *U.S. Army Transportation Museum website*. Undated.

CHAPTER 13

DAILY LIFE IN LONG KHANH

Page 105 - A LITTLE FOOD WHILE HUNGRY - (American idiom translation of Vietnamese quote by author). *AdoptVietnam*. http://www.adoptvietnam.org/vietnamese/proverbs.htm

CHAPTER 14

DEATH COMES

Page 110 - "WHERE LIFE IS EXHAUSTED" – Inspirational quotes.

PAGE 111 - BULLETS FIRED FROM A RIFLE OR PISTOLS – Author, personal experience and recounting by veterans.

Chapter 15

The Bottom of the Well

Page 118 - A FROG LIVING AT THE BOTTOM – Listofproverbs.com.

PAGE 120 - A BUILD-UP OF CARBON DIOXIDE - Roland Podlewski et al. "Carbon Dioxide as a Potential Danger to Medical Rescue Teams at Work - a Case Study. *Medycyna Pracy* (Occupational Medicine) Portal, January 1, 2017. https://www.highbeam.com/doc/1P3-4320813251.htmlPage 120 - IT FELT PAGE 120 - LIKE A KNIFE BEING THRUST INTO ONE'S GUT - Interview with Quoc Pham – personal recollection.

Chapter 16

Descent Into Despair

Page 123 - THE COMMUNISTS USE POLITICAL – Le Huu Tri, *Prisoner of the Word – A Memoir of the Vietnamese Reeducation Camps.* Seattle: Black Heron Press, 2001.

Chapter 17

The Daily Routine in the Camps

Page 130 - ALL HUMAN UNHAPPINESS - "Introduction to Buddhism," *Buddhist Studies.* See also "A Basic Buddhism Guide: 5 Minute Introduction."

Page 130 - NOBLE TRUTH Quotes - Ibid.

Chapter 18

Even to Live

Page 138 - SOMETIMES EVEN TO LIVE - GoodReads. http://www.goodreads.com/quotes/tag/survival

Page 138 - SOME COMPARE THE TASTE – "What DO scorpions taste like?" *Arachnoboards,* August 30, 2008. http://arachnoboards.com/threads/what-d o-scorpions-taste-like-here-is-your-answer.133442/

Page 142 - SKILLED OBSERVERS – William Branigin, "Forced 'Reeducation' Camps Continue in Vietnam, Laos," *The Washington Post,* December 23, 1982. See also Theodore Jacqueney, "They Are Us, Were We Vietnamese." *WorldView – Carnegie Council for Ethics in International Affairs.* Volume 20, Number 4, April 1, 1977.

CHAPTER 19

MURDER IN THE FOREST

Page 142 - REVENGE IS A CONFESSION - Inspirational quotes.

Page 149 - FLAT AS RICE PAPER – Interview with Quoc Pham – personal recollection.

CHAPTER 20

RETRIBUTION

Page 151 - INTELLIGENT MEN ARE CRUEL - Goodreads.

Page 151 - THUOC LAO – Thuoc Lao tobacco is finely ground and burned in a container and filtered through water. It is similar to a hookah in the Mideast and the bong, or water pipe in the West. The Vietnamese commonly used a shared bamboo pipe to draw the tobacco. Interview with Quoc Pham – personal recollection.

CHAPTER 21

THE CURRICULUM OF REEDUCATION

Page 180 - AT KATUM, EVERY PRISONER – Interview with Quoc Pham – personal recollection.

Page 180 - EVERY FIVE MONTHS ROUGHLY – Ibid.

Page 182 - CULT-DRIVEN HISTORY – Ibid.

Page 182 - WAS AN IMMORTAL SAINT – Ibid.

Page 182 - HO CHI MINH SONGS – Ibid.

Page 183 - HO WAS AS MUCH A COMMUNIST – Ibid. Other sources debate this statement. See, "Ho Chi Minh and the Vietnam War." *Society for Historians of American Foreign Relations*, undated. https://shafr.org/teaching/ho-chi-minh-and-vietnam-war) noting that allies and foes alike had difficulty discerning the true motivations of Ho Chi Minh. Nevertheless, the combatants in the South like Quoc had strong feelings about Ho that were informed by the experiences of their family members, like Quoc's father. Individuals like Xuong, who fought with the Viet Minh, but who did not embrace Communism, were routinely punished. Xuong spent more than a year in jail for his dissident actions. Also, the fact that Ho held his position as the president of North Vietnam for 15 years without holding free elections is another example noted by former South Vietnamese citizens. (Interview with Quoc Pham – personal recollection). The reality is, however, that Ho initially worked to free Indochina from colonialism. Did he do it to establish the basis for Communist hegemony over the country? Debates will likely continue among scholars, but the beliefs of Quoc and his fellow internees were created not by academic research. They suffered in the camps and saw the actions of those who supported Ho. That informs their worldview in a way markedly different from those of academics.

Page 184 - HO HAD REPRESSED THOSE – Interview with Quoc Pham – personal recollection.

PAGE 184 - HE HAD FORBIDDEN THE FREE PRESS – Ibid.

PAGE 184 - FRENCH AT DIEN BIEN PHU – Ted Morgan, *Valley of Death – The Tragedy at Dien Bien Phu That Led America into the Vietnam War.* p. 615. Also, see Nancy Bui, "50th Anniversary of the Vietnam War from a Vietnamese American Perspective."

PAGE 184 - VIET MINH – "Get Together Marks VFF's 70th Founding Anniversary." *Vietnamese News Agency,* May 19, 2011.

PAGE 184 - HOWEVER, THE TET OFFENSIVE – Interview with Quoc Pham – personal recollection.

PAGE 184 - VIETNAMESE HISTORY – Linda Trinh Vo, "Vietnamese American Trajectories – Dimension of Diaspora." *Amerasia Journal* 29:1 2003): ix-xviii. See also, "Annual festivities celebrate heritage." *Vietnamese News Agency*, February 16, 2011.

CHAPTER 22

VISITS

PAGE 185 - ADVERSITY BRINGS WISDOM – Pinterest.

CHAPTER 23

REMEMBERED

PAGE 194 - NEVER FORGET BENEFITS DONE YOU - Inspirationalquotes. com – Vietnamese quotes.

CHAPTER 24

A CHANGE IN THE WIND

PAGE 201 - GIVING JUST A CRUMB - Proverbatim – Vietnamese Quotes.

PAGE 209 - VIETNAM AND POL POT'S REGIME – Jimmy Lim Wei Chung, "Ethics and Leadership in Foreign Policy: The Case of Singapore," p. 2.

CHAPTER 25

JOURNEYS OF LOVE AND DETERMINATION

PAGE 211 - NO ONE SAVES US – Sourcesofinsight.com.

Chapter 26

A Second Camp in Bu Gia Map

Page 217 - JOY CAME BACK TO US – Interview with Quoc Pham – personal recollection.

Chapter 27

Journey Home

Page 222 - LIFE IS A TEMPORARY STOP – Proverbatim.com.

Chapter 28

Lai Khe – The New Economic Zone

Page 230 - PEOPLE SAY THAT TIME GOES BY – Proverbatim.com.

Chapter 29

Barbaric Weapons of War

Page 235 - LANDMINES ARE AMONG THE – AZ Quotes.

Page 236 - LIKE 122MM HOWITZERS - "122 mm gun M1931/37 (A-19), Wikipedia. https://en-wikipedia.org/wiki/122_mm_gun_M1931/37_(A-19)

Page 236 - CAMBODIAN CIVIL WAR - Keith B. Richburg, "Pol Pot Admits 'Mistakes' by his Regime; But Cambodian Insists, 'My Conscience is Clear.'" *The Washington Post*, October 23, 1997.

Page 236 - THE WAR REACHED A CRESCENDO – Ashbrook – *Boston Globe*.

Chapter 30

Quoc Escapes Into a New Role

Page 244 - I STILL DON'T KNOW – Carina Hoang, Editor. *Boat People – Personal Stories From the Vietnamese Exodus 1975-1996.* Cloverdale, W.A.: Carina Hoang Communications, 2010.

Page 245 - THE CHINESE USED DIETHYLENE GLYCOL - "FDA Advises Consumers to Avoid Toothpaste from China Containing Harmful Chemical." Press Release from FDA.gov, dated June 1, 2007.

Page 245 - THE UNITED STATES HAD ESTABLISHED – Ibid.

Page 250 - ALL THE WORLD'S A STAGE – William Shakespeare, "As You Like It," Act II, Scene VII.

Page 252 - THE VIETNAMESE INVASION BEGAN - Vietnamese Americans – lessons in American History. *Teaching Tolerance.* Undated.

Page 253 - THE INVASION CONTINUED – Tom Ashbrook, "In Cambodia, The War Shows No Signs of Ending." *The Boston Globe,* June 28, 1987.

Chapter 31

A Walk Down the Street

Page 256 - THE BIRD THAT ESCAPES – Vietnamese Proverbs.

Chapter 32

Captain Skills in Demand

Page 262 - DO THE THING YOU'RE GOOD AT – John Green. Goodreads.com.

Page 262 - THE GOVERNMENT, STILL IN THE MIDST – Connie Tran, "Vietnamese Boat People: The Stories of Vietnamese Refugees and their Journey in Seeking Asylum in Canada during the Late 1970s to the 1980s." *Mount Royal Undergraduate Humanities Review 3 (2015),* p 65.

Page 266 - THE UNITED NATIONS STEPPED IN – Interview with Quoc Pham – personal recollection.

Page 266 - REPLACE IT WITH AN ORDERLY – ""State of the World's Refugees 2000." Chapter 4 – Flight from Indochina." United Nations High Commission for Refugees, p. 79.

CHAPTER 33

WHAT MONEY CAN'T BUY

Page 268 - WHAT MONEY CAN'T BUY – Interview with Quoc Pham – personal recollection.

CHAPTER 34

CAPTAINCY FOR QUOC

Page 273 - THE REAL WEIGHT WE WERE – Cao Luu, *Boat People – Personal Stories From the Vietnamese Exodus 1975-1996.* Carina Hoang, Editor.

CHAPTER 35

HEART-BREAKING DECISIONS

Page 279 - IT IS VAIN FOR THE COWARD – Brainyquote.com.

Page 280 - THE LITTLE TWO-CYLINDER DIESEL'S - https://www.tuktukny. com. Note: Attempting to mimic the sound of a two-cylinder diesel engine is difficult. The most accurate approximation of the noise seems to be a rapid fire "tuk-tuk-tuk-tuk," which is similar to the noise made by a mechanized three-wheel taxi popular in Thailand.

CHAPTER 36

ESCAPE DOWN THE RIVER

Page 290 - GOODBYE MY LOVED ONES – Interview with Quoc Pham – personal recollection.

Page 290 - THAT DAY THE FRONT PAGE – *The New York Times,* January 1, 1980 reprint.

Page 291 - UN AUTHORITIES AT THAT TIME VERIFIED – "Report Says 12,368 Fled Vietnam in June." *The New York Times*, United Nations, NY, August 5, 1981.

Page 291 - THE UNITED NATIONS HIGH COMMISSIONER – Ibid.

CHAPTER 37

BOARDED BY MILITIA

Page 305 - IN ANY GAME, YOU SHOULD – Interview with Quoc Pham – personal recollection.

CHAPTER 38

THE OPEN OCEAN

Page 316 - THE OCEAN WAS WAITING – Goodreads.com.

Page 317 - BRITISH ROYAL NAVY OFFICER – Adrian Morgan, "FAQ Sir Francis Beaufort – It's an Ill Wind." *The Scotsman*, November 2, 2000.

Page 318 - IN 1978, THE SINGAPORE GOVERNMENT – Jerry Lewis, "Does Singapore Have a Reason to Refuse Refugees?" *Singapore Policy Journal,* May 21, 2015.

Page 323 - ALTHOUGH THE TEMPERATURE OF THE WATER WAS IN THE LOW 70'S – "Phan Thiet Average January Sea Temperature." SeaTemperature. org https://www.seatemperature.org/asia/vietnam/phan-thit-january.htm

CHAPTER 39

IMPRISONED BELOW DECKS

Page 328 - TIME IS LIKE THE OCEAN – Goodreads.com.

Page 328 - MOTION SICKNESS - "Motion Sickness," *Medical News Today*, September 8, 2015. http://www.medicalnewstoday.com/articles/176198.php

PAGE 333 - SEAFARERS ARE FULLY AWARE – Interview with Thomas Bushy, personal recollection.

PAGE 333 - FIRST YOU THINK YOU'RE GOING TO DIE – Ibid.

CHAPTER 40

THE EYES OF THE WORLD

PAGE 340 - FOR THOUGH THE STORY – Andrew Lam, *Perfume Dreams – Reflections on the Vietnamese Diaspora*. Berkeley, California: Heyday Books, 2005.

Page 345 - IT WAS CORE TO THE CULTURE HELD BY THE MEN WHO SERVED AT SEA. One American mariner who participated in a civilian rescue in the South China Sea still speaks passionately about what the rescue meant to him, his captain and the rest of the crew. "There was no doubt we were going to help those people." (Interview with author, Chief Engineer Dave Sexton.) There were reports from Boat People survivors, though, that some commercial vessels did not render assistance. There is little published in that regard. Concerning military rescues, there was at least one documented case of insufficient assistance being provided by military personnel. A U.S. Navy crew provided food and water, but not rescue to a boatload of escapees and the captain was later held accountable. See, "Navy to Try Captain for Not Aiding Refugees." *The Boston Globe*, August 24, 1988.

Page 346 - A QUICK AYE AYE, CAPTAIN – Reference to Lieutenant Derick (may also possibly be spelled Deryck), CWO2 Gavin and Seaman Mac Brown – This information was pieced together through San Jose references to the two rescues mentioned in: http://www.refugeecamps.net/Johnny_AFS7.html The author attempted to recreate the details of the whaleboat rescue accurately and completely, but was not able to locate the principals involved in order to verify details of the account.

Page 347 - JOHNSON ESTIMATED THAT THE BOAT – Interview with Admiral Jerome Johnson, personal recollection. Also, see Deck logs, USS Jan Jose (courtesy of *National Archives Research Administration*)

EPILOGUE

Page 359 - THE UN ESTIMATES THAT SOME - "Flight From Indochina" State of the World's Refugees, p. 98. Chapter 4 – Flight from Indochina." United Nations High Commission for Refugees, p 80.

Page 359 - HUMANITARIAN RESETTLEMENT PROGRAM - "Joint U.S. – Vietnamese Announcement of Humanitarian Resettlement Program," *Office of the Spokesman, U.S. Department of State,* November 15, 2005.

Page 359 - BY 2012, THERE WERE SOME 1.7 MILLION – Jeff Gammage, "Smithsonian's Vietnamese Exhibit Recalls Plight of Boat People." Philadelphia Inquirer, May 14, 2012.

SELECTED BIBLIOGRAPHY

AUTHOR INTERVIEWS

LTG (ret.) Malcolm B. Armstrong, USAF

Commodore Thomas L. Bushy, USMS (ret.)

Rear Admiral Eugene D. Conner, USN (ret.)

Admiral Jerome "Jerry" L. Johnson, USN (ret.)

Mr. Cuu Pham

Ms. Hong Ngoc

Mr. Hung Pham

Mr. Quoc Pham

Chief Engineer Dave Sexton, USMS (ret.)

COL Charles S. Tutt, USMCR (ret.)

BOOKS CONSULTED

Boykin, Richard. *Ride the Thunder – A Vietnam War Story of Honor and Triumph.* Los Angeles: WND Books, 2009.

Bowman, John, General Editor. *The Vietnam War – An Almanac.* New York: Bison Books Corporation, 1985.

Fullerton, Minh. *Thank You America! Memoir of an 18-year Journey to Freedom.* Lee M Vo, 1985.

Hoang, Carina, Editor. *Boat People – Personal Stories From the Vietnamese Exodus 1975-1996.* Cloverdale, Western Australia: Carina Hoang Communications, 2010.

Lam, Andrew. *Perfume Dreams – Reflections on the Vietnamese Diaspora.* Berkeley, California: Heyday Books, 2005.

Metzner, Edward P. et al. *Reeducation in Postwar Vietnam – Personal Postscripts to Peace.* College Station: Texas A&M University Press, 2001.

Morgan, Ted. *Valley of Death – The Tragedy at Dien Bien Phu That Led America into the Vietnam War.* New York: Random House, 2010.

Nguyen, Viet Thanh. *The Sympathizer – A Novel.* New York: Grove Press, 2015.

Templer, Robert. *Shadows and Wind – A View of Modern Vietnam.* New York: Penguin Books, 1998.

Tin, Bui. *Following Ho Chi Minh – Memoirs of a North Vietnamese Colonel.* Honolulu: University of Hawaii Press, 1995.

Tri, Le Huu. *Prisoner of the Word – A Memoir of the Vietnamese Reeducation Camps.* Seattle: Black Heron Press, 2001.

Vu, Tran Tri. *Lost Years – My 1,632 Days in Reeducation Camps.* Berkeley: Institute of East Asian Studies, University of California, 1988.

GOVERNMENT DOCUMENTS CONSULTED

Del Mundo, Fernando. "113 (Europe: The debate over asylum) – Vietnam: End of an era." United Nations High Commission on Refugees. http://unchr.org/en-us/publications/refugeemag/3b811t6e4/regug...ope-debate-asylum-viet-nam-end-era.html.

"FDA Advises Consumers to Avoid Toothpaste from China Containing Harmful Chemical." Press Release from FDA.gov, dated June 1, 2007. http://www/fda.gov/NewsEvents/Newsroom/PressAnouncements/2007/ucm108927.htm

Feller, Erika. "Asylum-seekers, refugees and Rescue-at-Sea." Presentation at International Shipping Federation Manning and Training Conference, The British Library, London, September 11, 2002.

"Joint U.S.–Vietnamese Announcement of Humanitarian Resettlement Program." Office of the Spokesman, Under Secretary for Public Diplomacy and Public Affairs, U.S. Department of State, November 15, 2005. https://2001-2009.state.gove/r/pa/prs/ps/2005/56936.htm

Lewis, Jerry. "Does Singapore Have a Reason to Refuse Refugees?" *Singapore Policy Journal,* May 21, 2015. https://singaporepolicyjournal.com/2015/05/21/does-singapore-have-a-reason-to-refuse-refugees/

Deck Logs, USS San Jose. January 1980. Courtesy *United States National Archives Research Administration.*

"State of the World's Refugees 2000." Chapter 4 – Flight from Indochina." United Nations High Commission for Refugees, pp. 79-103.

ARTICLES CONSULTED

"122 mm gun M1931/37 (A-19)." Wikipedia. https://en-wikipedia.org/wiki/122_mm_gun_M1931/37_(A-19)

"A Basic Buddhism Guide: 5 Minute Introduction." http://www.buddhanet.net/e-learning/5minbud.htm

"A Better War: The Unexamined Victories and Final Tragedy of America's Last Years in Vietnam (Review)." *Parameters,* September 22, 2000. https://www.highbeam.com/doc/1G1-67502116.html

"Admiral Jerome Lamarr Johnson." *Military Hall of Honor.* http://www.militaryhallofhonor.com/honoree-record.php?id=568

"A Forgotten Past – Vietnamese Boat People in Singapore." Remember Singapore. Posted July 1, 2011. https://remembersingapore.org/2011/07/01/vietnamese-boat-people-in-singapore/

"Alexander the Great." Encyclopedia Judaica, January 1, 2007. https://www.highbeam.com/doc/1G2-2587500753.html

"All that we are is the result of what we have thought." Goodreads. http://www.goodreads.com/quotes/1296640-all-that-we-are-is-the-result-of-what-we

Anh, Le Thi. "Second Anniversary – The New Vietnam." https://www.jim.com/ChomskyLiesCites/When_we_new_what_happened_in_Vietnam.htm

"Annual festivities celebrate heritage." *Vietnamese News Agency*, February 16, 2011. https://highbeam.com/doc/1G1-249268440.html

Ashbrook, Tom. "In Cambodia, The War Shows No Signs of Ending." *The Boston Globe*, June 28, 1987. https://www.highbeam.com/doc/1P2-8017279.html

"Boat 55 Rescue by USS San Jose." *Refugee Camps.net*. undated. http://www.refugeecamps.net/55Quocpham.html

"Boat People and Compassion Fatigue." *The New York Times*, July 14, 1988. http://www.nytimes.com/1988/07/14/opinion/boat-people-and-compassion-fatigue.html

Bonner, Kit. "LST – Otherwise Known as 'Large Slow Target.'" *Sea Classics*, September 1, 2010. https://www.highbeam.com/doc/1P3-2097714621.html

Bradlee, Ben Jr. "Vietnam Today Market Leninism - The Global Economy is Forcing Hanoi to Tiptoe Down a Free Market Track. But can an Aging, Calcified Politburo Control the Speed of Change and Keep Business from Reforming Itself Out of Business?" *The Boston Globe*, April 30, 2000, Sunday, Third Edition. http://www.benbradleejr.com/vietnam.php

Branigin, William. "Forced 'Reeducation' Camps Continue in Vietnam, Laos." *The Washington Post*, December 23, 1982. https://www.washingtonpost.com/archive/politics/1982/12/23/forced-reeducation-camps-continue-in-vietnam-laos/530b0f13-7982-4e96-8359-35ae3baed72c/?utm_term=.72193c2dcef3

Bui, Nancy. "50th Anniversary of the Vietnam War from a Vietnamese American Perspective." Undated. http://notevenpast.org/50th-anniversary-of-the-vietnam-war-remembrance-from-a-vietnamese-american-perspective/

Butterfield, Fox. "For Many from Vietnam, Life in U.S. is Still Hard." *The New York Times*, April 17, 1985. http://www.nytimes.com/1985/04/17/us/for-many-from-vietnam-life-in-us-is-still-hard.html?pagewanted=all

"Carbon Dioxide as a Potential Danger to Medical Rescue Teams at Work - a Case Study." *Medycyna Pracy* (Occupational Medicine) Portal, January 1, 2017 https://www.highbeam.com/doc/1P3-4320813251.html

Chung, Jimmy Lim Wei. "Ethics and Leadership in Foreign Policy: The Case of Singapore." Lee Kuan Yew – School of Public Policy, Copyright 2016 by the Lee Kuan Yew School of Public Policy at the National University of Singapore. https://lkyspp.nus.edu.sg/wp-content/uploads/2016/07/20160714 ethics and leader in foreign policy the case of singapore.pdf

Crossette, Barbara. "Thai Pirates Continuing Brutal Attacks on Vietnamese Boat People." Special to *The New York Times*, January 11, 1982. http://www.nytimes.com/1982/01/11/world/thai-pirates-continuing-brutal-attacks-on-vietnamese-boat-people.html

Do, Anh. "Camp Z30-D: The Survivors." *Dart Center for Journalism and Trauma.* March 1, 2002. http://dartcenter.org/content/camp-z30-d-survivors

Dodd, Jan. "List of Vietnamese proverbs, with English translations," *Adopt Vietnam*, undated. http://www.adoptvietnam.org/vietnamese/proverbs.htm

Esper, George. "Fall of Saigon was Death Knell for South Vietnam." *The Columbian* (Vancouver, WA), April 9, 1995. Https://www.highbeam.com/doc/1P2-23331536.html

"Famous Vietnamese Quotes." *Thinkexist.com.* Undated. http://thinkexist.com/quotes/top/nationality/vietnamese/

"Forest vs. Jungle." *Diffen.* http://www.diffen.com/difference/Forest vs Jungle

Friedman, Herbert A. (SGM, ret.) "The Armed Propaganda Teams of Vietnam." http://www.psywarrior.com/VNArmedPropTeams.html

Front page reprint, *The New York Times*, January 1, 1980. http://timesmachine.nytimes.com/timesmachine/1980/010/01/issue.html

Gammage, Jeff. "Smithsonian's Vietnamese Exhibit Recalls Plight of Boat People." *Philadelphia Inquirer*, May 14, 2012. http://vietnamtimesonline.com/2012/05/14/smithsonians-vietnamese-exhibit-recalls-plight-of-boat-people-philadelphia-inquirer-2/

"Gen. Duong Van Minh, 86; Briefly Led South Vietnam (Obituary)." *The Washington Post*, August 8, 2016. https://www.highbeam.com/doc/1P2-456317.html

Gershman, Carl. "After the Dominoes Fell." *Commentary Magazine*, May 1, 1978. https://commentarymagazine.com/articles/after-the-dominoes-fell//

"Get Together Marks VFF's 70th Founding Anniversary." *Vietnamese News Agency*, May 19, 2011. https://www.highbeam.com/doc/1G1-256816950.html

Goldberg, Aliza. "How the U.S. Sentiment Towards Refugees Shifted." Foreign Policy Association – *Foreign Policy Blogs Network*, December 28, 2016. http://foreignpolicyblogs.com/2016/12/28/u-s-sentiment-towards-refugees-shifted/

Grant, S. "9 Obscure Concentration Camps." *Listverse*, August 27, 2013. http://listverse.com/2013/08/27/9-obscure-concentration-camps/

Hiebert, Murray. "Vietnamese Reeducation Camp Victims Embark for U.S." *The Washington Post*, January 6, 1990. https://www.highbeam.com/doc/1P2-1103572.html

"History and Development of the Container – The 'Transporter' – Predecessor to the CONEX." U.S. Army Transportation Museum website. Undated. http://www.transportation.army.mil/museum/transportation%20museum/CONEX.htm

"Ho Chi Minh and the Vietnam War." Society for Historians of American Foreign Relations, undated. https://shafr.org/teaching/ho-chi-minh-and-vietnam-war

"Hypokalemic Periodic Paralysis FAQ." *Periodic Paralysis International*, June 21, 2011. http://hkpp.org/patients/hypokpp-FAQ

"Intelligent Men are Cruel. Stupid men are monstrously cruel." Jack London quote. *Goodreads.* http://www.goodreads.com/quotes/223275-intelligent-men-are-cruel-stupid-men-are-monstrously-cruel

"Introduction to Buddhism," Buddhist Studies. Buddha Dharma Education Association & BuddaNet. http://www.buddhanet.net/e-learning/intro_bud.htm

Jacoby, Jeff. "What Happened When U.S. Troops Left Too Soon." *The Boston Globe*, May 10, 2015.

http://www.jeffjacoby.com/16557/when-us-troops-left-too-soon

Jacqueney, Theodore. "They Are Us, Were We Vietnamese." *WorldView – Carnegie Council for Ethics in International Affairs.* Volume 20, Number 4, April 1, 1977. https://worldview.carnegiecouncil.org/archive/worldview/1977/04/2836.html/_res/id=-File1/v20_i004_a003.pdf

Kaiser, Robert G. "Surviving Communist 'Reeducation Camp' Series: REDISCOVERING VIETNAM Series Number: 1/2, *The Washington Post*, May 15, 1994. https://www.highbeam.com/doc/1P2-890791.html

Kirk, Donald. "Forty Years After Fall of Saigon, Vietnam Now Directs Anger at China." *The Christian Science Monitor,*" April 30, 2015. http://www.csmonitor.com/World/Asia-Pacific/2015/0430/Forty-years-after-fall-of-Saigon-Vietnam-now-directs-anger-at-China-video

Kleinman, Stuart, M.D. "Trauma and its Ramifications in Vietnamese Victims of Piracy." *Jefferson Journal of Psychiatry*, Volume 5, Issue 2, Article 4.

http://jdc.jefferson.edu/jeffjpsychiatry/vol5/iss2/4

Kramer, Tarrance, "Rotary Revelations: Managing Helicopter Operations around Fixed-Wing Aircraft Demands a Little Finesse and a Lot of Clarity on the Part of Pilots and Controllers." *IFR Magazine*, January 1, 2017.

https://www.highbeam.com/doc/1G1-476728159.html

Krause, Joshua. "Brace Yourself for the Frightening Symptoms of Starvation." *Health and Wellness*, Ready Nutrition, October 4, 2015. https://www.sott.net/article/303729-Brace-yourself-for-the-frightening-symptoms-of-starvation

Leona, Cate. "Asian Squats to Improve Health, Flexibility and Balance." *Udemyblog.* https://blog.udemy.com/asian-squats/

Le, Sonny. "Life in Commute – My Long Road to America." April 30, 2012 Blog. http://25hawkinsroad.blogspot.com/2010/11/escape-from-viet-nam-my-life-in-america.html

Maresca, Thomas. "40 Years Later, Vietnam still deeply divided over war." April 28, 2015, updated April 30, 2015. http://www.usatoday.com/story/news/world/2015/04/28/fall-of-saigon-vietnam-40-years-later/26447943/

Mason, Margie. "Vietnamese re-education camp prisoner kept promise." *AP Worldstream*, September 9, 2011. https://www.highbeam.com/doc/1A1-80f14d23c8214def9b6de4207375a9a0.html

Morgan, Adrian. "FAQ Sir Francis Beaufort – It's an Ill Wind." *The Scotsman*, November 2, 2000. https://www.highbeam.com/doc/1P2-18755170.html

"Motion Sickness." *Medical News Today,* September 8, 2015. http://www.medical-newstoday.com/articles/176198.php

"Navy to Try Captain for Not Aiding Refugees." *The Boston Globe,* August 24, 1988. https://www.highbeam.com/doc/1P2-8076113.html

"Nguyen Thi Dinh." *Vietnam War Reference Library,* January 1, 2001. https://www.highbeam.com/doc/1P2-18806624.html

"Nguyen Van Thieu (Obituary)." *The Scotsman,* October 2, 2001. https://www.highbeam.com/doc/1P2-18806624.html

"Phan Thiet Average January Sea Temperature." SeaTemperature.org https://www.seatemperature.org/asia/vietnam/phan-thit-january.htm

"President Minh's Inaugural Address in Saigon Palace." *The New York Times,* April 29, 1975. http://www.nytimes.com/library/world/asia/042875vietnam-minh-speech.html

Proctor, Pam. "Ordeal of the Boat People." *Boston Globe,* April 9, 1978. ProQuest Historical Newspapers, The Boston Globe.

Pinkerton, James P. "Echoes here of Watergate and Vietnam." *Star Tribune* (Minneapolis, MN), July 21, 2003. https://www.highbeam.com/doc/1G1-106759320.html

Proyect, Louis. "The Mirror of Vietnam." *Counterpunch,* February 13, 2015. http://www.counterpunch.org/2015/02/13/the-mirror-of-vietnam/

"Remember: an economist co-authored with Chomsky to write these." *Economics Job Market Rumors,* undated blog. https://www.econjobrumors.com/topic/remember-an-economist-co-authored-with-chomsky-to-write-these

"Report Says 12,368 Fled Vietnam in June." *The New York Times,* United Nations, NY, August 5, 1981. http://www.nytimes.com/1981/08/05/world/report-says-12368-fled-vietnam-in-june.html

"Republic of Vietnam Armed Forces." GlobalSecurity.org. http://www.globalsecurity.org/military/world/vietnam/rvn-af.htm

"Research Response – Keywords: Vietnam – Illegal Departure 1979 – Legal provisions – Orderly Departure Program." *Refugee Review Tribunal* – Australia, August 22, 2007.

"Rice in Vietnam." Vietnamese Culture Values. Undated. http://www.vietnam-culture.com/articles-218-34/Rice-in-Vietnam.aspx

Richburg, Keith B. "Former Saigon Official Adapts to Life After Camps." *The Washington Post*, July 19, 1988. https://www.highbeam.com/doc/1P2-1268627.html

Richburg, Keith B. "Pol Pot Admits 'Mistakes' by his Regime; But Cambodian Insists, 'My Conscience is Clear.'" *The Washington Post*, October 23, 1997. https://www.highbeam.com//doc/1P2-745467.html

Richburg, Keith B. "The Victory That Led to Defeat; Tet Altered Course of Vietnam War." *The Washington Post*, February 1, 1988. https://www.highbeam.com//doc/1P2-1237206.html

Rockstroh, Dennis. "Hidden Horrors of Vietnam's Re-Education Camps." *New SaiGon*, San Jose, California, April 2, 2005. http://vietfacts.com/VF_RECamp/hidden-horrors-of-vietnams-re%5B1%5D.htm

"Saigon Liberation: Witness recalls historic event." *Vietnamese News Agency*, April 22, 2010. https://www.highbeam.com/doc/1G1-224574732.html

"Saigon needs plan to preserve again street trees: expert." *Thanh Nien News*, August 10, 2014. http://www.thanhniennews.com/society/saigon-needs-plan-to-preserve-aging-street-trees-expert-29730.html

Sanchez, Nick. "5 Times US Welcomed Refugees from War-Torn Countries and How It Worked Out," *Newsmax.com*, September 11, 2015. http://www.newsmax.com/TheWire/america-welcomed-refugees-war/2015/09/11/id/688032/

Seidman, Gay. "Reconstruction & Revolution in Vietnam – The East is Red." *The Harvard Crimson*, February 20, 1976. http://www.thecrimson.com/article/1976/2/20/reconstruction-revolution-in-vietnam-pbwbhen/

Spector, Ronald H. "Vietnam War." Encyclopedia Britannica, last updated 10-28-2016. https://www.britannica.com/event/Vietnam-War

Swanson, Ana. "The Refugees Americans Have Fought Against Over 200 Years." *The Washington Post*, November 20, 2015. https://www.washingtonpost.com/news/wonk/wp/2015/11/20/what-refugees-to-america-looked-like-over-the-past-400-years/?utm_term=.aaf5306ebb48

Tillotson, Donna. "Treaty of Versailles: not exactly as planned: how the treaty "to end all wars" led instead to numerous new conflicts." (THE GREAT WAR), *Esprits De Corps*, July 1, 2009. https://www.highbeam.com/doc/1G1-203602880.html

"Thai Fishermen Admit to Killing 130 Vietnamese Boat People at Sea." *The Boston Globe*, June 27, 1989. https://www.highbeam.com/doc/1P2-8126987.html

"The Christmas Bombing. (President Richard M. Nixon ordered bombing of North Vietnam in 1972) (brief article)" *Newsweek*, March 1, 1999. https://www.highbeam.com/doc/1G1-54012235.html

"The Vietnam War – Allied Troop Levels."

http://www.americanwarlibrary.com/vietnam/vwatl.htm

"The Unwanted: Cambodia. (Vietnamese Settlers)." *The Economist (US)*, March 20, 1993. https://www.highbeam.com/doc/1G1-13526090.html

"Thieu Resigns, Calling U.S. Untrustworthy." *The New York Times*, April 22, 1975. http://www.nytimes.com/1975/04/22/archives/thieu-resigns-calling-us-untrustworthy-appoints-successor-to-seek.html

Thrower, Antony, "Paul Proposes New Theory on Young Minds." *Folkestone Herald*, June 6, 2013. https://www.highbeam.com/doc/1P2-34746406.html

Tran, Connie. "Vietnamese Boat People: The Stories of Vietnamese Refugees and their Journey in Seeking Asylum in Canada during the Late 1970s to the 1980s." *Mount Royal Undergraduate Humanities Review 3 (2015)*, pp. 65-77. http://mrujs.mtroyal.ca/index.php/mruhr/article/view/216

Truong, Quyen. "Vietnamese Re-Education Camps: A Brief History." *The Choices Program – Brown University.* http://www.choices.edu/resources/suppplemental_vietnam_camps.php

"USS San Jose (AFS-7) Submit by Mr. Johnson." Refugeecamps.net. http://www.refugeecamps.net/Johnny_AFS7.html

"Vietnam." Vietnam Facts - Encyclopedia Britannica, 2016.

"Vietnam War Info." http://vietnam-war.info/summary

"Vietnamese Americans Subject Guide." Texas Tech University, The Vietnam Center and Archive. Undated. http://www.vietnam.ttu.edu/resources/vietnamese-american.php

"Vietnam and Vietnamese Americans after 1975." Vietnamese Americans – lessons in American History. *Teaching Tolerance.* Undated. www.teachingtolerance/vietnamese

"Vietnamese Boat People." *Revolvy,* undated. https://www.revolvy.com/main/index.php?s=Vietnamese%20boat%20people

"Vietnamese Boat People." *History Learning Site,* March 27, 2015. historylearningsite.co.uk

"Vietnamese Boat People." *The Info List,* Website, undated. http://www.theinfolist.com/php/SummaryGet.php?FindGo=Vietnamese%20boat%20people

"Vietnamese boat people: living to tell the tale." The Guardian, March 19, 2016. https://www.theguardian.com/global/2016/mar/20/vietnamese-boat-people-survivors-families

"Vietnamese Re-education Camps." *The Vietnamwar.info,* November 6, 2014. http://thevietnamwar.info/vietnamese-re-education-camps/

"Vietnam's Political Hostages." The Economist (US), June 24, 1989. Htps://www.highbeam.com/doc/1G1-7707881.html

"Vietnam War 1954-1975." Encyclopedia Britannica. https://www.britannica.com/event/Vietnam-War

"Vietnam War Info." Website. http://vietnam-war.info

Vo, Linda Trinh. *"Vietnamese American Trajectories – Dimension of Diaspora."* *Amerasia Journal* 29:1 2003): ix-xviii. http://uclajournals.org/doi/pdf/10.17953/amer.29.1.t8kvv26307580520?code=ucla-site

Wee, Eric L. "Rising from the Ruins of War; Vietnamese Émigré Finds Niche in U.S." *The Washington Post,* May 20, 1999. https://www.highbeam.com/doc/1P2-597054.html

"What DO scorpions taste like?" *Arachnoboards,* August 30, 2008. http://arachnoboards.com/threads/what-do-scorpions-taste-like-here-is-your-answer.133442/

"What's the Difference Between Viet Minh and Viet Cong?" eNotes. https://www.enotes.com/homework-help/what-difference-between-viet-minh-viet-cong-359807

Will, George. "Marshall Still is Still Not Getting His Due." *The Buffalo News* (Buffalo, N.Y.), June 3, 1997. https://www.highbeam.com/doc/1P2-22917364.html

Zach, Paul. "Flood of Indochinese Refugees Ebbing." *The Washington Post*, March 11, 1980. https://www.washingtonpost.com/archive/politics/1980/03/11/flood-of-indochinese-refugees-ebbing/a7cf7105-1749-4bca-b230-febda9624136/?utm_term=.afb8056b584e

QUOTATION SOURCES CITED IN END NOTES

AdoptVietnam. http://www.adoptvietnam.org/vietnamese/proverbs.htm

AZQuotes. http://www.azquotes.com

Brainyquote. https://www.brainyquote.com

Goodreads. https://www.goodreads.com/quotes

Inspirational Quotes. https://www.values.com/inspirational-quotes

Listofproverbs.com. http://www.listofproverbs.com

Proverbatim.com. http://www.proverbatim.com

Sources of Insight. http://sourcesofinsight.com

Vietnamese Proverbs - Proverbicals. http://proverbicals.com/vietnamese-proverbs/

INDEX